THE MATURING OF
YIDDISH LITERATURE

ALSO BY SOL LIPTZIN

THE FLOWERING OF YIDDISH LITERATURE
THE JEW IN AMERICAN LITERATURE
GENERATION OF DECISION
GERMANY'S STEPCHILDREN
ARTHUR SCHNITZLER
SHELLEY IN GERMANY
RICHARD BEER-HOFMANN
THE WEAVERS IN GERMAN LITERATURE
LYRIC PIONEERS OF MODERN GERMANY
THE ENGLISH LEGEND OF HEINRICH HEINE
HISTORICAL SURVEY OF GERMAN LITERATURE
FROM NOVALIS TO NIETZSCHE
ELIAKUM ZUNSER
PERETZ
HEINE

THE MATURING OF
YIDDISH LITERATURE

by
Sol Liptzin

JONATHAN DAVID PUBLISHERS • New York

71-802

Contents

Preface

The Flowering of Yiddish Literature, published in 1963, dealt with the literary movements that arose before the First World War and with writers who made their initial impact upon the Yiddish scene before 1914.

The present volume deals with the generation that followed the classical flowering. Yiddish matured. Its horizon expanded to encompass every aspect of human experience on all continents. Between the two world wars Yiddish was the linguistic medium of no less than ten million Jews. Then came the catastrophe which damaged its vital roots. The Nazi Holocaust destroyed its Eastern European base. The Jewish State adopted Hebrew as the sole national language of the Jewish people and conceded to Yiddish merely academic significance. The offspring of Yiddish-speaking Jews in Russia, Western Europe, North America and Latin America gradually made the transition to the dominant tongues of the majority populations in whose midst they dwelt. In the final third of the twentieth century there is justified concern as to whether Yiddish can recover from these severe wounds. Though voices of foreboding were heard continually between 1914 and 1939, Yiddish literature nevertheless reached its apex during this quarter of a century and a rich harvest of literary treasures was garnered before the storm broke. This volume seeks to call attention to some of these treasures.

A concluding volume will deal with the interpreters of the tragic decade after 1939 and the two exhilarating decades that followed the founding of Israel in 1948. It will call attention to contemporary Yiddish writers now dispersed over many lands of Europe, North America and Latin America but also ingathered in Israel and still creating ever maturer works of wisdom and esthetic value.

Introduction

Yiddish literature arose when the Yiddish language was formed, in the late Middle Ages in Ashkenazic territory, out of Hebrew, Romance, Slavic and Germanic components. It flourished during the centuries of minstrelsy and attained a peak of artistry in the sixteenth and early seventeenth centuries in verse epics and prose narratives. It declined following the destruction of hundreds of Yiddish-speaking communities in the mid-seventeenth century. Its decline was accelerated in the eighteenth century by the spirit of Enlightenment. Jewish reformers and rationalists ultimately succeeded in supplanting Yiddish with German in Central Europe, except for a few pockets of resistance in the Rhineland and Switzerland. They degraded this tongue by labeling it *Jargon*.

By the mid-nineteenth century, its survival as a vehicle for literary creativity in Eastern Europe also appeared to be unlikely, even though Yiddish folksongs continued to be sung by the Jewish masses, women continued to pour out their hearts in Yiddish devotional prayers, and Hassidim retold in ever new variations Yiddish tales of their saintly rabbis.

When the first periodical in Yiddish, *Kol Mevasser*, was launched in 1862 by the Hebrew publicist Alexander Zederbaum, it was justified to the Russian authorities as an organ that would educate the unenlightened Jewish masses and prepare them for Russification. Yet, it was in this very periodical that Mendele Mocher Sforim, the Grandfather of Modern Yiddish Literature, began two years later the publication of his Yiddish stories and helped to develop an audience for sophisticated belles-lettres.

In the following decade, Abraham Goldfaden replaced the dramatic improvisations of the Purim players and of Yiddish bards such as Berl Broder, Velvel Zbarzher and Eliakum Zunser with theatrical performances based on texts through which flowed artistry of a high order. In the 1880's, the Russian poet S. S. Frug turned to Yiddish in order to weep with the victims of Czarist pogroms and to bring them comfort and new hope. A still higher level of creativity was reached by the end of this decade when Sholom Aleichem and Y. L. Peretz appeared upon the Yiddish scene.

The Classical Age of Yiddish literature was the quarter of a century between 1889 and 1914. From its base in Russia and Poland, Yiddish literature spread in all directions as mass migrations brought pogrom-fleeing, Yiddish-speaking Jews to distant lands. New York then became an ever more important center for Yiddish books, the Yiddish theater and the Yiddish press.

When writers from many countries gathered at the Czernovitz Yiddish Conference of 1908, they could proclaim Yiddish as a Jewish national language alongside of the older and more sacred Hebrew. Abraham Reisen, Sholem Asch and David Pinski opened wider horizons in various literary genres. Jacob Gordin ushered in the golden era of the Yiddish theater and was followed by Peretz Hirshbein, Leon Kobrin and Z. Libin. Ideological battles between original thinkers at the turn of the century, such as Chaim Zhitlowsky, Ahad-Haam and Shimon Dubnow, found repercussions in Yiddish prose and verse. Yehoash supplied readers inadequately versed in Hebrew with a Yiddish translation of the Bible comparable in quality to Martin Luther's German version or the King James' English rendering. Along with Joseph Rolnick and H. Rosenblatt, he paved the way on American soil for the first indigenous lyric movement in the New World, that of "Die Yunge," out of whose midst arose on the eve of the First World War, H. Leivick, the finest Yiddish poet and dramatist of the post-classical generation.

Until 1914, Jewish life was comparatively stable in Eastern Europe. Despite the stirring of new forces, the Jewish personality was still intact in the Yiddish-speaking areas. There was a complex of characteristics which defined the Jew of the era of Mendele, Peretz and Sholom Aleichem, even though the process of dissolution had already set in. Against this stable traditional Jew, the Yiddish writers, pre-classical *Maskilim* as well as their successors of the generation of Mendele, Goldfaden and Linetzky, leveled effective satiric barbs. These Yiddish writers saw in the somnolent communities, symbolized as Kasrilevke and Yehupetz, medieval nests of unenlightenment and obscurantism.

After 1914, however, the tradition-encrusted, Yiddish-speaking townlets were no longer viable. War, revolution, pogroms, emigration decimated the Jewish Pale. Faith in the power of pure reason proved to be a false faith and yet could not be rejected. Gradually, as doubts concerning the vaunted Western progress increased, Jewish cultural traditions began to assume a romantic, nostalgic attractiveness in all the centers of Jewish concentration outside the Soviet realm. Attacks upon Hassidism as a diseased fanaticism yielded to admiration for its colorful, cheer-inducing practices. The alliance of Socialism and anti-nationalism was weakened as Yiddish writers fought for Jewish minority rights in the Diaspora and a national base in the Jewish historic homeland. Though the enthusiasm which accompanied the Russian Revolution waned, though the hopes set upon the rise of an independent Poland, Lithuania and Greater Rumania were not fulfilled, though the longed-for Jewish commonwealth to which Zionists aspired ran into unforeseen difficulties soon after the Balfour Declaration of 1917, nevertheless the Jewish masses were saved from despondency and were repeatedly buoyed up by Yiddish poets and thinkers who kept them aware of the richness of the Jewish heritage, the unity of the Jewish people, the Messianic visions embedded in Jewish folklore.

As darkening clouds hovered over Europe's Jews, America became increasingly the center of Jewish creativity. Yiddish writers streamed to its shores in ever greater numbers and paved the way for the replacement of Warsaw, Vilna and Kiev by New York, Montreal and Buenos Aires. When the Eastern European cycle of Jewish history came to a tragic end, the regeneration of the Jewish people in other areas of the globe, above all in the United States and Israel, was in full swing.

Yiddish literature accompanied the Jewish people throughout the decades of vigorous growth, unprecedented horrors and glorious rebirth.

THE MATURING OF
YIDDISH LITERATURE

1

The Novel of Young America

YIDDISH LITERATURE IN AMERICA is coeval with the mass immigration of Yiddish-speaking Jews in the 1880's. For the first quarter of a century, the most popular Yiddish writers were the political and social agitators who saved the sweatshop toilers from flagging idealism and moral decay by holding up to them visions of socialistic and anarchistic Utopias which must inevitably dawn. Only very few works of these literary pioneers have retained enduring value. Even the finest poets among them, David Edelstadt (1866–1892), Joseph Bovshover (1873–1915), Morris Rosenfeld (1862–1923) and Morris Vinchevsky (1856-1933), are hardly known today.

These early radical writers were succeeded by a new wave of young intellectuals who arrived after the failure of the Russian Revolution of 1905, disillusioned with political and social panaceas, and who undertook to wean Yiddish readers from lachrymose sentimentalism and propaganda literature. They called themselves and were called by others "Die Yunge," a term which friendly critics translated as "Young America" and hostile critics as "Young Upstarts." Their best

1

poets were Moshe Leib Halpern (1886–1932), Mani-Leib (1884–1953), Zisha Landau (1889–1937), Reuben Iceland (1884–1955), Moshe Nadir (1885–1943), Berl Lapin (1889–1952), and I. I. Schwartz (born 1885).

Less known are the contributions of "Die Yunge" to narrative art. Only a few novels of Joseph Opatoshu (1886–1954) have as yet been translated into English, but the narratives of David Ignatoff (1885–1954), the most dynamic member of the group, Isaac Raboy (1882–1944), and M. J. Haimowitz (1881–1958) are still unknown to English readers.

Ignatoff was only twenty when he arrived in America and only twenty-two when he assumed the leadership of "Die Yunge," but the roots of his personality remained anchored throughout his life in the Hassidic earth of his parents and grandparents and in the revolutionary soil that nourished him at Kiev, where as a youth he participated in Socialist agitation, lived dangerously, and suffered arrest and imprisonment. His activity as a writer, therefore, alternated between a colorful romanticism which cast a halo about Jewish traditions and a radical realism which linked him with proletarian literature.

Ignatoff's romanticism was best expressed in his *Wondertales of Old Prague* (*Vundermases Fun Altn Prag*, 1916–1920) and in his adaptations of Nachman Bratslaver's stories in *The Hidden Light* (*Dos Farborgene Likht*, 1918).

The hero of the wondertales is a simple-hearted Jew, Berl Prager, a follower of the saintly Rabbi Loew of Prague. Berl faces innumerable perils as he wanders from land to land in search of a livelihood. He emerges unscathed because of his optimistic faith that God, whose cause he champions, will not let him perish. On his first adventure, he is shipwrecked and washed ashore on an unknown land, together with a sole companion. After three days, both come to the grazing grounds of a one-eyed, man-eating giant. This monster prefers the fat Turk to the lean Jew for his first meal. Before he is ready for a second meal, Berl Prager succeeds in blinding him and in escaping under the belly of the biggest sheep.

The adventure is easily recognizable as of Homeric origin, as the story of Odysseus and the one-eyed Cyclops. However, while the Greek hero depends solely upon his own craftiness, the Jewish wanderer puts his trust in God and in the beloved Rabbi of Prague, God's emissary on earth. Berl ascribes his ingenious plan of escape to God's inspiration and the success of his stratagem to his invincible faith that a homecoming to his wife and children and to the Rabbi is vouchsafed him.

In all of Berl's adventures in the Land of Purity and in the domains of the Queen of the Sabbath, in the belly of the Leviathan and on remote battlefields, he retains his humility and piety. After his victories over the giants who threatened Sabbathland, he puts away his armor, sword and spear. He remarks that he is no bear in the forest, out to frighten people. His weapons were lent to him by a kind Providence to execute the Divine Will and to cleanse holy earth from forces of evil. After his successful campaigns, the weapons are no longer needed. He is not ambitious for worldly success and he does not yearn for fame or dominion. He rather wants to find his way back from the realm of marvels to his waiting family in Old Prague and to the circle of the Rabbi. This wish is finally granted him just before he is gathered to his fathers, among whom he can then dwell forever in celestial palaces.

Ignatoff speaks of the whole world as a tale not yet entirely told. Each of us can experience but fragments of it. In the fantastic stories of *The Hidden Light,* he therefore weaves one incident into another, without at first completing a single one. This accords with his view that no object and no event is an entity in itself but rather a part of the universal structure. At the end, however, the strands of his stories are somehow tied together into a meaningful pattern and the chaos of the world is resolved into a moral edifice.

Ignatoff's search for loveliness via art is reflected in his symbolic tales with their emphasis on purity and light. He has been rebuked for overstraining the use of the word "light" in all his writings. Light is, for him, the symbol of the Sabbath brightness sought by all who dwell in the murky mists of weekdays. It is the symbol of the clarity desired by all who roam in the realm of doubt. It is the symbol of the celestial radiance envisaged in golden dreams as the true eternal abode of the mystic essence interpenetrating the universe. It occurs most frequently in Ignatoff's parables. The best of these is *The Golden Boy* (*Dos Goldene Yingele*, 1921), a vision of the glory perceived in young days, pursued throughout life, and rediscovered by the inner eye after the sun-drenched outer eye has been blinded.

In addition to romantic tales, Ignatoff also composed significant novels of the New York he knew so well both as a shopworker and as a union organizer. Above all his realistic descriptions of slums and tenements, however, there tower dream-turrets reaching up to a mystic heaven. Through the filthy streets with their stale air there still blows a breath of divine purity, and the decay of the soul is constantly arrested by an ideal of personal and national regeneration.

In the Cauldron (*In Kesselgrub*, 1918) he depicts the struggle between degeneracy and spiritual rebirth among the young Jewish immigrants. The writer Baruch, in whom Ignatoff portrays himself, is derided as a naive fool when he wants to take his group out of New York's crippling shops onto homesteads in the free spaces of the Western prairies. Nevertheless, he has a beneficent influence upon the skeptical young men and is adored by the troubled young women. All of them sense his inner goodness and are impressed by his unselfish devotion to a moral cause.

Ignatoff's fictional trilogy *Vistas* (*Oif Veite Vegn*, 1932) describes the rise of the Jewish labor movement. Revolutionary idealists, defeated in their efforts to bring about a better order in Russia and uprooted from their native land, try to grow new roots in the United States and to unite against exploitation there. The hero, Berman, is again easily recognizable as Ignatoff himself. He is attracted to radical Socialism but also repelled by its militant atheism. He holds that human beings who don't have God in their heart are like mirrors in which nothing is mirrored. At the same time, he is isolated among religious Jews and stoned by Orthodox fanatics because of his radical social views. He strives for a synthesis of religion and Socialism, of traditional piety and cooperative idealism.

Ignatoff skillfully makes the real seem unreal and the unreal seem real. When he paints in words New York's Broadway on a weekday morning while workers are on their way to the shops, we see this avenue as a long river into which rivulets from side streets pour their human waves. Above this river of countless human droplets, we see the gigantic skyscrapers towering with their thousands of windows which are illumined by the red and golden rays of the setting sun. These skyscrapers in turn are held in leash by a titanic monster who directs their teeming industrial activities. Each human droplet, however, still retains individual features. One man is solemn and careworn, as he is borne along on the human tide, while another is smiling and self-satisfied. One girl, rushing and rushed on to her shop, is pale and embittered, while another still trembles with delight, recalling kisses of the preceding night.

Ignatoff's later works include the biblical tragedy *Jephta* (1939) and the longer tragedy *Gideon* (1953). These were little read, because the militant movement he led in the early decades of the century had lost its influence by the mid-century. Its young writers aged and scattered far and wide.

Among these young writers, Ignatoff's most faithful disciple was the novelist Isaac Raboy. Ignatoff called him a pillar of "Die Yunge."

Raboy introduced into Yiddish literature the Jewish farmer of the American prairies, even though the greater part of his life was spent among the slums and factories of New York. Born in the Ukrainian province of Podolia and growing up in Bessarabia, he yearned to escape from his Hassidic home and from the cramped townlet of Rishkon to a more natural existence in intimate contact with the soil. He found, however, that Jews were excluded from acquiring farmland and did not normally engage in health-giving, productive toil. Consorting with young intellectuals who had bright visions of catching up with modern trends of thought, he began to write at seventeen. However, when he sent his first story to Russian, Hebrew and Yiddish magazines, he received from all of them the same discouraging reply. Even his adored Bialik wrote him the single sentence: "You are absolutely without talent."

The Kishinev Pogrom of 1903 convinced his family that there was no future for Jews in the midst of hostile govern-ment officials and superstition-ridden peasants. Nor was young Raboy anxious to be drafted into the Czarist army to fight in the Russo-Japanese War, which erupted in 1904. He, therefore, escaped across the border and made his way to America.

In Raboy's two-volume autobiography, published posthu-mously in 1947, he related in fascinating detail the story of his flight from Bessarabia, his experiences enroute in Lemberg, Vienna, Trieste, his arrival in Castle Garden, and his first impressions of New York's East Side. Two brothers had preceded him and six others, as well as his parents, were soon to follow.

The dream of a literary career, which he entertained, dissolved within a few weeks, as Raboy made the rounds of all the Yiddish newspapers and was everywhere rebuffed. He then had to reconcile himself to toil from dawn to dusk in a hat factory. Only during late hours of the night and in periods of unemployment could he indulge in his passion for literary expression. Not only in his first immigrant years but also throughout most of his later years, he was forced to continue to earn his bread either at his specialty of making wire frames for ladies' hats or as a furrier. This hard toil, even while his fame as a writer spread, exhausted his strength, ruined his eyesight and undermined his health.

David Pinski, as editor of the weekly *Der Arbeiter*, en-couraged the new immigrant by publishing three of his short stories. Mani-Leib, who was his neighbor, and Ignatoff, who worked in the same hat factory, recognized his talent and introduced him to the literary group they were assembling. The anthologies of "Die Yunge" became the principal me-dium for the publication of Raboy's narratives.

In 1908, weary of the sweatshop and the verbal acrobatics indulged in by the Yiddish literary practitioners of New

York's East Broadway, Raboy followed the example of his friend Jacob J. Jaffe, afterwards Professor of Soil Sciences at Rutgers University. Jaffe had given up a job at a New York factory in order to study farming at the Jewish Agricultural School set up near Woodbine, New Jersey, with funds supplied by Baron de Hirsch. He invited Raboy to join him. For two years Raboy studied various aspects of agriculture. After graduating in 1910, he made his way to a ranch in North Dakota which specialized in horse breeding.

Raboy's experiences as a farmhand supplied him with rich, original subject matter for short stories and for his longer novels *Mr. Goldenbarg* (1913) and *The Jewish Cowboy* (1942). For a time he seriously considered establishing a homestead in the prairie state. A few unpleasant incidents, however, convinced him that his neighbors, despite much good will, could not entirely forgive him his Jewish origin. Strong family attachment and longing for Jewish companionship hastened his decision to return to the Atlantic seaboard. The single effort of his family to make a living as farmers in Connecticut ended in failure and doomed Raboy to a difficult existence thereafter in New York factories.

In his imagination, however, he still roamed the prairies on horseback. He cast a halo about his two years of freedom from the stifling metropolis. In his idealizing novel of the farmer and rancher *Mr. Goldenbarg,* he foreshadowed the characters and themes of his most important work *The Jewish Cowboy.* In both novels, the hero bears the name Isaac and is obviously Isaac Raboy himself. Mr. Goldenbarg is Jewish and sympathetic, in contrast to the boss of the later novel, who is non-Jewish, brutal, avaricious. The hero's supersensitive Jewish conscience prevents him from feeling entirely at ease among the various types of ranchers. He is consumed by a longing for Palestine. Though Mr. Goldenbarg, aware of Isaac's love for his daughter, offers him the ownership of the successful ranch and a productive life on the fat earth of the prairie, the farmhand cannot renounce his dream of cultivating Jewish dunams in a Jewish homeland.

Raboy's first novel, later adapted for the stage and produced in 1926 under the direction of Peretz Hirshbein, was hailed as a pioneering work which broadened the horizon of American Yiddish literature and which introduced a new type of Jewish toiler, one whose heart went out to horses and cows, forests and prairies. Raboy's second novel *Seaside* (*Der Pas fun Yam,* 1918) was more sober in tone. It was based upon his family's unsuccessful venture on a neglected Connecticut farm. It dealt entirely with Jews who left urban occupations, unprepared for rugged country living, who therefore found adjustment to the rural environment very difficult, but who nevertheless held out.

Raboy's realistic novels of Bessarabia and of his grandparents' experiences after exchanging Bessarabia for New York at the turn of the century did not measure up to the quality of his last masterpiece of fiction *The Jewish Cowboy.* Largely autobiographic and going beyond realism, this narrative contrasted the beauty of the prairies throughout the changing seasons with the cruelty of man to man.

Isaac, the Jewish farmhand on a rich ranch in North Dakota, fathoms in his boss the abyss of cruelty and duplicity to which a person who is in the grip of greed can descend. He witnesses in the latter's wife, an aging, lonely woman, the struggle between hellish passion and nobility of soul. In the first Indian he meets, he becomes aware of the injustice done to the Red Men by the White Men, the degradation of the peaceful, trusting aborigines. These were deprived of their broad prairies and grazing fields and concentrated on small reservations, where a continuation of the rich, native cultural existence they had long been accustomed to was impossible for them. Isaac gets to know Ellen, the girl sold into servitude by her poor parents, because they have no other resource with which to pay for the pair of horses needed on their homestead. He senses kindness and self-sacrificing love beneath the girl's taciturn, morose exterior. At no time is he allowed to forget that, though he may be liked as an individual, he cannot escape unreasoning antipathy toward the Jew in him. In whatever work he does, he feels that he must excel excessively in order to prove that a Jew can also engage in hard physical labor and in order to be accepted as an equal. When he rides a horse or sharpens an axe, all eyes are upon him to see whether he behaves or does not behave as clumsily as the imaginary Jew should. He wonders, finally, whether the horse he tends would continue to respond to him affectionately if it too knew of his Jewish origin. Throughout the year Isaac toils faithfully for his stern boss. Both seem to be getting along well with each other. When in a moment of anger, however, his boss gives vent to a deeply ingrained prejudice and calls Isaac a dirty Jew, then he is almost strangled by this normally calm assistant. Isaac returns east but not again to a sweatshop. On a Connecticut farm, not entirely isolated from his ethnic kind, he hopes to live the productive, healthy life of a dignified human being, one who neither exploits others nor is himself exploited.

Raboy is a lyricist in prose. The fresh air of the prairies courses through his novels, and the growth of the soil is depicted by him with ardent affection. He was, therefore, often likened to Knut Hamsun, long before he read this novelist of the untamed Scandinavian North, a comparison which became odious to him when Hamsun began his flirtation with the Nazis.

M. J. Haimowitz was far more prolific as a narrator than either Raboy or Ignatoff and yet only a few of his stories and novels appeared in book form. Most of his work is scattered in Yiddish periodicals. Coeditor of anthologies of "Die Yunge," he lacked the dynamism of Ignatoff and the robustness which attracts followers. A gifted storyteller, he steered clear of pure Naturalism, which he condemned as brutal, clinical, unimaginative. On the other hand, he could not lose himself in romantic visions and refused to spin out wonder tales which lacked a basis in reality. He rather sought to enrich carefully observed facts by an injection of lyricism and by an emphasis on the emotional motivation for happenings. He was, therefore, drawn from the very beginning of his long career to the Impressionism of the Viennese esthetes, especially Arthur Schnitzler.

Under the influence of Schnitzler, Haimowitz tried to delve into the psychology of the modern woman and to unravel the subconscious layers of her soul. However, he lacked the light touch, the melancholy humor and the tolerant wisdom of the Viennese master. His emancipated characters were still plagued by a Jewish conscience. As a result, his radical girls of New York are less fascinating than Schnitzler's sweet Danubian maidens, and his irreligious heroes retain a dull stodginess and a censoring moral monitor even in the midst of questionable amorous experiences.

Haimowitz best portrayed himself as Levin in the novel *En Route* (*Oifn Veg*, 1914). This weak-willed hero let himself be tempted by his friend's estranged wife, Frieda. After considerable hesitation, he yielded to her on a wild night. When Frieda and her unsuspecting husband were about to be reconciled somewhat later, Levin stepped in to prevent their reconciliation. Upon Frieda's questioning his right to interfere and to reveal her recent past, he replied that he had a right to shield his friend from being a deceived and betrayed husband. His meddling in his friend's life in the name of absolute truth resulted in Frieda's suicide and in her husband's breaking with him. After this experience, Levin decided to return to his own wife, from whom he had been separated for seven years. When she told him, however, that she had not been entirely faithful to him during this long period of separation, he flared up in anger and again rejected her as an unworthy mate. This double standard of morality, condoning the man's infidelity and punishing harshly the infidelity of both women, was logically indefensible. Nevertheless, Haimowitz accepted it despite its inconsistencies. He was no innovator in morals as was Ibsen, who had dramatized a similar situation in *The Wild Duck*, but merely an observer of life with its contradictions and failings. His characters were endowed with a conscience which was only partly flexible. They were never completely amoral. They lacked lustre and fire. Even famed adventurers, such as Casanova and Cagliostro in the narrative collection *Merry-Go-Round* (*Karusel*, 1946), were but pale imitations of Arthur Schnitzler's Casanova and Stefan Zweig's Cagliostro.

The most gifted novelist of "Die Yunge" was undoubtedly Joseph Opatoshu, who commanded a worldwide audience both with his short stories and his long historical novels.

Opatoshu traced his ancestry on his father's side to Reb Meir of Tannhausen, a sixteenth-century follower of Shlomo Molcho, the Messianic visionary who was burned by the Inquisition in 1532. This earliest known ancestor left Franconia in 1552 and settled in the Polish city of Posen. His descendants were rabbis and scholars in Hildesheim, Lask, Warsaw. Opatoshu stemmed on his mother's side from well-to-do villagers who dwelt on the edge of forests and engaged in lumbering.

In his childhood he imbibed from his mother the folklore of Polish woods and streams and from his father the stories of the Hassidic rebbes of Kotzk. During the decade following his birth, his father was active in the pre-Herzlian movement "Lovers of Zion" and composed Hebrew lyrics. At the same time that the young boy attended a Russian elementary school, the father provided him with an intensive Hebrew education at home. The growing lad came in contact with Jewish and non-Jewish playmates from all strata of society and accumulated a vast storehouse of memories upon which he later drew for stories and sketches.

Among strange acquaintances who left a deep impress upon him in his early years was a horse thief who made a living smuggling horses across the border from Poland to Germany. This thief was killed while defending Jews who were being harassed and beaten at the marketplace by their Polish neighbors. Opatoshu later depicted him in his first novel, *Romance of a Horse-Thief* (*A Roman fun a Ferd-Ganef*, 1917), both in the opening chapter as Eliahu Vilner, a Robin Hood who robbed aristocrats and priests but who never stole from Jews, and in the following chapters as Zanvel, the hero with a rough exterior and a soft heart, who dreamed of respectability even while engaged in his not-so-respectable profession of horse-thievery.

At nineteen, Opatoshu left for France to study engineering at Nancy, but within a year, when his financial resources were exhausted, he had to return home. At twenty, he began to write. When he showed his first short story to Peretz at Warsaw, he was encouraged to continue.

The bleak reaction in Russia, after the failure of the Revolution of 1905, and the wave of pogroms, which brought about a mass flight of Jews from the Czarist realm, also swept young Opatoshu on to America. He landed in New York in 1907. After brief experiences as a worker in a shoe factory and as a newspaper vendor, he was able to resume his study of engineering. He attended classes at Cooper Union, while supporting himself by teaching in a Hebrew school on Sundays and during afternoon hours. His years of trying to hammer Jewish knowledge into the heads of reluctant pupils and under the supervision of unscrupulous principals and ignorant lay administrators were described by him in a novel published in 1919 under the title *Hebrew* and republished three years later under the title *Lost Persons* (*Farlorene Menshen*).

The main characters in this novel were indeed lost souls. Their prototypes were Opatoshu's colleagues, teachers in New York's Talmud Torahs. He described them as having given up earlier ideals, as having become morally corrupt, intellectually dishonest, emotionally decayed, and as having accustomed themselves to live cynically and to indulge in follies and trivial jealousies. Their pupils, in whom they were supposed to implant a love of Jewishness, grew up hating the Hebrew school, the Hebrew language and the Hebrew pedagogues, and preferred the exciting liberation of ball playing to dull hours of bondage to a heritage unsuited to New York's raw reality.

From 1910 on, Opatoshu participated in the annuals and anthologies of "Die Yunge." His narrative of the horse thief appeared in the anthology of 1912 and aroused great interest. It introduced a new area of Jewish life, an area avoided until then by his predecessors—the underworld with its joys and dangers, its tremendous vitality, hot passions and not altogether respectable moral values.

Opatoshu's full-blooded, earth-rooted, ignorant, fearless, crafty thieves, smugglers and drunkards were far removed from the frail, impractical, heaven-gazing paupers of Sholom

Aleichem or the over-idealized, God-fearing patricians of Sholem Asch's romantic townlets. Opatoshu's hero Zanvel, horse dealer and horse smuggler, can neither read nor write, but he is resourceful in overcoming difficulties, overpowering opponents, eluding border police. He can also win the hearts of maidens, the timid daughter of a Hassid no less than the more sensual, laughter-loving types.

Opatoshu does not condemn his pariahs. His characters feel that their actions are justified according to their standard of values. If momentarily they are led astray and act contrary to their own moral code, they are sincere in their repentance and ready to atone. Though they revel in sensuality, it is for them rarely an end in itself. It is rather a stage in their personal development, a steppingstone in their ascent to a more complete life which embraces body and soul.

Opatoshu is faithful to reality. In his many stories no word is spoken and no detail is introduced which is not in consonance with character, environment and era. Nevertheless, though rooted in realism, Opatoshu often transports his readers to an inner world in which dreams, longings, sublimated intuitions seek expression. *In Polish Woods* (1921) best illustrates his approach, his undeviating devotion to factual reality. This novel depicts the decay of a Hassidic court which is overladen with superstitious excrescences, but it also offers glimpses of fervent faith and visions of Jewish and world redemption.

This historical narrative paints the whole gamut of Jewish life in the post-Napoleonic generation, from the lowest depths of degeneracy to the highest summit where saints wrestle with God. It was translated into English, German, Spanish, Hebrew, Russian, Polish, Ukrainian, Rumanian, and thus established Opatoshu's international fame. Based upon thorough research but also upon the author's recollections of incidents narrated to him by grandparents, granduncles and grandaunts, it unrolls a rich panorama of Polish-Jewish interrelations up to the Revolt of 1863. Mordecai, who grows up in a forest hamlet and consorts with woodsmen and fishermen, becomes the spokesman for the novelist's views on eternal and specifically Jewish problems. Mordecai's observations at the decaying Hassidic court of Kotzk forms the central part of the narrative. Mordecai witnesses the death throes of a great mystic movement, the disintegration of a famous religious brotherhood, the wrestling of a mighty pillar of Hassidism, Reb Mendele Kotzker, with doubt and despair. He is also introduced to the pioneers of enlightenment, the early *Maskilim,* who were burrowing with the tools of logic and skepticism into the structure of traditional beliefs. Toward the end, he is fascinated by the glamorous mirage of Polish–Jewish brotherhood, which is to point the way to universal fraternity and world salvation. He, therefore, participates with Polish patriots in the movement for the liberation of his native land from Russian domination and is forced to seek safety abroad.

In a sequel to the novel, entitled *1863* and published in 1929, Opatoshu transports this hunted refugee to Paris, the center for exiled Polish patriots. There Mordecai, who can no longer retain his faith in the God of his childhood, seeks the divine in striving for universal justice on earth. He consorts with Moses Hess, Michael Bakunin and Western thinkers as well as with Polish poets and Polish apostles of the brotherhood of nations. From Parisian exile he then makes his way back to his native land as revolutionary plans explode into action. The rebellion of 1863 fails and Mordecai's father, who has also become involved, is hanged by the Cossacks. At the last moment, when Reb Abraham is led to the gallows, a doubt flashes through his mind. He was sacrificing his life for the cause of Poland, his cause and yet not his cause. He was dying for the sanctification of God's name. Which God? The Jewish or the Polish? The narrative closes with the crows flying from the still warm, dangling body of this old Jew of the forest to the prostrate corpse of a murdered Polish aristocrat and back again to the Jewish patriot.

Mordecai, wounded in battle, was kept alive by the author in order to figure as the central character of the third part of the fictional trilogy, but this third part was never written.

Opatoshu's interest was shifting more and more from the

land of his birth to the New World and from the century
of his birth to all the previous centuries of Jewish history.
In describing the Jewish personality in its various transformations, he felt that he was also describing a universal personality, since Jews were not merely residents of a specific
land but also members of a world people whose capital was
Jerusalem. Jewish history was, in his opinion, the history of
almost all lands on this globe in whose midst Jews dwelt for
centuries and millennia. As a Jew, he was international,
cosmopolitan. Sitting beside the Hudson, he saw the Jordan
and the Vistula. In his imagination, he saw himself walking
with Rabbi Akiva along the shores of the Mediterranean
and with the Jewish minstrels in sixteenth-century Regensburg. Cordova, Rome, Paris, Worms, Prague, Posen, Lublin
and Warsaw lived in him no less than his birthplace, Mlave,
or his more recent abode, New York. As a novelist, he was
less chained to facts than were academic historians. He could
intuitively apprehend the truth of an era, while scholars were
obsessed by mere facts and helpless when suffering from a
dirth of recorded facts. Fascinated by the vast vista of the
Jewish past, Opatoshu held that this past was not adequately
interpreted even by Graetz and Dubnow, the ablest historians. They were unduly emphasizing persecutions and martyrdom. Surely there must have been also happy aspects to
Jewish existence in earlier eras even as there were in his
own era of pogroms but also achievements. Such happy
aspects he set out to depict in a series of historical tales.

Opatoshu's joyous narrative, *A Day in Regensburg*, appeared in the catastrophic year 1933, when Hitler rose to
power. It recalled to life the vanished world of Yiddish minstrels and merrymakers, the popular bards of the sixteenth
century who sang of King Arthur and his knights or of
Dietrich von Bern and Master Hildebrand. The research
workers of YIVO, the newly founded Yiddish Scientific Institute, had uncovered old Yiddish manuscripts, had reprinted the earliest printed poetic booklets, and had proved
that Jews were never hermetically sealed off from their non-
Jewish neighbors. Opatoshu undertook to compose a fictional antidote to the gloomy chronicle of Graetz. In a

stylized archaic Yiddish, he unrolled colorful episodes of a single day in Regensburg, the happy day when one of its richest Jews, Shlomo Belaser, married off his daughter to the son of the patrician of Worms, Eliahu Margolis. For this glamorous occasion wandering mendicants from many communities in Ashkenazic territory streamed into town. They filled the ghetto streets with jest, laughter, song and dance. Famed merrymakers of Prague arrived for the festival. Flutes and cymbals resounded. Beer and wine flowed in abundance. Even the Prince-Elector and his retinue of knights joined in when merriment reached its climax at the wedding ceremony. Despite gathering clouds and rumors of a threatening expulsion from the town, Jews were not to be restrained from enjoying in full measure their interlude of peace and prosperity.

The same historic era was again portrayed by Opatoshu in three scenes from the life of Elia Levita, the author of the *Bovo-Bukh* and the most talented of the Jewish romancers of the sixteenth century. The first scene showed Elia in the midst of a dispute with a fellow minstrel in Venice, whom he accused of plagiarizing one of his songs. The second scene brought him to the patrician home of a Jewish lady, who commissioned him to write a *siddur* for her daughter in which he was to include not only a Yiddish translation of the sacred prayers but also secular songs and ballads. The third scene presented the sixty-year-old Elia as secretary of the Italian Cardinal Egidio di Viterbo, residing with his family in the palace and disturbed by the fact that his own grandchildren no longer spoke Yiddish and were consorting with Christians on too intimate terms.

Shortly before his death in 1954, Opatoshu completed his most important historical narrative, *The Last Revolt (Der Letzter Oyfshtand),* upon which he had worked for many years. The first volume, *Rabbi Akiva,* appeared in 1948, the year of the founding of the Jewish State, and the second volume, *Bar Kochba,* appeared posthumously in 1955. In the former the novelist deals with the preparations for the liberation of the Jewish homeland from Roman rule during the reign of Emperor Hadrian and in the latter with the revolt itself and its tragic outcome.

As the accumulated dust of ages is brushed away, Judea of the second century comes to life in town and countryside, and Jewish figures, from donkey drivers and hermits to patricians and scholars, emerge in full-blooded vigor. Three score years after the fall of the Second Kingdom, Jews have recovered materially but still suffer spiritual hurt. While Jerusalem lies desolate, Jericho and Caesarea harbor Jewish merchant-princes who carry on large trading operations throughout the far-flung Roman Empire. Yet, even the richest families respect learning based on Torah and send their sons to the Jewish schools of Yavne and Bnei Brak. Some of these sons are also well grounded in Hellenistic lore. They speak Greek and Latin as well as Aramaic. They can quote Homer, Sophocles and Virgil no less than their beloved teacher Rabbi Akiva. The heads of the prominent families counsel patience and submission to the Roman authorities. The disciples of Rabbi Akiva, however, gather arms and provisions, and prepare for the overthrow of the hated pagan regime.

In Bar Kochba, the aged Rabbi Akiva finds the warrior-leader who can rouse the Jews to self-sacrificing heroism and who can outmaneuver and outfight famed Roman legions. Ultimately, however, Bar Kochba's moral flaws disappoint and estrange many who saw in him the Messiah of the House of David. His depleted forces are penned up in the fortress of Betar and their desperate resistance ends in defeat. This defeat is, however, only a temporary one, if measured on the scale of Jewish history. As long as Jews continue to survive anywhere on earth, their Messianic hope still lives on. It will accompany them throughout the ages. Just as Yochanan ben Zakai built a haven for the Jewish spirit at Yavne after the destruction of Jerusalem in the days of Vespasian and Titus, so Rabbi Joshua ben Hanina continues with Jewish learning after the catastrophe at Betar.

The novels were written during the years of Jewish martyrdom and the heroic rise of the Jewish State. They mirror, despite their historical setting, events of the Warsaw Ghetto

Revolt against the Nazis and the resistance to the mighty British Empire and the Arab kingdoms by the outnumbered Jews of Palestine. The novels voice faith in the survival of the Jews as a world people and of the Jewish Messianic idea as a world-saving force.

The novelists of "Die Yunge," Ignatoff, Raboy, Haimowitz and Opatoshu, were transition figures, spokesmen of the Eastern European Jewish generation which immigrated to America during the early twentieth century, a generation which believed itself to be emancipated from the religious, moral and social values of the Old World but which, nevertheless, retained these values within its subconsciousness. These writers were not alienated souls brooding over their alienation from Jewishness, as were far too many of their articulate descendants whose medium of expression was no longer Yiddish but English. They were members of a group that in its strident youth discovered the wonder of America, and they voiced the group's yearning to be embedded in a meaningful Jewishness and a meaningful Americanism. They matured and enriched Yiddish literature with valuable insights into new horizons and with a few masterpieces of narrative art which are able to withstand the ravages of time.

2

New Lyric
Voices in America

THE MASS EXODUS of Jews from Eastern European, Yiddish-speaking townlets to North American metropolises, beginning in the 1880's, included at first only a minute proportion of intellectuals. Even most of these were subjected to the purgatory of sweatshops and could devote themselves to literary pursuits only during periods of unemployment and in spare moments after long, wearisome hours of service to machines. Not until the decade preceding the First World War did "Die Yunge" offer a congenial home and platform for the creative products of young writers; not until after this war did a second group of Yiddish writers, the "Insichisten," join in a manifesto outlining a common literary striving.

There were, however, other writers who kept aloof from coteries and who trod a lonely way through the labyrinth of ideas. They peered into their inner souls and found original modes of expressing what they saw within themselves. Such lyricists were Menahem Boraisha (1888–1949) and Ephraim Auerbach (b. 1892).

Born in Brest-Litovsk as the son of a Hebrew teacher,

Menahem Goldberg came to Warsaw in 1905 and was encouraged by Peretz to publish his first lyrics in Yiddish rather than in Russian. He did so under the name of Menahem, and only much later did he add his mother's maiden name of Boraisha as his adopted name.

These early poems consisted mainly of rhapsodic odes filled with longing for God and Holiness. Some were in the form of prayers in which he wrestled with the Creator of the Universe and begged for a revelation that would make comprehensible the mysteries of heaven and earth, life and death. Others sensed the presence of God in the fire of passion consuming men and women. Still others emphasized the ancestral roots and the tradition-drenched earth that gave sustenance to the poet.

Peretz reminded the aspiring young man that the God of the Jews could not be forcibly dragged down to earth nor exhibited on wooden beams along village roads. Menahem, however, continued to wrestle with God throughout all later years. He never accepted the doctrine of art for art's sake. He could not envisage lyric beauty as an end in itself. Poetry was for him inseparable from religion, philosophy, history. It was for him primarily intuitive apprehension of truth in contrast to the logical apprehension sought by the exact sciences. It was cosmic knowledge welling up from the subconscious in contrast to factual knowledge based on minute observation. It was recovery of the Greater Memory possessed before birth and persisting outside of time—a concept basic to Platonic philosophy.

Menahem did not, however, invoke Plato, Wordsworth or Shelley as his forerunners and allies in this approach to the function of poetry. He found his inspiration in Jewish sources. His symbol for the supreme poet was Moses, to whom the Infinite was first revealed in the Burning Bush. Maintaining that revelation was as legitimate a gate to the realm of the Absolute as were the calculations of reason, Menahem held that in Moses, the most creative of poets, were embodied the powers of revelation, national vision, Messianic faith, and the urge to holiness. Menahem's dramatic poem *Moses,* posthumously published in 1950, was the final expression of his religious, philosophic and poetic insight.

Meanwhile, the aspiring lyricist had gone through many disappointments with transitory ideals. The seventeen-year-old youth, who came to the Polish metropolis from Lithuania, was dazzled by the cultural life of Warsaw. He saw in the Poles an ethnic group oppressed by the Russians even as were the Jews. He equated the melancholy of the Poles, which stemmed from a loss of national independence, with his own sadness and that of his coreligionists who were forced to be homeless wanderers. He therefore dreamed of a symbiosis of Poles and Jews. But this dream did not last long. He discovered that the Poles were engaged in an economic boycott against Jews in order to compel the emigration of this unwanted minority. In blistering verses he then hurled lacerating accusations against every sector of the Polish population, until his mentor Peretz had to remind him that it was unseemly to talk to an entire people in such bitter tones. After the appearance of his poem *Poland* in 1914, he left that land.

He arrived in the United States shortly after the outbreak of the First World War. Here too he suffered keen disappointment. Though surrounded by two million Jews in the largest American metropolis, he felt repelled by the growth of secularism among his coreligionists, by their abandonment of long-preserved traditions, by their acceptance of the tinsel values of a commercial, industrial order. For more than a third of a century he was active as a journalist in Yiddish dailies and English weeklies. He participated in Jewish cultural organizations and occupied an influential position in the Joint Distribution Committee and later in the American Jewish Congress. Nevertheless, he remained a lonely wayfarer, ever in search of deepest insight and ever dissatisfied with the fragmentary wisdom within his reach.

To the poems he published in 1920 he gave the symbolic title *Sand*, because he held that Jews were dispersed everywhere like the sand on the seashores. Apparently, it was their fate to wander on and on, buffeted by storms of hate throughout the Old World. Yet, their fate was no less tragic in the

New World, even though they did manage to escape from hate and to pioneer successfully. There the mild sun of freedom and the warmth of prosperity melted away and dissolved their Jewishness. Ultimately, as depicted in his poem *By the Sea,* only a fenced-in tombstone with a half-faded inscription remained as testimony of a Jew's former presence in an American frontier community. The Jew's Americanized Christian descendants knew him no more. The poet concluded: "At your lone tomb I stand and ask: who will come after us and who will revive our heritage?"

Menahem is melancholy but not pessimistic. He is sad but not nihilistic. He never doubts that there is purpose and direction in this universe of which we human beings are an integral part, but he experiences difficulty in ferreting out the precise meaning implicit in our existence. His main philosophic verse epic, upon which he worked for nine years and in which he recorded his adventures in the realm of ideas, was *The Wayfarer (Der Geher,* 1943). Its motto was taken from a Hassidic dictum: "A saint falls seven times and rises again each time. Man is a wayfarer and not a stationary bit of creation. He must go on from level to level."

Menahem relates the ascent from level to level of Noah, a nineteenth-century Jewish wayfarer, who combines traits and experiences both of the poet and the poet's brooding father.

The odyssey of Noah, the Jewish Faust, begins at infancy. His mother dies at childbirth and his nineteen-year-old father puts him into a knapsack and goes forth with him into the strange world. When the father remarries, the child, unwanted by the stepmother, is shunted back to an uncle. At thirteen, Noah is on his own and resumes his wandering. Thirsting for knowledge of God and all creation, the poor youth must content himself with black bread at charitable tables and with a hard bench at a synagogue for his weary head. In his dreams, however, he consorts with the angels who ascend and descend the ladder that leads to heaven. At sixteen he gets to the court of the Habad Hassidim and immerses himself in cabalistic lore. But he does not drown in this ocean of mysticism.

In the midst of his studies, temptations of the flesh assail him and he escapes from them by marrying, at twenty, a bride of the finest lineage of scholars. His father finds the long-lost son and urges him to settle down as a rabbi in some community and interpret the Jewish law to parishioners. Noah, however, seeks not stability but learning without end. He therefore leaves wife and child and as a wandering scholar continues to adventure in the realm of reason and then beyond reason. He makes his way past Maimonides and Aristotle. He ascends ever higher on the ladder that leads to perfection.

When the realization comes to him that he ought not to evade family responsibilities, he returns from his distant roaming. He teaches Torah to the children of his pious community but is unable to make a living and suffers from the injustice of the rich and the powerful. Employed as a night watchman, he acquires a better understanding of nature. Creatures of air and earth, who were mute for him hitherto, voice to him their pain, their terror, their joy, their wisdom. Lilith tries to convince him that the flame she kindles in man is not sin but redemption, that she too fulfills God's command, that through her body a path also leads to unity, salvation, eternity.

Noah continues his wayfaring, his questioning, his searching for clarity of perception, for the key that will unlock eternal mysteries and resolve all his doubts. As a salesman, he gains access to homes of the rich and the poor, the virtuous and the sinful, the kind and the hard-hearted, the normal and the abnormal, the dissident and the submissive. His insight grows and deepens but is still inadequate to pierce the mystery at the heart of things.

After reaching an abyss of poverty and burying his emaciated child, he temporarily experiences a change of fortune and becomes a storekeeper. He makes contact with the Men of Enlightenment, the Russian followers of Moses Mendelssohn. They teach him that Jews must live in harmony with their neighbors, must make concessions, must leave isolation, must interchange ideas. This approach of Mendelssohn, who sought to fashion peace between *tallit* and Cross, loses its glamor, however, when he learns that this philosopher's children ended by embracing the Cross. In a vision he witnesses a similar earlier approach by Elisha ben Abuya to mediate between the Hebraic and the Roman ways in the days of Bar Kochba, an approach which also failed utterly. When Noah's teacher ends as a convert to the Russian Church, he recognizes the danger of the manna of Enlightenment and betakes himself back to the synagogue and the Talmud.

To the argument of his friends, the *Maskilim,* that their mentor Mendelssohn did not reject the yoke of the Torah but rather that he brought the Torah with him from the ghetto of provincial Dessau to the intellectual metropolis of Prussia, Noah counters with the question: why then are Mendelssohn's descendants today to be found in non-Jewish cemeteries? His own explanation is that the German reformer did indeed bring the Torah to Berlin but that he left the Jews behind in Dessau. Torah without Jews dies even as do Jews as Jews without Torah.

Noah's wayfaring again brings him to Hassidic circles. His debate with a widely adored Hassidic *rebbe* does not resolve his doubts. Just as he could not accept the reasoned wisdom of the *Maskilim,* which was not grounded in faith, so too he cannot accept the faith of the Hassidim that is not grounded in reasoned wisdom.

A brief encounter with a Christian missionary leads him to study the New Testament. He finds its insistence upon blind belief in an intermediary between man and God even more distasteful than Hassidic efforts to interpose the *Tzaddik* as such an intermediary. He wants to break through directly to God, who is for him absolute truth and absolute righteousness.

Pursuing his life's quest, he consorts with Socialists and with peasants, the supposedly unspoiled natural creatures. Under the spell of Rousseauism, he seeks salvation in physical labor as a woodcutter. At the hands of his rough fellow workers, he experiences cruelty, beatings, brutality. He learns that whosoever seeks truth must be able to endure torments. Soon thereafter he sees remorse assailing his tormentors and he arrives at the conclusion that, just as the righteous are not wholly righteous, so too the wicked are not entirely evil.

When Czar Alexander II is murdered, Jews are sought as scapegoats. Although the hanged conspirators all bear Russian names, the incited masses are most easily appeased with Jewish blood. Pogroms spread like an epidemic. Noah wonders whether it is a tradition since time immemorial that the robbers remain with their booty and the victims with their hurt. Or whether there is indeed retribution and expiation.

Meanwhile, as a reaction to the massacres, Zionist ideology finds receptive ears in Noah's town. The call of Daniel Deronda for a reconstitution of the Jewish nation on its historic soil of Palestine reaches him. It is followed by Lawrence Oliphant's call to the people of the Bible to return to the land of the Bible. The Jewish magnates fear that endorsement of a Jewish exodus from the pogrom-ridden land might cast doubt upon their own loyalty to their Russian fatherland. Although Oliphant fails to win the rich and the influential Jews to his vision, young Jewish idealists do set out for the Promised Land under the banner of Bilu. Noah joins such a group and gets as far as Istambul. In the course of his weeks of traveling and waiting, however, he has a change of heart. He becomes conscience-stricken when he recalls his abandoned wife and children. He is not as free as his companions of Bilu. They may proceed to carve out a national Jewish existence in the Holy Land. He has no right to shed his responsibilities towards his family. He must return. Nevertheless, this return is not a retreat or a descent. It too is a dedication and a service to his people.

Just as the earth returns every morning to its position of previous mornings and just as the sun returns every spring to its spring location of earlier years, and yet with each return a new day and a new year is born, so too the wayfarer, completing his round of duties and accepting normal responsibilities, was venturing ever further and further on the road to holiness and to an understanding of God's universal order. Noah, the Jewish Faust, who set out in search of knowledge

without limit and righteousness without any trace of wickedness, thus ends by accepting the fact that there is a boundary
to human knowledge and that there is no righteousness
without some taint of evil, or wickedness without some kernel
of goodness. A superior power does exist. We must bow to
it and do its bidding, even if we do not entirely comprehend
its design or purpose.

Menahem Boraisha's philosophic and religious brooding
reaches its climax in this epic of a simple individual's efforts
to rise to moral eminence and to obtain a glimpse of pure
essential truths. During the poet's last years, two other major
poems were completed. These reflected new doubts that
arose in him during the years of the Holocaust and they
reaffirmed his hard-won faith in the meaningfulness of Jewish
and human existence.

In one poem, Menahem attempted a moral stocktaking
of his own generation. Above the ashes of Warsaw's ruined
ghetto, he engaged in a dialogue with his mentor I. L.
Peretz, whom he invoked from the Beyond. Both relive scenes
of horror, moral degradation, extermination and desperate
heroism. They emerge with faith in God and man unshaken.

In *Moses,* a dramatic poem not entirely completed at
the time of Menahem's death in 1949, the poet was still
engaged in reaching out to God. His Moses had caught a
glimpse of the nameless, eternal "I Am" and it became his
task to raise his people from slavery in Egypt to holiness in
their Promised Land. This task required superhuman patience and fortitude, since physical enslavement had also
resulted in moral decay. Though Moses succeeded in bringing his people out of the land of the Pharaohs and in having
them sense the nearness of God at Sinai, he could not eradi-
cate their longing for Egyptian fleshpots nor prevent their
relapsing into defilement again and again. Besides, in the
very effort to uproot evil in their midst, he had to exercise
utmost severity and wade in blood. Even the God-intoxicated
Moses could not always scourge with the fire of wrath. As
a human being he made concessions to human frailties. He
yielded on occasion to his people's weaknesses, though less
so than his gentler brother Aaron, for he too was blood of

their blood and bone of their bone. The process of evolving a group of liberated slaves into a holy people, God's people, was a gradual process and, after forty years in the wilderness, Moses had only begun it. His successor, Joshua, would continue it and the hundred generations after Joshua would still not succeed in completing it. Yet Moses had set his people on the right path and they would march on and on as the moral vanguard of the human species.

Menahem lived to see the founding of Israel. He hailed enthusiastically this historic event. But he also recognized that many physical pitfalls and many moral temptations faced this young state of an old people. Would it strive for normalcy and an end of wayfaring? Or would it continue to pioneer on the road set for God's people by Moses, the Prophets, and all the later seekers of a moral realm on earth?

These questions were also asked during the same time by Ephraim Auerbach, a poet of no less distinction and originality than Menahem. He also found inspiration in the past of his people and in the present of the reborn Jewish homeland. His longing for Israel was intense throughout half a century of lyric creativity and found repeated expression in his works. But only on rare occasions could he sate this longing by temporarily sojourning there.

Auerbach began as the singer of Bessarabian Jewry. Born in 1892 in the town of Beltz, he could trace his paternal ancestry back to the family of Rashi, the famous biblical commentator. The Auerbach home resounded with song and dance on Sabbaths and holidays. In his youngest years, Ephraim chanted portions of the Bible and Talmud. Soon he learned to insert his own words into rhythmic molds and to find joy and emotional release in creating lyrics. From the age of seventeen, his Yiddish verses and tales were published in Vilna, Warsaw and Odessa.

Auerbach's ancestors had been the town's ritual slaughterers—*shochtim*—for several generations. His father had to yield to family pressure and continue the profession, despite his distaste for it, since it conferred social prestige upon its practitioners in that Orthodox community.

The sensitive poet, however, succeeded in escaping. In

his lyrics in *The Red Thread* (*Der Roiter Fodem,* 1927), he wrote how, as a child, he felt the pain of the gentle doves whose throats were slit to provide meat. He heard the moaning of the oxen when the red river of life flowed out of their necks, and he saw their terror-frozen eyes fixed upon him with mute questioning. His joy in dancing with the calf in the springtime was tempered by awareness of the gory end destined for it at the hands of his father.

In 1911, Auerbach left for Warsaw, and a year later, fascinated by Zionist idealism, he joined the pioneers who set out for Palestine. He worked there in Judean colonies until the Turks compelled the evacuation of the young Russian Jewish immigrants to Egypt. He then joined the newly formed Jewish Legion and fought under Josef Trumpeldor at Gallipoli. When he fell ill, he was sent back to Alexandria and from there, in 1915, made his way to the United States, which became his home.

Caravans (*Karavanen*), his first volume of verse, appeared in 1918. A few of its lyrics harked back to idyllic moods of early years along the Dniester, but most dealt with his impressions of Palestine. Included is his farewell to his mother, whom he comforts with the thought that he is leaving a realm of frost and ice for a warm and verdant land, a land always remembered in her devotional prayers, a land where he would not have to trade and haggle but could plant and harvest the almonds about which she sang in her lullabies. An unbreakable thread led from the distant, desolated land of his forefathers to his longing heart. This thread tugged at him until it brought him to Judean shores, caves and hills, well-known to him from dreams and *cheder* memories.

The poet saw the Palestinian landscape with romantic eyes: a shepherd playing on a flute while grazing his flock; the brown Yemenite maiden bearing her earthenware jar to the well; the chanting cameleer swinging past along fig trees; the Arab lover serenading the beautiful Fatima. But Auerbach also sang of the joy of physical labor, his delight in reaping golden barley, cutting grape clusters from vines, planting saplings for a new forest, and accompanying them with hope and love and a prayer for dew and rain. A youthful freshness permeates these verses, with the word "joy" constantly repeated.

Throughout Auerbach's long career as a poet, he sought out themes, images and thought-associations based on Jewish sources. His subjects ranged from Adam and Cain to contemporary Jewish events. In his early lyrics, the landscape and picturesque figures of Bessarabian Jewish communities fascinated him. In his middle period, the American Jewish experience became important. In his later period, the European Jewish catastrophe and the rise of the Jewish State became an obsession. In his last lyrics, he reverted to Bessarabian Jewry, now annihilated, but which once teemed with vitality and continued to live in his imagination. Despite half a century on American soil, he was haunted by the melodies of Beltz. As late as 1963, his poems in the volume *The Steppe Is Awake (Vakh Is Der Step)* still dealt exclusively with the cultural milieu of his childhood years in Bessarabia.

Auerbach accepted the basic doctrine of Hassidism that to be a Jew was good per se and that goodness was synonymous with happiness. In *Pure Is the Old Source (Loiter Is Der Alter Kval,* 1940), he contrasted the joy of goodness with the sadness of evil. He held that just as trees obtained their vital essence from deep roots in good earth, so too man derived his sustenance from deep-rooted optimistic faith in justice and goodness. Happy were those who sat in the dwellings of goodness and were warmed by the light of God. Pure was the biblical source and it supplied him with ever new inspiration. Beyond the ageless biblical figures, Auerbach also recalled to life legendary figures ranging from Baal-Shem, father of Hassidism, to Hershele Ostropoler, the Jewish Till Eulenspiegel, as well as by such picturesque figures of his native Beltz as the Red Flutist and Pusi the Water Carrier.

Auerbach's most cheerful volume of verse was *Ada's Songbook (Ada's Liederbukh,* 1934). It consisted of songs composed for his six-year-old daughter Ada and featured as characters the dog Hintl-Vintl, the cat Kitzele-Ketzele, the goat Tzigele-Migele, and the horse Ferdl-Berdl. The poet animated the inanimate. Windowpanes smiled. Raindrops danced with glee and were scolded by a child for not waiting with their dance until she got home. A half-baked, half-burned loaf of bread suffered rejection all day long but found appreciation at the hands of a poor little girl at the close of the day. The girl bought it for a pitttance and shared it with her brothers and sisters, all of them singing as they sated themselves with its goodness before dropping off to sleep.

Auerbach's lyrics of the American scene centered about New York. In the volume *The Red Thread,* he sang of the immigrant quarters in more cheerful tones than did his predecessors, Yiddish social poets like David Edelstadt or Morris Rosenfeld. In Orchard Street, located in the heart of New York's Lower East Side, it was not the filth and poverty that he observed but the merry mingling of peddlers and customers, the glances and colorful phrases of man and maid, the play of a bit of sunlight on tousled heads and eloquent beards. In a cycle of fifteen sonnets, he reproduced the mood of the Bowery and its tramps. The denizens of the gutter and sidewalks lived truthfully even if shabbily. Theirs was lucid pain, naked honesty, disillusioned understanding, strange charm. Wallowing in dirt, at the edge of the abyss, they fathomed the deep, pure meaning of human existence.

Under the influence of the European catastrophe, Auerbach composed religious lyrics. In the volume *The Tents of Jacob* (*Yakov's Getseltn,* 1945), he comforted the survivors of the Holocaust and beseeched the mercy of heaven for the Jews, living and dead, all of whom had been purified by their unfathomable suffering. He lamented with his coreligionists who were weeping by the waters of the Vistula and with those who were penned within ghetto walls. He recalled the heroism of the Jews of Tulchin who, almost three centuries before the revolt of Warsaw's ghetto dwellers, defended Jewish honor against Cossack hordes and died for the sanctification of God's name.

During the war years, sadness engulfed this lyricist of joy, a recurrent weeping in the stillness of the night, a moaning for a generation prematurely cut off from life. Never did he yield to despair, however, or question that all creation was imbued with the Creator's will. As an antidote to despair, he invoked the spirit of Rabbi Nachman of Bratslav from the Beyond and he had this Hassidic sage and storyteller fortify the faith of contemporary disciples by relating to them a still untold tale: the redemption of the Land of Evil by contact with the Land of Goodness.

The Tents of Jacob also contained an adaptation of the Song of Songs, interpreted, in accordance with tradition, as an allegorical dialogue between God and Israel, God's beloved people. In addition, there was a poetic drama based on a legend of Beltz. During the Turkish occupation, cells had been chiseled into the walls of a cave in this town so that it might serve as a prison. Jews regarded this cave with awe and whispered that it led on and on, coming to the surface in the land of Israel. In the first two scenes of the poetic drama, Auerbach depicted the privations of the surviving Jews who escaped annihilation by taking refuge in the dark, damp, dreary cave. But in the final scene, they found the far exit in the land where vines and almonds grew. They emerged from the darkness in which they had long been entombed to the sunlit radiance of the Holy Land, where a new life could blossom for them. There, on their own soil, the remnants of Israel would again plow and sow and reap.

After the founding of the Jewish State, the poet revisited the land which he had first experienced as a young pioneer on the eve of the First World War. His rapture in witnessing in Tel Aviv the first-anniversary celebration of Israel's independence was reflected in *The White City,* composed in 1949 and published in a Hebrew-Yiddish bilingual edition in 1960. He recalled the days in 1913 when, barefoot and hungry, he trod the sandy dunes of Tel Aviv, kneaded the loam, and planted the cool shade for the first boulevards. Now the proud, white metropolis was full grown, its colorful populace, drawn from all tribes, was dancing in the streets, and its veterans were heading a Jewish government.

A decade later, in the volume *Golden Sunset (Gildene Shkiye,* 1959), he sang a song beyond all his songs, a hymn to his people's return from the thorny roads of exile. He saw the new life blossoming in redeemed towns and villages and he blessed his Bessarabian contemporaries who had found their way to the Emek, Galilee, Jerusalem. He saw himself as the chronicler of the desert generation, doomed to die in the wilderness en route to the Promised Land. Yet, it had been granted him to catch a vision of his reinvigorated, rejuvenated people. "It is evening. I sit beside the Mediterranean. Waves with foaming lips kiss the stones. Here I am a guest, soon to leave. How shall I tie together my here with my there?"

As a late reaper in the Yiddish field, Auerbach was well aware that his rhymes would not set many spirits afire or change the course of galloping events, but perhaps they would brighten a thought in an individual mind or send a moment's thrill through a human heart. This sufficed him in his later years when, sated with slogans, he sipped sadness drop by drop and found compensation in mating moods to words, ever quieter moods to ever lower-toned words.

Zishe Weinper (1892–1957) was born in the same year as Auerbach, grew up in a similar Hassidic environment in the townlet of Trisk in Volynia, and also fought with the Jewish Legion at Gallipoli. His father was a cantor at the court of the Rebbe of Trisk. After a traditional education up to his sixteenth year, young Weinper became interested in the new Hebrew and Yiddish literatures and began to wander from town to town throughout Ukraine and Poland in search of bread and learning.

In 1913 he landed in New York and came under the spell of "Die Yunge." Soon there gathered about him a group of poets, who thought of themselves as the youngest of the young. They included Aaron Nissenson, B. J. Bialostotsky, and Naftoli Gross. They published their earliest contributions in a magazine edited by Weinper under the revealing title *Beginning* (*Der Onheib,* 1918). However, when the editor joined the Jewish Legion to fight for a Jewish homeland, this venture came to a premature end.

Weinper's first volume of lyrics, *From Our Land* (*Fun Undzer Land,* 1920), dealt with his impressions, emotions and experiences as a legionnaire, his boundless joy as his ship neared the shores of the Holy Land, his longing for a

Messiah who would lead the vanguard of Jewish redeemers, his sadness and animation amidst the ruins of Jerusalem.

Disillusioned with the British overlords of Palestine who had replaced the Turkish overlords but who did not redeem the land for the Jews, Weinper returned to the United States at the end of 1919. His year and a half in Palestine, however, remained engraved upon his mind and heart and found expression in many later lyrics and in his book *With the Jewish Legion,* published in 1942 at the height of the Second World War, when again a movement for a Jewish army was taking shape.

Weinper had, on the whole, an optimistic attitude toward life, until 1929. His gayest lyrics were his songs for children, written in the 1920's when he was a teacher in Yiddish schools. Many of these were set to music by outstanding Jewish composers and were sung on the concert stage as well as in Yiddish classrooms. Weinper's optimism, however, was subjected to great strain during the years of the Great Depression in America and of Nazi dominance in Europe. The carefree singer was disconcerted by the cynical tolerance of intolerance, by the prevalence of poverty amidst plenty, and by the widespread indifference to injustice toward his people.

Called upon to react in verse to the ever worsening political and social scene, he became the poet of the radical left and a moving spirit of "Ykuf," the Yiddish Cultural Federation, from 1938 on. This led to his alienation from the mainstream of Yiddish letters, an alienation under which he suffered intensely and to which he reacted vigorously in the lyric volume *Pain and Joy (Laid un Fraid,* 1954). He arrived at the conclusion that not only in Judea but also in every hill and in every dale, from Birobidjan to Arizona, wherever the Jewish tongue was heard in song and lamentation, there was the holy land of Israel. He sought comfort by identifying his own striving with that of the ancient prophets in his *Poems of the Prophets (Poemen Vegn Die Neviim,* 1951) and in visions of grandiose natural phenomena such as he described in lyrics of the Grand Canyon and the Canadian Rockies. In vain! Weinper's unreciprocated love for the Jewish people left him disconsolate and frustrated at the end.

A harsher fate befell a poet far more talented than Weinper and hurled him from a high summit of adulation to a profounder depth of misery and abject loneliness. He was Yitzkhok Reiss, one of the earliest members of "Die Yunge," who attained greater fame under the pseudonym of Moshe Nadir (1885–1943). Brought to New York from a small town in Eastern Galicia at the age of thirteen, he voiced his disappointment with his new environment in lyrics which began to appear in print before he was sixteen. In later years, nostalgia often overcame him for the ecstasy and dirt which he associated with Rivington Street on New York's Lower East Side, but in his earliest sketches, he emphasized only the travails of the immigrant generation and caricatured its efforts to graft townlet values onto the great metropolis.

Nadir's youthful poems, filled with *Weltschmerz*, were reminiscent of young Heine. Soon he mastered Heine's technique of reversing the flow of emotions in the course of a lyric, of shocking trusting readers with sobering irony just as they were succumbing to sweet sentimentalism. This mixture of gentle lyricism and biting irony remained with Nadir throughout the four decades of his creative career and was reflected in his prose and verse, in his dramas and sketches, in his essays and aphorisms. Under various pseudonyms and in many literary genres, he acted the clown, the lover, the intoxicated idealist, the despairing cynic, and all his poses were assumed to be genuine. In the deepest reaches of his soul, however, he found life empty, barren of meaning, vanity of vanities.

From abysmal loneliness and nihilistic moodiness, he fled back to the Galicia of his boyhood dreams, he roamed on to Vienna and Paris, but soon found that the beauty he sought in Europe was only a surface varnish masking a decaying civilization. He thereupon returned to New York and to Philadelphia, participated in the strident literary innovations of "Die Yunge," edited humorous periodicals such as *Der Grosser Kundus* and *Der Yidisher Gazlen*, published his first book of erotic miniatures, *Wild Roses (Vilde Rozen,*

1915), and contributed lyric, philosophic sketches to the liberal daily *Der Tog*. Translating Peter Altenberg, Jerome K. Jerome and Mark Twain, he also assimilated into his own Yiddish style some of their characteristics and was soon hailed as the greatest Yiddish humorist since Sholom Aleichem.

While delighting others with flashes of his wit and the brilliance of his paradoxes, however, Nadir himself was weighed down by a constant awareness of the senselessness of life and death and the transitoriness of all values and ideals. His bohemianism turned into an unnatural affectation. His laughter at all existing institutions and conventional ideas turned to bitter sarcasm. His extreme individualism prevented his becoming rooted anywhere. He yawned at the world, sneered at his contemporaries, succumbed to a philosophy of pantragism, and entitled an entire collection of his lyrics *Delusions*. He confessed that tragic happenings no longer moved him since they occurred so often, women no longer impressed him since he knew too many of them too well, art was for him a beautiful word useful chiefly in salons, science pained him like rheumatism, readers were laughable jackasses, the whole world was hopelessly boring. From this universal ennui there was no escape unless one could forget oneself. But, as an egocentric poet, he could not do so. He was ever immersed in introspection, in brooding over the ebb and flow of his emotions, in analyzing the products of his thinking, the fragmentation of his ego, the dissolution of his kaleidoscopic impressions and fleeting memories. Angry at life, he still loved it in all its capricious, banal and contradictory manifestations.

Flight to Communist circles for a time brought him release from deepest pessimism. In 1922 he became associated with the Communist daily *Freiheit* and through its columns he directed the darts of his venomous sarcasm against all who did not share his new vision. In 1926 he undertook a trip to Russia and returned a confirmed adherent of its Messianic gospel.

When the Communists in 1929 justified the Arab massacre of the Jews of Hebron, some of his associates on the

Freiheit could not stomach this daily's headline "Jewish Fascists and Englishmen Make Pogroms on Arabs," and resigned as a group. Nadir thereupon attacked them mercilessly. His vitriolic outbursts against his erstwhile colleagues Menahem Boraisha, Abraham Reisen, H. Leivick and Isaac Raboy, as well as against his earlier victims Abraham Cahan, S. Niger and dozens of prominent Jewish men of letters who eschewed Communism were collected in three volumes in 1935 and 1936. Outraged literary critics refused to review his books or even to reply to his attacks. Not until 1939 did disillusionment with his ideal set in.

When his adored Russians entered into a pact with Hitler's Germany, then he recognized that he had been led astray by a utopian will-o'-the-wisp and sought to atone for his literary misdeeds of many years. In an autobiographic confession written in April 1940, he pleaded for understanding of his predicament: "For every drop of blood that I drew with my pen, I paid with two drops from my heart's blood. This is no excuse for all those I attacked with such blind fanaticism and my heart weeps because of my deeds." By then, he was anathema to both Communists and non-Communists.

If Nadir's early poems echoed young Heine, his last poems were reminiscent of the dying German poet, to whom he repeatedly paid tribute and to whose fate he likened his own. Like Heine, the penitent Yiddish poet also sought to make his peace with the God of Israel from whom he had been estranged since his fifteenth year. He recognized that he had sinned against individual human beings even while he was engaged in a so-called holy war for a better humanity. He realized in the hellish flare of a world conflagration that force, bloodshed, revolution, despotism of right or left could not create a better society, but that only through a long process of education in tolerance, democracy, humanism could man ascend to a higher stage of civilization.

Broken-hearted, the most talented humorist among "Die Yunge" bade farewell to God and man in the final poems, published posthumously under the title *I Confess* (*Mode Ani*, 1944).

I. I. Schwartz, who was born in a Lithuanian townlet in 1885, the same year as Moshe Nadir, and who arrived in the United States in 1906, also participated in the publications of "Die Yunge," but always steered clear of the group's rebellious militancy. Just as in his superb translations of Bialik, Tchernikhovsky, Milton and Whitman he subordinated himself to these Hebrew and English poets, reproducing their spirit faithfully rather than imposing his own spirit upon the Yiddish text, so too in his original lyrics he preferred to let landscape, people and situations impose their will and their moods upon him. This is true also of his two longest poems, *Kentucky* (1925) and *Young Years* (*Yunge Yorn,* 1952), even though these are autobiographic in essence.

The latter poem affords an insight into the poet's childhood and youth until his departure for New York. It begins with his earliest memories of his Lithuanian birthplace and weaves a web of enchantment about his townlet along the banks of the Nieman. In this community Jews had been rooted for many generations, making a living as skilled craftsmen and busy tradesmen. Throughout adult life, they found some time each day for Talmud study at the communal houses of learning, their preferred relaxation and delight.

Nostalgically the poet recalls the closing years of the nineteenth century when the fountain of Jewishness streamed bright, clear and fresh. Time obliterated whatever bitterness, harshness and cruelty he had experienced and left a residue of mild sadness and here and there bits of pure joy. He remembered his father, the revered rabbi, dispensing justice and learning, and his mother sanctifying each holiday with her special cooking and baking. As a Jewish child, he was no less familiar with the Nile of the Book of Exodus than with his native streams, and the warmth of Galilee was as much his as were the snowstorms of the Baltic. At thirteen, Schwartz was sent away to study at Kovno's Yeshiva. Together with half a hundred other semi-starved youngsters, he studied, from seven in the morning to nine at night, the many tomes in which the heritage of all the older generations was contained. Beyond traditional subjects, there blossomed the new Hebrew of Bialik and the Yiddish of Frug, Morris Rosenfeld and Abraham Reisen, and found a way to young hearts. Above all, the royal figure of Herzl dawned upon Kovno's youth like a ray of light in the *Galut* darkness. But the path of the aspiring poet led him westward, despite yearning for the land of the Patriarchs and the Prophets.

The verse narrative ends with his parting from home and with his father's admonition: "Remain a Jew!"

Schwartz remained a Jew and a poet. Landing in America with the torrent of penniless Jewish immigrants, he soon found congenial spirits who were seeking expression for their uniqueness in melodious songs and in the visual arts. Escaping from the knout of Cossacks, they felt fire coursing through their veins as they stepped on the New World's blessed soil. Schwartz felt happy in their midst, since their striving was not for fortunes of gold but rather for the riches of the spirit. Unwilling to submit to the hellish sweatshops in New York's maelstrom, he wandered westward in 1918. He stayed in Kentucky for a few years and engaged in business on a small scale with his meager capital. His experiences and observations were recorded in *Kentucky,* his poetic epic of the Jewish pioneering peddler.

The honest, intelligent, persevering hero of this narrative also began by walking from town to town with a pack on his back, sleeping in haystacks and barns, until he finally found a desirable home among kind neighbors. These helped him to dispose of his wares and encouraged him to settle among them. His store, started in an abandoned shack, prospered. With his first savings, he brought over his family from Europe. As the community grew, it attracted other Jewish pioneers, a cobbler, a tailor, a capmaker. These Jewish settlers were not content to remain merely craftsmen. Restless and venturesome, they risked expansion and diversification, until their hovels became the town's department stores. Soon they felt the need of a synagogue, not only as a religious center but also as a warm communal Jewish home. With the passing of years, their children grew into adulthood, liberated from the harried sadness which had plagued the youth of the preceding generation. With frank eyes and sensitive ears, these children grasped at opportunities constantly opening up in Dixieland. They had no scruples about mating with non-Jewish neighbors and striking out on new roads. Orthodox practices no longer satisfied them. For their religious requirements they needed a pastor's sermons on Sundays and a Reform temple with organ and choir on Saturdays. The pioneering peddler, having become a prosperous pillar of Kentucky society, saw children and grandchildren flocking about him. And when the final hour struck for him, the tired old patriarch, he was lulled to eternal sleep by golden dreams in which were commingled Psalms of David and melodies of Dixie.

Schwartz's epic called attention to tendencies and forces in American Jewish life which were to gather momentum in later decades of ever greater dispersion beyond the Atlantic seaboard. But it was the Introspective movement after World War I that widened still further the horizon of Yiddish poetry and brought to it innovations which were then being introduced by American lyricists writing in English.

3

The Introspective Poets

THE INTROSPECTIVE MOVEMENT in poetry, for which the Yiddish designation is "Insichism," arose in 1919, when the three young poets A. Glanz-Leyeles (1889–1966), Jacob Glatstein (b. 1896) and N. B. Minkoff (1893–1958) agreed upon a common program and upon the founding of the literary organ *In Sich* for the propagation of their credo and the publication of their works and those of allied spirits.

Older poets, such as Yehoash (1870–1927) and H. Leivick (1888–1962) encouraged them. Soon there rallied to their standard the young immigrant poets B. Alquit (1896–1963), Bernard Lewis (1889–1925), Kalman Heisler (1899–1966), Reuben Ludwig (1895–1926), Jacob Stodolsky (1890–1962) and Alef Katz (1898–1969). Contributors to later issues of *In Sich* included the poets J. I. Segal (1896–1954), Michel Licht (1893–1953), Eliezer Greenberg (b. 1896), A. Lutzky (1894–1957), Aaron Kurtz (1891–1964), Shloime Schwartz (b. 1912), Celia Drapkin (1888–1956), Esther Shumiacher (b. 1899) and Anna Margolin (1887–1952). Shortly before *In Sich* ceased publication in 1940, the first writers of a still newer group known as "Young Vilna," Abraham Sutzkever

(b. 1913) and Leiser Wolf (1910–1943), made their American debut in its monthly issues. By then, the original founders of the movement had matured, had discarded flamboyant proclamations, and were engaged in defending their non-political devotion to art against the onslaughts of aggressive so-called proletarian poets.

The American Yiddish lyric had been in a state of revolt against traditionalism since 1907, when "Die Yunge" had challenged the social and moralizing poets dominant during the pioneering generation and had succeeded in emancipating the Yiddish muse from servitude to anarchist and socialist causes and in replacing utopian visions, calls to revolution, and sweatshop elegies with the reproduction of individual moods and longings. Now a lyric group, younger than the "youngsters" of a dozen years earlier, was demanding attention.

In contrast to "Die Yunge," who had emphasized art for art's sake and who had sought to communicate faithfully impressions that impinged upon them from the world without, the new group of Insichism stressed poetry as the expression of emotionalized thought or intellectualized emotion and sought to reshape and to reinterpret the environment in accordance with the individual's *Gestalt* or psychic configuration.

Introspectivism meant peering into oneself. The Insichists wished to give a structure to the chaotic multiplicity of phenomena, an organic form based upon their own uniqueness. Their earliest manifesto of January 1920 proclaimed: "The world exists for us only insofar as it is mirrored in us, insofar as it touches us. The world is a non-existent category, a fiction, if it is not related to us. It becomes a reality only in us and through us."

Leyeles questioned the existence of an objective world. Even if such a world did exist in some chaotic, amorphic way, we could not possibly know it. All we know is ourselves. It is our soul that organizes the chaos. We create or recreate the world in our image. In us are all worlds, past, present and future. What we see within ourselves is the only truth for us.

Minkoff, too, despaired of objective reality. He did not trust facts. He sought the truth behind and beyond the facts. "All that we see with our eyes has deceived us. We no longer believe in the reality of the world about us. We believe only in what our inner will can create. This is our true world." He, therefore, called upon poets to find their way through the chaos of apparent facts to the absolute, dazzling, creative clarity which pulsated in their innermost being.

The Insichist concept of poetry as the expression of a poet's inner panorama, no matter how kaleidoscopic, contradictory or unclear it might be, paralleled the egocentric formulation of the Expressionists dominant in Central Europe during and after World War I. Like the Expressionist poets, the Yiddish group found existing metrical and stanzaic patterns too confining. The inner melody of a poem was for them the essential element. They therefore preferred to experiment with free verse as practiced in American poetry from Walt Whitman to Amy Lowell. They felt that every lyric must have its own individual rhythm.

If a poet wrote about a subway, about the sand of the sea in summer, and about his love for a girl in the same rhythm or meter, then at least two of his poems must be false, probably all three. Without entirely rejecting the straitjacket of regular rhythms, the Insichists believed that free verse could better reproduce the accelerated, irregular, noisy tempo of the metropolis and the machine civilization. Seeking to narrow the boundary between prose and verse, they refused to accept rhyme as an essential ingredient, but they were willing to use it for special effects in combination with free verse, even as Vachel Lindsay, whom they admired, was using it.

Although the Insichists called also for a widening of the lyric horizon to include any and every subject, and although they claimed the urbanization of the Yiddish lyric as one of their supreme achievements, their chief contribution resided in innovations of style and not of content: their creation of ever newer and subtler rhythms, their concentration on essential traits rather than heaping of detail upon detail, their emphasis on the simple word rather than the decorative one, their stress on the exact, sculptured phrase and the concrete, sharply delineated image rather than the dreamy diffusiveness preferred by their Impressionist forerunners.

Aaron Glanz, who in 1914 adopted the pseudonym of A. Leyeles for his verse but not for his prose, was the oldest member of the Insichists. In 1905, at the age of sixteen, he emigrated from Poland to London in search of higher education, and four years later he continued on to New York. During his student years at Columbia University, from 1910 to 1913, he obtained a thorough knowledge of American literature. Afterwards he proved, by his superb renderings of Edgar Allan Poe's "The Raven," "Annabel Lee," and other lyrics, his ability to translate complex English rhythms into equally effective Yiddish rhythms.

His first original volume, *Labyrinth* (1918), showed the influence of the American Modernists but also his mastery of intricate traditional forms. It preceded the founding of Insichism and did not spurn Impressionistic effects. In one poem, "Rain," he aimed at imitating in trochaic dimeters the harsh fall of heavy raindrops. In another poem, "Snow," he sought to reproduce in trochaic stanzas of varying length the soft fall of snowflakes. In "Nocturne," he tried to convey through an accumulation of adjectives the mood of night —a mood of weariness, satiety, melancholy, uncanniness, ghostliness. In "Rest," he joined various colors from pale blue and pale violet to orange and tender rose, and various images from a soft sofa with silver-silken cover to dying flowers and medieval magic in order to create a unitary impression of autumnal tiredness.

Leyeles, however, also sang in strident tones of the sights and sounds of New York, its haste and confusion, its Bowery figures and asphalt pavements, its streetcars and granite skyscrapers. His subject matter was universal rather than specifically Jewish, with the single exception of his final poem, "Yehuda Halevi." This poem related the story of the medieval Sephardic minstrel's longing for his ideally envisaged Zion and his death at the gates of Jerusalem when he attempted to realize his dream.

In the lyrics of *Young Autumn* (*Yungharbst*, 1922), the

Introspectivism of Leyeles was full grown. When he now composed a new poem on "Snow," he sought to capture in images the essence of a mound of snow and not the temporary mood it evoked. As he compressed the frosty whiteness of the snow in his hand, he felt its soul running down in cold tears. This evoked the image of an expired infant whose mother was still wiping the last tears from its pale, chilled cheeks. When he now composed a "Nocturne," the emphasis was on images and thought associations that spanned many years and not on the immediate impression of a New York night under the cold shimmer of an electric lamp. The subjects of Leyeles now ranged from cats and worms, chaos, madness, and pogroms to maidens with musical, exotic names by the shores of the Ganges, along the sands of the desert, and within the harems of fabled Samarkand. Free verse was now his normal medium.

As the chief theoretician of Insichism, Leyeles continued throughout later decades to battle for his concept of poetry as rhythmically disciplined thinking, feeling, experiencing. He prefaced his lyric volume *Fabius Lind* (1937) with a vigorous restatement of his creed.

Fabius Lind, the title hero, is Leyeles. In him are commingled two main streams which had their origins in Lodz and in New York. His ancestry and childhood experiences molded him into a Jewish personality to whom every aspect of his people's past and present was precious. But his adult years were spent in the American metropolis. Hence New York also became his spiritual no less than his physical home. He loves and sings of its teeming life from the Battery and Bowery to Crotona Park and Bronx Park. If he reacts in anger and in sadness to Hitler's anti-Jewishness, he reacts no less intensely to the hurt inflicted upon America by reactionary forces. He cannot cavort in the roundelay of carefree life as do others. He dreams throughout his days and nights of a non-existent utopian land and of human beings as they should be and not as they are.

Jews, whom others despise and drag through horrors, come closest to his ideal of man because amidst their suffering they still scorn the might of their oppressors. For a brief moment he puts his faith in the Birobidjan pioneers as symbols of Jewish rejuvenation in the land of the Soviets. But he is quickly disillusioned by Stalinist reality. He is no less shocked by American injustice and laments the fate of Sacco and Vanzetti in a poem of 1927, the year of their execution. His disappointment with America, however, is only temporary and he emerges with renewed faith in America's historic ideals, a faith he documents most eloquently in the lyrics of *America and I* (*Amerika Un Ich*, 1963).

The lyrics of *A Jew at Sea* (*A Yied Oifn Yam*, 1947) were composed mainly under the impact of the Jewish catastrophe in Eastern Europe. This catastrophe cries out in him. He is ashamed to walk in the sunlight along the banks of the Hudson while his kinsmen are being ground to dung along the Vistula. He is pursued by nightmares of the horror being perpetrated at Maidanek and Treblinka. After a moment of weakness in calling for vengeance upon those who desecrated the face of man, he recovers and calls upon the surviving Jews to react rather in typically Jewish fashion to the evil which has spread over the globe—by becoming better, purer, holier.

A verse preface to this volume opens with the line: "In the beginning was the melody." Only a person who has an ear for a poem's inner cadence is at home in the mystic land of poesy. A decade later, in the introduction to the lyrics of *At the Foot of the Mountain* (*Beim Fuss Fun Barg*, 1957), Leyeles restates his opposition both to pure abstract poetry stripped of emotional content and to poetry as the expression of untamed feeling utterly devoid of ideas. He continues to insist that poetry is always concrete, the direct or indirect expression of a real experience in which thought and feeling, feeling and thought, rise together at the same time like two leaves from a single root. He holds that the best Jewish poets have always sung of the meaning and purpose of life, the omnipresence and splendor of God, the destiny of the Jewish people, and, above all, man's submission to a higher entity. Non-Jews might content themselves with songs of unbridled emotions and unfettered instincts. Jews believe in the taming of emotions and in the fettering of instincts by reason.

Of Leyeles's experiments in poetic drama, only *Shlomo Molcho* (1926) aroused considerable interest. This drama centers about the Portuguese Marrano of the early sixteenth century who returned to Judaism and who was regarded by many as the Messiah. The drama is overrich in ideas. It moves from the royal palace at Lisbon and the synagogue of Joseph Caro in Safed to the ghetto of Rome, the chambers of the Pope, and the emperor's court at Regensburg. The basic conflict of ideas rages between the two Messianic aspirants, David Reubeni and Shlomo Molcho.

Reubeni wants to redeem the Jewish people by the power of the sword and to restore them to a normal existence on their ancient soil. Molcho, a disciple of cabalistic lore, wants the Jews to remain in the Diaspora and to become the self-sacrificing redeemers of all mankind. In this ideological conflict, Molcho triumphs over Reubeni, his teacher who becomes his follower. But other dramatic conflicts also come to the fore in which Molcho becomes the victim. In one scene the extreme demands of young Molcho for absolute sincerity and holiness in word and deed are opposed by a wise, aged Marrano who has become a Prince of the Church and the king's confessor and who uses his influence to mitigate somewhat Jewish suffering and to ward off threatening, more stringent anti-Jewish decrees. In another scene Molcho's efforts to convince Jews and non-Jews of an impending Messianic salvation are opposed by the Jewish leaders along the Tiber, who bear responsibility for the survival of the endangered, oppressed community and who fear that his arousal of unjustified and unrealizable Jewish hopes might lead to an irreparable catastrophe. In still another scene the intense otherworldly faith of the Jewish visionary is juxtaposed with the lack of faith of the all-too-worldly Pope Clement VII, scion of the House of Medici.

The climactic scene, in which Molcho the Jew calls upon Emperor Charles V, mightiest ruler of Christendom, to give up illusions of temporal power, to dissolve the empire, and to initiate the return of man to God, is strongly reminiscent of Friedrich Schiller's climactic scene in *Don Carlos,* when Marquis Posa calls upon King Philip of Spain to establish a reign of religious tolerance, freedom of thought, and human fraternity in all his realms. In both plays the monarch is deeply moved for a moment by the splendor of the grandiose vision, but both conclude by turning over the Messianic dreamers to the Inquisition.

The most memorable performance of the drama took place in the doomed ghetto of Vilna toward the close of 1941 before an audience of *morituri.* The poet Abraham Sutzkever, who composed a prologue for this occasion, reported that he saw the performance through a veil of tears.

Leyeles also deals with Jewish Messianic longing in a second drama, *Asher Lemlen* (1928). On the eve of the Lutheran Reformation, when a peasant revolt threatens, Messianic visions come to the Jew Asher Lemlen. These visions help to fan the rebellion. However, when Lemlen's followers wish to join in the struggle against oppressive aristocrats and landowners, he opposes the use of brute force. He counsels delay until God's will is made more manifest. He opposes bloodshed under any circumstances. He cannot face reality, in which pure and impure ingredients are tangled. He can only sacrifice himself and fall a victim.

In his seventy-fifth year, Leyeles visited Israel for the first time and was stimulated to a new burst of lyric creativity. The poet, who had been entranced throughout his life by beauty as a goal, saw in Israel a free, sovereign Jewish community to which, as in days of old, beauty came, if at all, as a byproduct and not as an objective of group activity.

In a poem *Joseph and Judah,* penned in Israel, he contrasted the dazzling beauty of Joseph with the earthbound virility of Judah. Joseph, the favorite of Jacob, saw in dream-visions lords bowing low before him and peoples subjected to his will; but now Joseph's descendants, even as those of Reuben and Simeon, have disappeared from the face of the globe, and Joseph himself is but a legend of beauty, sad and nostalgic. Judah, on the other hand, less beloved by his father and less intent on dominating others, still lives a life of service. His descendants still wander over the earth bearing his burden of pain and memories, and are still attached to his heaven and his inward vision of service to his fellow men. Now and then Judah betakes himself to his old home, kisses its soil, builds anew structures of stone and loam, but soon thereafter he resumes his roaming over the world. He is, he exists, he carries on.

A similar refrain "We are here, we are here," concluded Leyeles's cycle of poems on *En Gedi,* composed after his visit to this Israel outpost on the Dead Sea. He described his rapture in the new vineyards of En Gedi, vineyards that re-called memories of Saul, David and Solomon, that looked out upon the heroic ramparts of Massada, and now re-echo the sound of cymbals, tambourines and the gay songs of youths and maidens.

Leyeles's songs of Israel appeared in the Israel quarterly *Die Goldene Keyt* shortly before and after his death. Its editor, Abraham Sutzkever, called them miracles of poetic renewal, fresh, clairvoyant, melodious, even though composed in the poet's late seventies, reminiscent of the young, pure rhythms of the earliest songs, but more symphonic and more Jewish.

Far more intense than in the case of Leyeles was the transformation of his Introspectivist co-founder Jacob Glatstein from a beauty-intoxicated cosmopolite to a lyric spokes-man of Jewish tragedy and Jewish rebirth.

Glatstein, too, ranks among the finest lyricists in the Yid-dish tongue. His earliest book of verse appeared in 1921, seven years after his arrival in the United States from his native Lublin, in Poland. He had begun to write at thirteen and published his first short story soon after landing in New York in 1914. Fascinated by the unlimited opportunities for higher education which opened up to immigrants, he quickly acquired a knowledge of English and was admitted to the law school of New York University. There he struck up a friendship with a fellow student, N. B. Minkoff and soon both came under the influence of Leyeles, slightly older, who had already attracted wide attention with his lyric volume *Labyrinth* (1918).

In 1921, a year after the three poets published their credo

71 - 80 *y*

of Introspectivism, Glatstein's first volume, applying this credo, appeared. The book bore no title but only the name of the young author. Seeking to avoid parochialism in the choice of subject matter, he preferred to invoke Buddha and Brahma rather than Jehovah, and to sing of Nirvana and of proud monarchs who rode victoriously into conquered towns at the head of sword-flashing warriors. He delighted in original sound effects. He replaced rhyme and metrical stanzas with complex assonances, alliteration and onomatopoeia.

Free Verses (Freie Fersen, 1926) was the title of Glatstein's second volume. Jewish themes were still muted but did break through now and then. The poet spoke not only through the voice of King Canute, who vainly bade the waves of time to stand still, but also through the voice of King Saul, who would gladly have exchanged his care-filled throne for the earlier carefree guardianship of his father's flocks. The poet bewailed the poor lot of a Chinese family and also the mournful end of King David over whose dying nights Abishag, the young Shunamite, maintained vigil.

Two other booklets of verse followed, in which the poet's mastery of Yiddish ripened. But it was not until tragedy broke upon the Jewish people that he became the lyric interpreter of their woe and grandeur.

In 1934, after an absence of two decades, Glatstein revisited his native Lublin. His trip from New York to his arrival in Poland was recorded in the prose volume *When Yash Set Out (Venn Yash Is Gefuhrn,* 1938). Most chapters dealt with his five days on board ship and the international assortment of travelers encountered. Some were returning to their permanent home in Europe while others were vacationing abroad, but all were released from normal inhibitions as they floated between heaven and the watery depths. They readily communicated memories and emotions, even such as were usually kept out of sight when on solid land. Their revelations provided insight into the various currents of thought, national and social stratification, as well as individual yearnings and ambitions in the 1930's.

The later chapters dealt with the train trip across the European continent, over which the shadow of Hitlerism was then spreading. While non-Jews made their way to pleasure-resorts in France, Italy, Spain and Switzerland, Jews were en route to relatives in Poland, Rumania, Lithuania and Soviet Russia. "I look upon their darkened faces and the thought occurs to me that twenty-five years from now, this type of traveler will have disappeared completely. The last survivors of an older generation are on their way to ancestral graves. Almost all their fathers and grandfathers have already passed away and soon the sons will also be gone. When grandsons will later travel to Soviet Russia, Poland, Lithuania or Rumania, it will be for them a summer resort like Paris, Switzerland, or Italy. For none of them will it constitute a homecoming. They will be journeying to those distant lands in order to affix foreign tags to their valises. They will not be seeking their old roots. The Poland which was will have died and the longing or hatred for that Poland will also have faded. They will be touring and not hastening to dying or dead fathers and mothers. In a quarter of a century something will be missing on these train-carriages."

Homecoming at Twilight (*Venn Yash Is Gekumen,* 1940), a second volume, mirrored Glatstein's impressions during his stay in Poland and the reactions of the Polish Jews toward this visitor from a happier clime. In Buchlerner's rest home he created a Jewish parallel to Thomas Mann's Magic Mountain sanatorium. Here the Jewish sick arrive in various stages of physical decay and spiritual dissolution. They have a foreboding that their days are numbered and that death will overtake them ere long, as indeed it does overtake Steinman, the lustiest character among them.

The mood of the novel is autumnal throughout. The melancholy guests are aware, even in the midst of their open-air waltzing, that winter is on the way, the winter of the year as well as of their lives. They reminisce about the past, when Jews were supposedly of a stronger mettle, great personalities who saw themselves as God's emissaries on earth. In Poland between two world wars, however, even Hassidic rebbes were embittered, taciturn, worried about the increasing impoverishment of the Jewish flock. Every Jew sensed the accumulated hatred of his Polish neighbors. "They hate

us for observing the Sabbath and they hate us for violating
the Sabbath. They hate pious Jews and they hate free-think-
ing Jews who eat lobster. They hate our capitalists and they
hate our beggars. They hate our reactionaries and they hate
our radicals. They hate Jews who earn their bread and those
who die three times a day from starvation."

Steinman, who in his childhood survived a pogrom by
hiding in a synagogue book closet, interpreted this hatred
as a continuation of Cain's hatred of Abel, an enduring hatred beyond logical explanation. To escape it, he once
dreamed of joining the movement to build a Jewish state.
He recalled Herzl's appearance upon the Jewish scene, when
Jewish backs straightened and Messianic visions floated before
ghetto eyes. Jewish misery lingered on, however, and was
intensified decade after decade, while the state was still
unborn.

This misery paraded before Glatstein's eyes: a steady
stream of the poor who saw in him the messenger from a
mythical paradise, a messenger holding out the possibility
of salvation from crushing penury. Each of the supplicants
was described with his past history, his present aches, his
dreary future. Only a miracle could save the Jewish masses
in Poland from deepening despair. This miracle was not
forthcoming: Hitler's march into Eastern Europe ended their
hopes and lives.

In the post-Hitler period Glatstein concentrated on specifically Jewish themes. He was not averse to Jewish lyricists
joining in all battles for a better humanity, but he felt that
their position in such battles should be on the Jewish barri-
cades. They should sing out their faith in a moral tomorrow
in Jewish tones and should trust that these tones would reach
beyond their own borders.

In his *Memorial Songs* (*Gedenklieder,* 1943), Glatstein
sought to recapture the simple Sabbath holiness of the Jew
rooted in tradition, the melody of the Yiddish word that
blossomed on the lips of grandmothers, the awesome mood
of the *shofar* and the comforting delight of a Goldfaden
melody. The poet bade farewell to the "wide, great, stinking
world," even to the effete democracies with their cold sym-

pathy-compresses. He put on the yellow badge as his emblem, and he groped his way back to the narrow, dust-covered lanes of his bearded coreligionists locked in ghettos.

Glatstein sang of these coreligionists in his cycle *Radiant Jews (Shtralendike Yidn,* 1946) , after the Holocaust. At night in a vision he saw millions of outstretched dead hands imploring him to cry out the Jewish pain, to be the intermediary between martyred sires and their living descendants. He no longer defined the Jews as a people, a race, a religion. They had become a sect of mourners bearing mute urns, a legion of survivors marching in an unending funeral procession memorializing their perished relatives. The Torah which Jews received at Sinai from the Lord of heaven and earth and with which they lived for millennia was returned by them at Lublin when they died in the gas chambers; the dead could no longer praise God.

Enveloping himself in the cloak of Rabbi Nachman of Bratzlav, the poet begged God to let him share in the punishment being meted out to Jews. Why should he be spared when so many of his coreligionists endured so much? After seven years of mourning, however, his lamentations subsided and he turned his attention to comfort his people.

In the cycle *Father's Shadow (Dem Tatens Shutn,* 1953), Glatstein held that the time had come both for the maimed God as well as his surviving bard to give up pretensions of universality and for both to betake themselves from the seven continents to the tiny land of their origin. For it was far better to be the intimate deity of a *minyan* of Jews than to be the mighty God of countless brigands. It was far better to dwell in the tabernacle of Israel than to be Lord of the world, especially such a world. When Jehovah set out from His people's tent and became international, His Jews followed suit and became a world-shaking, world-inflaming group. Now they were sick of that world and of their role in it. "Save yourself, O God, return with us to our little land, become once more the Jewish God." A people that was convalescing and regaining its youth would also help its God to rejuvenate Himself.

In many variations Glatstein reiterated his preference to

be remembered in the small vineyard of the Jewish people rather than on the broad highways of the non-Jewish world. Let others emphasize their cosmopolitanism, his emphasis would continue to be on his Jewishness. He illustrated this in his last lyric volumes *The Joy of the Yiddish Word (Die Freid Fun Yidishen Vort,* 1961) and *A Jew of Lublin (A Yid Fun Lublin,* 1966).

The former volume begins with memorial verses for departed poets of his circle, elegies for the souls of ravaged cities, satiric jibes at tired humanity. Then the poet bursts forth with joyous hymns to the re-arisen Jewish homeland whose flags flutter in the free air, a state built on the basis of shared poverty, cooperative fraternity, and warm with hope of redemption. Through thunder and lightning, out of the ashes of the recent conflagration, a new beginning has emerged. After commemorating so many tragic events of the past, the old people of wanderers can at last celebrate on *Yom Ha-atzmaut* a young holiday of rejoicing, a new holiness.

Despite affirmation of the dynamic Jewish reality symbolized by Israel, Glatstein nevertheless cannot tear himself away in his creative imagination from the vanished world of his youth. In *A Jew of Lublin,* published in his seventieth year, he continues to revert to his native Lublin and its more moral civilization. He dips his pen in misanthropic gall when he writes of the present coarse, wicked, oversexed Occident. He lashes out sardonically at the wild insanities of the avant-garde literature which interprets it, which crashes the privacy of the bedroom and which dissects and embalms the still living flesh. He sees in the Beatnik a caricature of the filthy, obnoxious, contemporary man, an angry nihilistic protester against sick, false respectability. He can understand such negative characters even though he does not sympathize with them. His own preference is to escape from maledictions, unbelief, and skepticism even to a Hassidic booth, if necessary. There he can at least pray with a handful of genuine, old-fashioned Jews and sense a breath of God's nearness.

Looking back upon a life of service as a guardian of the shrinking Yiddish heritage, Glatstein finds his chief joy in the Yiddish word and he wishes to continue with it until his last hour. His verses are magnificent tributes to the richness of Yiddish as a linguistic medium.

The third of the founders of Insichism was N. B. Minkoff, who began as a poet but who was more influential as editor, literary critic, scholar and lecturer.

Raised in Warsaw, in a home where Russian and Polish were esteemed far more than Yiddish, it was not until after he emigrated to the United States in 1914 and came into contact with Yiddish writers, actors and composers that he began to write Yiddish songs. Leyeles, his mentor, and Glatstein, his classmate at New York University's law school, roused his interest in the Insichist movement they were about to launch and he joined them from 1920 on in common literary ventures.

Minkoff remained faithful to the Insichist credo. His poetry is indeed intellectualized emotion. He rarely permits the cry that wells up from the heart to find untamed expression, and even the dream-visions that float up from his subconscious are filtered through the clear logic of thought before they are compressed into words and tangible images. Nevertheless, not all his mystic insights emerge unshrouded by obscurity despite his straining for clarity.

As a trained musician, Minkoff has an impeccable ear for tonal effects and he experiments with subtle rhythms of free verse, as do all Insichist poets. But, like Leyeles, he too likes equally well the discipline imposed upon his roving imagination by the sonnet. His first volume, *Songs* (*Lieder,* 1924), reaches its climax in the wreath of sonnets "Alone Am I." A tired melancholy whispers in him, but it never descends to the depth of cynicism. He often invokes the concept of joy, but his longing for joy fails to find fulfillment and he lacks real cheerfulness. The shadowy domain of night is more congenial to him than the glare of daylight. Typical titles of the poems in the first volume are: "Autumn," "November Nights," "The Weeping of Winterland," "Weeping of Pure Reason," "Sleepless Nights."

Minkoff's second lyric volume, *At the Edge* (*Beim Rand,* 1945), is even more thoroughly saturated with the imagery of death and desolation. It is written under the impact of the

Hitler years. But the finest lyric of this mature volume deals with the thought-associations and conjectures that come upon him "Upon Hearing Beethoven's *For Elise.*" The music impinging upon his ear and penetrating into his heart of hearts evokes a mood of reverie. In this dream state he has an awareness that his journey betwixt birth and death is merely half the road that his soul travels and that there is another half between death and rebirth which he must have traversed earlier and which he will traverse later. There come to him intimations of immortality, a feeling that he has been here before, though when or how he cannot tell, a possibility that there is no end to the renewal of lives, a wondering whether his precious lost existences do not stream back to him in his semi-conscious reveries as last spasms of recollections beyond space and time.

Minkoff seeks and fails to find a meaning in the suffering imposed upon his people. He wants to retain his faith in God but finds it most difficult to do so amidst war and catastrophe. Yet, even as he drives God from himself, God returns as creator and renewer, and the poet's heart, tired of raging and rebelling, finally accepts Him, though without hope of ever comprehending His mysterious ways.

Minkoff, who stresses subjectivity in his verse, is a most objective critic and scholar in his prose. His studies *Eliahu Bocher* (1950), dealing with the sixteenth-century Yiddish minstrel, and *Glickl Hamel* (1952), dealing with the matronly memoirist of the early eighteenth century, display great erudition and meticulous accuracy in interpretation. His books of essays *Yiddish Classical Poets* (1937) and *Six Yiddish Critics* (1954) show his understanding and tolerance of widely different attitudes to life and letters. His main contributions to literary scholarship, however, are the three volumes comprising *Pioneers of Yiddish Poetry in America* (1956). These volumes trace the growth and development of the social lyric, dominant in America during the closing decades of the nineteenth century.

Although Minkoff as a poet fought for pure poetry undiluted by propaganda or party programs, nevertheless as a literary historian, he appreciates the value of the Yiddish lyric pioneers who placed their talent at the service of social-istic, anarchistic and revolutionary causes. He correctly rec-ognizes that Yiddish literature from its very origin was oriented toward the common man and on the whole rejected the "art for art's sake" philosophy. If the Jewish immigrants who faced exploitation in sweatshops or near starvation as peddlers and small shopkeepers were saved from despair and moral disintegration by faith in a better tomorrow, they owed this faith to a large extent to the social poets whose verses ranged over a wide field, from naturalistic depiction of con-temporary evils to romantic, Messianic visions of a classless utopia. Minkoff is at his best in tracing the intellectual growth and the literary characteristics of Moritz Vinchevsky, David Edelstadt and Joseph Bovshover, the three most gifted and most popular poets who pioneered in singing of the sorrows and hopes of the working masses, even though they themselves were not of proletarian origin. But Minkoff also revivifies both as writers and as human beings nineteen other social poets who had become in the course of half a century shadowy figures. Some of these fervent idealists and somber cynics he knew in his early years when in the exuber-ance of youth he fought for Insichism and against their excessive didacticism.

According to Minkoff, the most erratic and extreme fol-lower of Insichism was Bernard Lewis, who began with Eng-lish verses but whose chief claim to fame are the Yiddish lyr-ics of his Insichist year, 1920. Minkoff describes him as a Byronic type, pessimistic but not resigned, dynamic in his hatred and scorn, theatrical in his speech and behavior.

Before Lewis came to America in 1906, at the age of sev-enteen, he had already participated in the Jewish self-defense organization which resisted the perpetrators of a pogrom in Odessa and he had joined a revolutionary cell which planned and executed the assassination of a Czarist official in Slonim. After escaping to America, he continued an adventurous existence, roaming as a hobo over the entire continent, im-pressing vagabonds with his bravado, and hatching imprac-tical, idealistic castles in the air.

In Insichism, Lewis found a movement which apparently

endorsed his egocentrism and let him give vent to his self-glorification and to indulge in eccentricities. Yet, before a year had passed, he took leave of his fellow poets in a misanthropic poem in which Nietzschean tones are audible. He told them that his Asiatic blood could not stand their inferior species. He disclaimed communion with them on the ground that they were born to be servile and would soon pass away. He, on the other hand, would watch their disappearance from his lofty pedestal and would sing a hymn of triumph.

Lewis's versified phantasmagorias often bordered on the absurd and the insane, but they did show flashes of greatness. In the imaginary land of his "own madness," which he called Flamtalin, he let the skeletons of his thoughts dance their infernal dance on the edge of the abyss, until he sickened of himself, "his wretched, wild blood," his aimless wandering. He then·let mocking laughter resound in his lyrics. "My heart rattles towards the lawless grass, the decaying rocks and the red orgy of death, as a snake rattles to its prey."

After spending his last years in a sanatorium for consumptives and denying premature reports of death's arrival, death caught up with him in Colorado Springs at the age of thirty-six. Two years later his poems were collected in the slender volume *Flamtalin* (1927), with an introductory tribute by Leyeles.

Reuben Ludwig also made a meteoric appearance among the Insichists with poems that emphasized the imminence of death. Before death claimed this consumptive poet in his thirty-first year, however, he sought to escape the deterioration of his health by sojourning in dry areas of New Mexico, Arizona and California. His few well-constructed lyrics dealt with the Far West. He discovered the silence of the snow-covered Rockies and the desolation of the yellow Southwestern deserts. Throughout his lyrics there coursed the refrain that for him there would soon be darkness and nothing more. His three short stories also dealt with the sick who yearned for the sun and for whom the damp, cold grave was waiting.

Ludwig experienced America, to which he came at fifteen, as his own and yet not his own. His sympathy was with the old Indian who had given way to white intruders, the Negro torn from the wilds of Africa to serve white masters, the melancholy, guitar-playing Mexican, the exotic Chinese, and other underprivileged characters. The poet was prematurely sad, pale and stripped of hope, even while his heart ached for joy, robustness and the intoxication of love and glorious adventuring. A single volume, containing his *Collected Poems (Gezamelte Lieder),* appeared posthumously in 1927.

The quietest of the Insichists was Eliezer Blum, who wrote under the pseudonym of B. Alquit and who was one of the editors of *In Sich.* Orphaned at an early age, he left his native Chelm in Poland at twelve, wandered on to Lublin, Warsaw, Vienna, and at seventeen arrived in New York. There he experienced the grueling fate of a sweatshop worker.

A posthumous slender volume, *Songs (Lieder,* 1964), contains the sum total of his lyric efforts of forty years, and a collection of short stories, *En Route to Peretz Square* (1958), contains his best narratives. His lyrics are compassionate and gentle, lucid and barely audible. They express the eternal melancholy that, in his opinion, hovers over shadows of nothingness. His metaphors are startling, his imagery is grotesque, his thought-associations are bold and original, his melodious verses with their subtle assonances drift gently onto the inner ear. He concretizes abstractions. His themes range from memories and figures of Chelm, the town of his childhood, to recurring premonitions of death. He sings of the silence of night, the sadness of the earth, the loneliness of the sea, the fading of dreams, the ebbing of desire, the autumn of life, the coolness of the grave. He does not struggle against adversity or resist the encroachment of age. His characters do not find much meaning in existence. He fathoms the fruitless longing of the girl who sees her youth wasting away in the factory and he peers into the withering eyes and hearts of middle-aged ladies who frequent picture galleries. These frustrated beings understand far better than the sixteen-year-olds the transitoriness of all existence and that even

God has become tired of fruitless activity and is therefore resting in the clouds.

Alquit belongs neither to the victors nor to the defeated but rather to those who stand on the sidelines and observe the passing scene. From the wine of life, he sips drops of melancholy. From the parade of the years, he extracts verses of haunting loveliness.

Jacob Stodolsky, publisher, bookseller, editor, poet, participated in the publications of the Insichists, but left only few lyrics of value. His volume of free verse bears the symbolic title *Will-O'-the Wisp* (*Irrlicht,* 1933). In it, he, the son of a Hassid, describes himself as having pursued deceptive lights before finally returning with Hassidic fervor to the God of his fathers and accepting a humble role as a guardian of his people's traditions. The will-o'-the-wisp he refers to is the anarchist philosophy which he followed in his earlier years in Warsaw and Paris before coming to New York in 1912. He wants to atone for former blasphemies by devoting himself entirely to the Yiddish word. He captures in verse the uniqueness of Jewish boulevards, such as Manhattan's Second Avenue and Brooklyn's Ocean Parkway. He sometimes dazzles the mind with his heaping of colorful image upon colorful image but he rarely succeeds in moving the heart, a common failing of the minor Insichist poets who, in seeking to combine intellectualism with emotional sensitivity, lose themselves in artificial, barren abstractions from which the emotions have oozed away.

Aaron Kurtz came from a Hassidic home in a Vitebsk townlet. He began his wandering and struggling for a livelihood at thirteen. He arrived in the United States in 1911, worked in factories and wrote poetry. When the Insichist movement arose, he was at first attracted by it and contributed to its journals, but before long he felt drawn more closely to the proletarian writers who sought to change America's social and economic structure. Insichism did not involve its followers in the struggle between capital and labor. Kurtz felt that poets should take their place at the vanguard of this struggle, inspiring, conjuring, suffering with the underprivileged masses. In *Placard* (1927), he introduced an original poetic style, which he designated as "placard style." Its dynamic rhythms were designed to reproduce the kaleidoscopic metropolis, the raw, chaotic manifestations of industrial capitalism, the striving of the red-hearted, black-breaded plebeians. In *The Golden City* (*Die Goldene Shtot,* 1935), he sang of strikes, mass protests, the Negro slums of New York's Harlem, the derelicts of its Bowery, the angry rebels of its Union Square. In *No Pasarán* (1938), he identified himself with the Spanish Republicans in their desperate struggle against Fascism. In *Marc Chagall* (1947), he paid lyric tribute to the painter of the fantastic whose soul, even as his own, was rooted in Jewish Vitebsk and who placed his talent at the disposal of all fighters for freedom. Like Chagall, he too was battling for a world of social justice and pure love, but used the rhythmic word rather than the brush as his weapon.

Shloime Schwartz identified himself with the Insichists in the preface to his first volume, *Blue Monday* (*Bloimontik,* 1938). Indeed, most of the lyrics in this volume originally appeared in their organs. These lyrics are consciously conceived and then draped in images and besprinkled with emotions. In the title poem, for example, Sunday sighs out its holidayness and only burnt-out tallow is left of its festive light; the blueness of Monday ushers in the tower-high, spiralling problems which wrap themselves around the weekdays. Schwartz prefers melancholy moods and autumnal visions. He reproduces the nuances of various months but his preference is for October, November and December. Even in his New Year's poem, he emphasizes the loss of the faded year rather than the promise of the coming one. His love poems forfeit immediacy of feeling as his emotions are intellectualized and frozen into crystalline images.

In his second volume, *America* (1940), Schwartz frees himself to some extent from dogmatic adherence to Insichist theories. His artificial straining for original word combinations is less marked. The poet of Chicago sings of sights and sounds in his midwestern metropolis and discovers in the ranges of Wyoming and the deserts of Arizona scenes and figures new to Yiddish poetry. But the worsening Jewish situation on the eve of the Second World War compels him to take cognizance of Jewish woes earlier untouched by him. Poetry cannot any longer remain for him merely playful variations on exotic and impersonal themes. Flaming ghettos and ships with unwanted Jewish refugees adrift on the high seas recall him to his people's destiny, to biblical subjects, and to legends of his grandfather.

Michel Licht contributed to *In Sich* and edited literary journals in 1925 and 1926 together with Jacob Glatstein and N. B. Minkoff. His earliest lyrics, which go back to 1917, show Impressionistic characteristics in their emphasis on the communication of moods and in their vague symbolism. His preference then is for the echoes of sounds, cool shadows, gentle reveries, twilight and demi-night. He lets paintings, symphonies, the gyrations of dancers and acrobats, the movements of birds and swanlike maidens, impinge upon the senses and tries to reproduce the effect in words. But soon he becomes dissatisfied with the mere reproduction of impressions and feelings. Under the influence of the Insichists, he filters these through his intellect and dissolves them in irony. His metaphors become too refined, his neologisms not entirely comprehensible. He assimilates influences from avant-garde French and American poetry and adores Ezra Pound. His cerebral rhythms astound with their virtuosity but leave the reader unmoved. He revolts against the concept that art should mirror life and that the Jewish artist should mirror Jewish reality. He prefers universal themes, often far removed from his own immediate experiences. He loses himself in abstractions and versifies pure ideas. He is rationally sober even in the midst of dreams. He pacifies his turbulently beating heart with the cold medicine of logic.

After publishing three volumes of lyrics during the decade 1922–1932, Licht was chained by illness for twenty years and, only after his death in 1953, did his *Collected Poems* (*Gezamelte Lieder*) appear. By then his tamed ecstasies and allegorical chimeras were even less intelligible to his few readers.

Kalman Heisler stemmed from Kymarno, eastern Galicia, and experienced the First World War in Prague. He arrived in New York in 1921, when the Insichists were propounding their new literary insights, and he attracted the attention of Jacob Glatstein. In 1927 he published his first lyric booklet, *People (Menshen)*, with an introduction by Glatstein, who compared Heisler's gallery of Galician characters to Edgar Lee Masters' unheroic heroes of *Spoon River Anthology*.

The young poet sketched portraits of his ancestors and his townsmen with nostalgic affection and with subtle humor. There was his great-grandfather, who tailored before the days of specialization and mechanization, singing and humming as he worked, content with God and man, and with his most precious possessions: children and grandchildren, needles and scissors, *tallit* and *tfillin*. There was his grandfather, also skilled in tailoring but no longer disdaining the help of the new machines, a reputable master who brought the latest Parisian styles to the Galician outpost and who retained the pious, stable habits bequeathed to him by tradition. There were his father and mother, who still accepted as apparently God-ordained their status on a low rung of the social ladder. In his own generation, however, the tailor lads were infected with doctrines of class struggles and hoped for a social revolution. They proudly evaluated their profession as superior to that of the idle bourgeoisie. After adolescence, many of them made their way to American shops, even as did their poetic chronicler, but they retained the traits of their native Kymarno.

In the lyrics of a subsequent volume, *Kymarno Types (Kymarno Parshoinen, 1930)*, Heisler continued to delineate the townsmen he had known in his boyhood years, each an individual with unique characteristics but all enveloped in an east Galician Jewish atmosphere. Under the influence of Moshe Nadir, a satiric undertone accompanied these crotchety types with their picturesque nicknames. This satiric tone subsided, however, when a quarter of a century later he reverted to lyric sketches of additional townsmen in the booklet *Alas, My Kymarner (Maine Kymarner Nebikh, 1953)*. By then, this centuries-old Jewish settlement survived only in his memory, since its men had been machine-gunned in 1941 and its women and children set afire in 1942.

Alef Katz, a far more versatile poet than Heisler, also was encouraged by Glatstein and also had his early poems published in the organ of the Insichists. His first lyric volume, *A Tale of the Sea* (*A Mayse Fun Yam,* 1925) incorporated Insichist innovations. The opening poem, "A Leaf," lets us view in lucid images the movement of a leaf from the instant it parts from its branch, even as a dream from a sleeper's brain, until it finally touches the earth and comes to rest. Other poems, in the manner of the American Imagists, let us experience New York by directing our gaze to single specific objects which are delineated with utmost clarity. Katz shows not a mass of skyscrapers but the single Woolworth Building, not a multiplicity of streets but the Bowery only, not the majesty of rivers but the Hudson River as perceived from a definite point on the upper Manhattan bank where street lamps cast braids of light upon the water.

In his second volume, *Plowing Time* (*Akertzeit,* 1929), the poet again emphasizes New York subjects. He is again fascinated by the picturesqueness of the Bowery. In the manner of Edwin Markham's *Man with the Hoe,* he describes the man of the Bowery, cast out by society, unable to find his way back or to advance forward to respectability, a severed link of the human chain, a derelict devoured by hatred, his burning brain cooled by the sad melody of nighing death.

In the poetic booklet *Heavenly Saucer* (*Dos Tellerl Fun Himl,* 1934), Katz emancipates himself from Imagism and Insichism, only to fall under the spell of the then fashionable proletarian practices. He shows starving workers becoming class conscious and revolting against their sated plunderers.

Not until the lyrics of *Once There Was a Story* (*Amol Is Geven A Mayse,* 1944), written under the impact of the European Jewish tragedy, does Katz find his own, original tone and the subject matter closest to his heart. He tells of his disillusionment with the proletarian panaceas. The eagles he followed to the desired land of pure humanity turned into terrifying, wild, screeching bats. He was left lonely and bereft of his wings. Recovery from his temporary paralysis came when he linked himself again to the healthy trunk of the Jewish generations, past and future. "My father is in me and I am in my children. We are all one, in a single, complex truth."

Katz then pens children's poems, playlets, stories for the coming generation and finds real happiness in this activity, because these are sung, played and recited in Yiddish schools and thrill young Jewish hearts. A playlet, *Good Morning, Alef* (1946) has as its dramatis personae the letters of the Hebrew alphabet. These letters are indestructible. When Houses of Learning went up in flames in the Hitler decade, the letters floated up and wandered about in the air. *Alef* and *Bet* set out in search of their dispersed comrades and, when all of them were found, the question arose as to who could use them after the conflagration. A child was discovered that survived the night of the long knives and Elijah descended on earth to teach it the alphabet. Jewish learning was thus resumed and the Hebrew letters again had a home and a new lease of life in Jewish hearts. This dramatic poem was produced in camps of post-war survivors and brought much needed cheer.

The lyrics and playlets of the following volumes—*Dreams Be With You* (*Cholem Aleichem*, 1958) and *Quite a Wedding* (*Die Emesse Khassene*, 1964)—are singable and playful, a delight for adults and children. The best of the included poetic tales are based on stories of the Hassidic Rabbi Nachman Bratslaver.

"An Old Portrait," with its suggestive symbolism, is typical of Katz's mature style in his last volume. After years of silence, a portrait in a museum suddenly begins to talk. It recalls the moment when it was created, the painter who created it, and the whole world that once was. Now it looks out of its frame upon an entirely strange world in which the painter and the subject portrayed are no more. As the solitary hero of a wordless drama, as the shadowy survivor of a faded era, it alone lives on. In this apparently simple lyric of a portrait, there obviously peers through the face of the aging poet and of his entire Yiddish-speaking generation. This is Alef Katz at his best.

His uniqueness, late arrived at, lies in his ability to bridge with laughter life's yawning abysses and tragic canyons. Amidst the maze of symbols, the ever-changing rhythmic patterns, the virtuosity of startling rhymes, the capricious whirl of metaphors, serious meaning trickles through or is hinted at. The poet's weeping becomes music; his tears dissolve into songs; his sad memories skirt along the edge of humor; he hides behind supernatural creatures and animated objects. He is aware that words alone are inadequate to express a reality beyond observed phenomena and he even entitles one of his mystic poems "What Cannot Be Uttered in Words." But he hopes that this reality can be hinted at through allegorical symbols.

Insichism was primarily an American movement of young Yiddish poets. It flourished in the 1920's and brought excitement and experimentation. Its vogue receded in the 1930's. Some of its followers returned to traditionalism. Others became infatuated with proletarian poetry as practiced in Kiev, Minsk and Moscow. Still others discovered their own uniqueness and followed a lonely path, removed from the main currents. But all had been enriched by the temporary enthusiasm which Insichist striving had called forth.

4

The Rise of
Literary Criticism

LITERARY CRITICISM was practiced by Yiddish writers
ever since the first modern Yiddish organ, *Kol Mevasser,*
was founded in 1862 by Alexander Zederbaum. But it was
not until the physician Isidor Eliashev (1873–1924) appeared
upon the Yiddish scene that literary criticism was accepted
as a legitimate artistic genre alongside of poetry, drama and
fiction.

Eliashev, who wrote under the symbolic pseudonym
"Baal-Makhshoves" (the Man of Thought), was the creator
of Yiddish esthetic criticism. Educated in a traditional home
and in a Yeshiva that stood under the influence of the ethical
movement inspired by Rabbi Israel Salanter (1810–1883),
the *Musar* movement, he found his way from his native
Lithuania to Switzerland, where he completed preparatory
studies for admission to the universities of Heidelberg and
Berlin. After imbibing the best of European culture and
graduating as a doctor of medicine, he left Berlin in 1901
for Kovno, then moved on to Riga, and finally settled in
Warsaw. Literary interests gradually eclipsed his interest in
medicine.

In Warsaw, he came under the influence of Peretz and hailed with great enthusiasm the efforts of the Peretz Circle to strengthen Jewish national rebirth by means of creative works in Yiddish. His love of Yiddish, however, did not exclude a love of Hebrew. In a famous essay, "Two Tongues —One Literature," he preached the unity of Jewish literary expression, regardless as to whether the author used either language. He did not share the view of his enlightened friends or of the nascent Zionist movement that Yiddish was a transitional linguistic medium useful for educating the masses so that these could rise in the cultural level and ultimately change to Hebrew, Russian, German, Spanish or English. He rather felt that literary works being created in Yiddish were of such high artistic calibre and mirrored the Jewish soul so well that even estranged Jewish intellectuals could be brought back through such works to a love of their people.

His essays on Mendele revived the flagging interest in this master of Yiddish. His essays on Peretz, Sholom Aleichem, Bialik, Dineson and Nomberg were sensitive appraisals of established writers. No less important, however, was his impact as the discoverer and furtherer of talented new writers such as Leivick, Bergelson and the Kiev group of Soviet authors.

As a critic, Baal-Makhshoves combined both clarity of insight and the ability to recreate the mood about all of his subjects. We see them, we hear them, we taste them, we touch them, we sense the uniqueness inherent in each of their works. And he does this in a style so pleasant, so calm, so rich in imagery. For him, the critic was an essential pillar of the literary structure and especially necessary as a midwife at the birth or revival of a literary movement. He noted that Lessing in Germany, Byelinski in Russia, and Sainte-Beuve in France were held in no less esteem by their contemporaries than were poets or novelists. A critic's role should not, in his opinion, be restricted merely to passing judgment, voicing approval or disapproval. It was also incumbent upon the critic to prepare the atmosphere for the reception of a new original work and to supply the sunlight so that young, good, fresh literary shoots might grow and prosper. The critic was the trumpeter who broke down the wall of indifference among prospective readers. He was the herald announcing the arrival of kings of thought. Far from being a cold inquisitor who sought out blemishes in works of art and who castigated artists for their inadequacies, he was rather himself a passionate lover of art who opened the eyes of the less discerning and the hearts of the less sensitive to the magnificence and loveliness which moved him.

Baal-Makhshoves was the Jew and the Good European. Upon the substratum of his Jewish heredity and early environment, there were superimposed in his personality Germanic and Slavic influences and, as a result, he interpreted Jewish life both as an intimate participant and as an objective observer from without. This dualism in his personality gave his essays an original flavor: a rich sympathy for the old forms of Jewish life, an awareness of their non-viability amidst the new social upheavals, a longing for a Jewish national and cultural rebirth, an emphasis upon the need for quality rivaling the dominant European groups, a stress upon both Jewish languages as necessary vehicles for intensifying Jewishness in all lands.

Baal-Makhshoves was both rationalist and sentimentalist. As he grew older, his optimistic Messianism yielded to an increasingly pessimistic and satiric appraisal of the changing social and political scene and he gave vent to his melancholy moods in his *Ironic Tales (Ironishe Maaselekh),* rich in disillusioned wisdom.

Baal-Makhshoves was fascinated by the magnificent personality of Herzl. He saw in the Zionist leader a living example of the historic Hebrew who had once led an harmonious existence, as well as a dignified forerunner of the envisaged new Jew who yearned to return to a healthy existence in a regenerated homeland. He devoted three essays to Herzl upon the latter's death and he incorporated Herzlian ideas in several of his *Ironic Tales.* In one of these tales, "The Island of Shrouds," he pointed out how difficult it was for a community which was skilled in the art of dying to respond to a prophet of reinvigorated life such as Herzl.

In another tale for Purim of 1901, composed as a sequel to the *Book of Esther,* he stressed Herzl's idea of a return to the cradle of the Jewish people as the sole permanent solution to Jewish homelessness. This sequel centered about Parshendatha, Haman's oldest son. Since Parshendatha was of prodigious weight, the rope used for his hanging broke and he fell to the ground only half dead. At night he awoke from his swoon and fled to a forest. There, in the course of time, he assumed the leadership of all the surviving anti-Jewish families of Persia. The conspirators longed for revenge and bided their time. As anti-Jewish sentiments rearose and continued to mount, two young men, Ezra and Nehemiah, suggested to their fellow Jews mass flight from the Persian capital before the situation deteriorated even further. They formed groups for the purpose of emigrating to the land of Israel. They tried to convince Mordecai that it was far better to hew stones and to draw water in their own land than to live prosperously under the shadow of eternal fear of an unpredictable tomorrow. Mordecai, however, had faith in the constitution of the Persian realm, which guaranteed his rights. One day King Ahasverus, in a happy mood, offered to let Mordecai and his people return to their native land from which they had been exiled by King Nebuchadnezzar. But Mordecai, the great Persian patriot, answered: "My land is the soil over which your sublime steps float and I am your servant." Ahasverus became angry when he saw his generous offer spurned; he withdrew his golden scepter from Mordecai and restored Parshendatha, son of Haman, to the premiership. Then pogroms broke out and the streets ran red with Jewish blood. Only the followers of Ezra and Nehemiah survived, since they had already left the rich, prosperous capital Shushan and were en route to the land of Israel.

Baal-Makhshoves realized, however, that in his own century most Jews still had to continue to live in the Diaspora and that for them a longing for Zion and an interest in Hebrew were insufficient props to guarantee their group survival. He therefore advocated converting religious holidays into Jewish national holidays in order to meet the need of the irreligious and the intellectuals. He urged that on Hanukkah the struggle for national liberation should be stressed and on Lag B'Omer the heroism of Bar Kochba should be emphasized. Above all, he saw in the Sabbath the finest surviving pillar of ancient Jewish culture, the one day each week when Jews would be purified of materialism, a day of balm for the heart of a battered, scattered nationality. This insight formed the theme of his most memorable essay, *The Sabbath.*

After the Russian Revolution, restlessness overcame Baal-Makhshoves. He wandered from one Jewish center to another, happy nowhere. In 1917 he lived in St. Petersburg, in 1919 in Kiev, in 1921 in Kovno, in 1922 in Berlin. Increasing fame and increasing influence did not, however, lessen his melancholy.

Abraham Coralnik, who was in many respects his most talented disciple, characterized him as a critic in whom were united traditional Judaism of the Kovno Yeshiva, ethical culture of Slobodka, Russian education, German scientific training, Jewish nationalism and European supra-nationalism, Lithuanian acuity and Berlin wit, Nietzschean paradoxical seriousness and Solomonic awareness that all was vanity of vanities.

Coralnick (1883–1937) himself combined many of these disparate elements in his own personality. He too was a Good European and a Jewish intellectual, a lover of Hebrew and Yiddish but without real faith in the future of Diaspora creativity, a Zionist working for Jewish renewal in Palestine and yet nostalgic for the culture of the East European Jewish townlet, a pessimist who was saved from cynicism and despair by an ironic contemplation of life, a rationalist with a yearning for mysticism.

Born in the Ukrainian town of Uman, Coralnik was able to enter the University of Kiev, despite the severe quota system imposed upon Jews, but soon left for universities abroad. At Florence he imbibed the spirit of classical and Mediterranean cultures and at Berlin, Bonn and Vienna he came in contact with German romanticism and realism. His main interest was in philosophy and his doctoral thesis, completed in 1908, dealt with the philosophy of skepticism.

From his twentieth year on, he was active in Zionism. He edited the Viennese Zionist organ *Die Welt* during Herzl's last and stormiest year and he contributed to leading Russian and German newspapers and periodicals. Although he felt more at ease writing in Russian and German, nevertheless he early recognized that only through Yiddish could he reach the Jewish masses. He schooled himself to develop a Yiddish style which could communicate the profoundest ideas with utmost clarity and simplicity. But the communication of ideas never sufficed him. He also sought to clothe ideas in properly fitting moods, to transmit aromas, overtones and feelings that accompanied living thoughts.

After the outbreak of the First World War, Coralnik came to the United States and was invited in 1915 by the newly founded daily *Der Tog* to become a permanent contributor. It was through this Yiddish organ that he reached hundreds of thousands of readers during the following two decades and helped to improve their literary taste and to direct their thinking on eternal problems and on specific Jewish matters.

In 1917 he was swept up in the general enthusiasm at the birth of freedom in Russia and returned to his native land. His enthusiasm quickly waned, however, when he saw the oppressed turning into oppressors and violence rampant everywhere. He then returned to New York a disillusioned humanist but still clinging to his love for Jewishness and his love for pure ideas.

Throughout his creative life, Coralnik wrestled with the question: what is Jewishness? Or, more specifically, what can Jewishness, howsoever defined, mean to contemporary man? In an essay of 1909 on the essence and future of Jewishness, he expressed both fear that dominant trends were inimical to Jewish survival and hope that, out of still undimmed Messianic longing, movements for Jewish salvation might yet arise. He saw such a movement in Zionism, which might offer redemption to the Jewish people and also to all mankind. In later years, as he accumulated ever greater knowledge and as ultimate answers still eluded him, he learned to content himself with illuminating fragments of the vast complex of Jewishness without seeking for a general panacea.

Coralnik's sympathy abided with the thinkers who asked basic questions and who were not content with easy, conventional answers. His heart went out to Elisha ben Abuya, the lonely heretic who wrestled with God and remained with skepticism, far more than to Rabbi Akiva, who sought compromises and temporary answers which enabled people somehow to live on. Coralnik was fond of Koheleth, the ironic sage who smiled at the world through the mask of King Solomon. He was fond of Esdras, the prince of the Apocrypha who wanted to know why there was undeserved suffering here below and who was not satisfied with the replies that satisfied Job.

Coralnik's essays stressed mood, atmosphere, inner rhythm. Often he wrote with a heavy heart, unsure of himself. He feared that he could not satisfy his Yiddish readers, who demanded of him definitive criteria by which they could live. He distrusted generalizations. Thinking was for him a playing with ideas, a dialogue with himself, a pleasurable technique for dissecting apparent reality and rebuilding its fragments in ever new forms. But he did not overemphasize the role of logical thinking in the realm of practical human affairs. Thinking might suffice to illuminate the uppermost layers of the soul but it could not penetrate to the deepest layers, there where multi-dimensional, super-individual psychic abysses yawned, where maelstroms of emotional energy whirled, and chaotic, instinctive elements yearned to be encased in structures. He knew that culture included far more irrational entities than rational ones. He therefore preferred the myth and the legend to the historical fact.

Coralnik's essay on Georg Brandes revealed more of himself and his own approach to critical writing than it did of Brandes. While recognizing the achievements of Denmark's greatest literary critic, whose fame was then worldwide, he asserted that Brandes failed to grasp the essence of artistic creativity. Why? Because Brandes, who understood everything, could not leap beyond the boundaries of mere un-understanding. Brandes never lived art. For example, he understood the trappings of Shakespeare and Goethe, to whom he devoted voluminous tomes. But the real Shakespeare who was hidden behind the facade of the Elizabethan stage eluded him and the real Goethe who was lonely amidst the adulations of the Weimar Court was a mystery to him. Brandes had a keen eye for the environment encircling an author. He saw the candlestick upon which the candle was perched, the tallow of which the candle was made, and even the circle of light at the edge of the candle's flame, but he never pierced with his glance to the innermost heart of the flame. He knew the facts but not the truth behind the facts. He possessed sound common sense, an unbiased outlook, a liberal temperament, but he lacked the seer's mystic insight into the soul's irrational core.

Coralnik himself possessed this mystic insight but could only communicate small fragments of it. He was ecstatic when he caught a glimpse of a writer's true essence and was sad that he could not convey the full intensity of this ecstasy to his readers. He sensed the radiance of beauty which poured as a flood of sunlight about him and he despaired of containing more than a meager shimmer of this radiance within the straitjacket of words.

Coralnik loved life. He loved man and the works of man. Above all, he loved his Jewish people. But he covered his love with a cloak of irony. He was a sentimentalist, but because he feared the ridicule normally heaped upon sentimentalists he hid his feelings behind a stylized mask.

Books opened up to Coralnik the entire past of peoples and civilizations. Books brought him the wisdom of gifted individuals and gave him insight into diverse patterns of experience. Books were for him a source of strength, security, hope. He lived in books and from them he extracted showpieces to display to his readers.

In 1928, two decades before Melech Ravitch proposed the canonization of the post-biblical treasures of Jewish learning and literature, Coralnik called for the collection of the best products of the Jewish mind and their incorporation within a single, comprehensive volume, a volume which should be revised and brought up to date every half century. In his essay on "The Jewish Intellect," he advocated the immortalization of the spirit of the post-exilic generations within the covers of a supplementary Bible. Until the present, such tomes were prepared by individuals and bore the stamp of their prejudices and predilections. The authoritative book should be prepared by an authoritative body, by an academy of scholars, thinkers, poets and critics, since no one individual could today claim mastery of all fields of Jewish culture. This supplementary Bible should mirror the Jewish intellect in all its aspects. It should be designed not only for Jews but also for non-Jews who ought to know Jews as they really were and are. The vast material of two thousand years should be sifted by responsible, competent, learned Jewish representatives and the final product should be published not alone in the Jewish national languages, Hebrew and Yiddish, but also in the major world languages.

Coralnik urged that in such a book there should be included, in the first place, the early post-exilic thinkers Josephus and Philo, the medieval poets and philosophers Yehuda Halevi, Solomon ibn Gabirol, Maimonides, Saadia Gaon, and the finest minds of more recent centuries down to Heinrich Heine, Abraham Reisen, Hermann Cohen, Disraeli, Herzl and Rathenau. Coralnik then suggested going further afield and also incorporating, within the Jewish treasury of thought, letters and experience, the products of heretics, dissenters and scientists which carry in some way the stamp of Jewishness: an *Epistle* of Paul, polemics of the Sabbatai Zvi movement, a chapter of Moses Mendelssohn's *Phaedon,* selections from Georg Simmel, Marcel Schwob, Ludwig Börne, Spinoza, Henri Bergson, Heinrich Herz and Albert Einstein.

Coralnik could not accept the view that Jews should strive to become a normal people. He felt that Jews did not experience a millennial tragic fate unequalled by any other historic group in order to end as a normal people. Jews could not afford to become old and sated. The smile of self-contentment did not befit the Jewish face. They were chained to their past and to the land of their origin.

When Coralnik visited Palestine in 1926, he felt the land to be his. He walked along the streets of Jerusalem not as a tourist who gazes at novel attractions but as a son of the land who returned after sojourning abroad for a while. This while had lasted a few thousand years but in the relativity of time those thousands of years in exile were but as days. Now he was back home. He sloughed his usual ironic contemplation of scenes and wrote with unrestrained emotions of this center of his longing. Jerusalem was not for him a little oriental mountain community but his own history and the ultimate root of his personality. Nevertheless, he returned to the American metropolis and spent the last decade of his life raising the cultural level of his Yiddish readers with his critical articles on literature and philosophy. But the hope of a return to Zion never died within him.

Shmaryahu Gorelik (1877–1943) began, like Coralnik, as a multilingual essayist, participating in Russian, German, Hebrew and Yiddish publications. Under the impact of Herzl's death and the pogroms of 1905, he gave up his early Bundist, Socialist and anti-Zionist orientation. In 1908, he joined A. Veiter and S. Niger in editing the Vilna Yiddish monthly *Literarishe Monatshriften,* a purely literary organ in which writers of diverse ideologies could cooperate in working for a Yiddish cultural renaissance. During the First World War, he lived in Switzerland and participated in the pacifist movement centering about Romain Rolland. After the war he resided in Berlin until 1933 and thereafter in Tel Aviv.

Gorelik had a wide knowledge of European literature and, in his critical articles, he was more interested in the insights of modern writers than in their stylistic innovations. The essay was, in his opinion, an educational medium. It was concentrated spiritual energy converted into noble form, a flashlight illuminating for a brief moment dark and hidden corners of the human soul.

As an ardent convert to Zionism, he sought to tear his readers away from their drab daily pursuits and lead them to the more inspiring goal of rebuilding a national Jewish life. He loved the irrational aspects of the Zionist approach: the resurrection of an ancient tongue to new vitality, the transformation of stagnant European slum dwellers to healthy agriculturists on oriental plantations and fragrant orange groves. He wanted Jews to grow wings, and meanwhile he carried them on the wings of his own imagination.

In his literary criticism, Gorelik distinguished between three types of literature. The first was the objective description of reality by honest, talented writers. Such writers revealed accurately what they saw. They communicated sensations and impressions. They provided esthetic pleasure. Yiddish literature, he held, was rich in such works.

The second type, a higher type, embodied in portrayed characters the ideas, moods, struggles and stirrings of the age in which the writers lived. Not content with merely reproducing the environment and surface reality, these writers had their characters engage in debates in which the conflicting currents of the social order and the deepest layers of the group soul were brought to the fore. Readers became involved more intensely and were influenced to change their own reactions and their own views of the current scene through their experiencing of literary works embodying philosophic and religious content and providing insight into the spiritual essence of a people and an era. Turgenev, Ibsen, Knut Hamsun and Romain Rolland exemplified this second type of literature for European readers, while Mendele Mocher Sforim, Sholom Aleichem and Peretz did so for Yiddish readers.

There was, however, still a third type of literature, the highest type. It included not only a reservoir of ideas dominant in a writer's generation but it also opened up horizons of a new world and envisaged possibilities for future human relationships unperceived or only dimly perceived until then. Such writers wrestled with eternal problems, with the meaning of existence itself. Having made their way up the ladder of human suffering and having surveyed an ever expanding panorama of human experience, they sought to elevate their readers to their level of insight and to communicate moral and intellectual vistas attainable to our species if we but willed it. Goethe, Rousseau, Tolstoi, Dostoevsky represented this highest type in modern European literature. They helped the individual to understand his relationship not only to his own specific contemporary society but also to all super-individual entities regardless of space and time; they taught him how to escape cosmic loneliness, how to overcome the fear of death, how to find lasting meaning in his transient years on earth. While academic philosophers also sought answers to these eternal questions, they did so via cold logic. Great writers explored these regions through the creation of characters with whom we could identify ourselves, characters who traversed the entire gamut of emotions from despair to ecstasy, who worked their way up from the abyss of confusion to final clarity. Such literature was a reading of life at the deepest, most intimate strata of the soul. Through literary characters like Koheleth, Job, Don Quixote, Hamlet, Faust coursed the thoughts and dreams of the human species. Yiddish literature should now be ready to rise to this highest level. It had already mastered the art of depicting the collective soul of the townlet. It should now essay to depict the complex, tragic Jewish individual who leaves the shelter of the townlet and goes out into the great world beyond in order to seek ultimate meaning and fulfillment. It should deal with the Jew as man per se. Gorelick, therefore, called upon Yiddish writers to dare grandly, to enter the holy tabernacle of the highest type of literature, to incorporate themselves in lasting figures created to hand down eternal Jewish visions as an inspiration to all humankind down the generations.

While Gorelik's strength lay in his appeal to the imagination and Coralnik's in the communication of moods, Shmuel Niger (1883–1955), who for almost half a century exercised enormous influence as the arbiter of literary taste, preferred to reason with his readers and used logic as the yardstick for literary evaluation.

Niger, who was born as Shmuel Charney, was the oldest of three brothers who rose to prominence in Yiddish letters. One of them, Baruch Charney (1886–1938), became a leader of the Bund and acquired a reputation before his twentieth year as a second Lassalle because of his oratorical skill and indomitable courage. He participated in the Revolution of 1905 under the name of Vladeck and then retained this name when he was forced to flee to the United States in 1907. In the Yiddish literary monthly *Die Zukunft,* Vladeck found a congenial organ for his poems, feuilletons, short stories, travel sketches, drama and critical essays. He also influenced the American Jewish community as manager of the largest Yiddish daily, *Forverts,* from 1918 to 1938, as a Socialist member of New York's Board of Aldermen from 1917 to 1922, and as a founder of the American Labor Party.

Niger's youngest brother, Daniel Charney (1888–1959), began his literary career in Poland, edited Yiddish journals in post-revolutionary Moscow, lived in Berlin from 1922 to 1934, in Paris from 1934 to 1941, and in the United States thereafter. He wrote love lyrics, travel sketches and essays, but is best remembered for his several volumes of memoirs and family chronicles.

Niger came under the influence of Hassidism, Zionism, Socialism in his boyhood, amassed a great deal of miscellaneous knowledge in his youth, participated in subversive activities against the Czarist regime, was arrested and tortured in Russian prisons. During and after the Revolution of 1905, he wrote in Russian, Hebrew and Yiddish on current political issues.

He made his debut as a literary critic in 1907 with an essay on Sholem Asch which aroused a great deal of attention. A year later, he joined S. Gorelik and A. Veiter (1878–1919) in founding the Vilna *Literarishe Monatshriften,* a periodical which was influential in the Yiddish cultural resurgence after the Czernowitz Conference of Yiddishists.

During the First World War, when a clamor arose for new themes and new moods that would reflect the more immediate reality, Niger opposed the slogan of the modernists and insisted that the concern of great literature was not the ever changing present but rather the eternal problems of the human spirit, problems of life and death, free will and determinism, causation and purposefulness. The best of his essays of the war decade were included in the volume *Talks on Books (Shmuesn Vegn Bikher,* 1922).

In April 1919, during the conflict between Russia and Poland, Niger was sharing an apartment in Vilna with A. Veiter and Leib Yaffe (1876–1948), when Polish legionnaires broke in, shot Veiter, and transported the other two writers to jail. After their release, due to Marshal Pilsudski's intervention after he was convinced of their political non-involvement in the conflict between the two opposing powers, Yaffe left for Palestine. There he edited Hebrew journals, wrote lyrics in Hebrew and Yiddish, agitated for Zionism as an emissary to many lands, and was killed when the Jewish Agency building in Jerusalem was dynamited during the struggle for Israel's independence. Niger emigrated to the United States. There, during his thirty-five years in New York, he came to be recognized as the outstanding literary critic, as the spokesman for the Yiddish cultural movement. There his dictum made and unmade reputations.

According to Niger, a critic must have sympathy for every variety and every level of creative expression, provided that it was genuine expression. He must possess the traits of patience, curiosity, sensitivity, many-sidedness. A critic who could understand and react only to works of a single, specific tendency would fail to grasp even these works in their entirety. Whatever esthetic or philosophic approach a critic might himself espouse, he must not be deaf to other approaches, he must be able to acclimatize himself to all territories of the spirit, he must immerse himself in the essence of each literary personality he portrayed. His realm was not raw reality but rather reality after it had been given a definite esthetic form by a talented, creative personality. A critic must be as objective in his judgments as was humanly possible and must be fearless in their expression. He must emphasize those books which conveyed unforgettable pleasures and enduring values.

Without such books an individual experienced only one life, but through them he experienced many lives. Books were emissaries that brought messages from all corners of the earth, from distant stars, from the wisest men of all eras.

Books enriched, purified, lit up new roads to mysterious realms of being. Books deepened comprehension of the present by linking it to innumerable yesterdays and tomorrows. Books therefore extended our years beyond the normal span of three score and ten by revivifying the generations of our forefathers and by envisaging utopias and apocalypses of coming generations. Books also liberated us from the narrow confines of the self and opened up a boundless universe of freedom and pure delight.

Although Niger was often accused of being a dictator of taste, he himself placed little value on a critic's apportioning of praise and blame. A critic, he held, was neither an author's press agent nor a literary prosecutor. A critic was an artist in his own right, giving expression to thoughts, feelings and visions aroused in him by a literary product. He was a seeker of beauty. Having fallen under the spell of a work of beauty and having penetrated to its essence, he then showed others its basic configuration and taught others how to garner from it more joy and more wisdom.

A critic's function was primarily the interpretation of the text, its meaning, its basic structure, and only secondarily historical, psychological, or sociological analysis. Literary history, psychology, sociology were at best aids to the main purpose. They supplied a framework for a critic's elucidation of the text itself, for his penetration into the innermost world of the artist. They helped to illumine the uniqueness of a writer who brought to life characters able to outlast time and to transcend a specific spatial environment.

Niger put his theory of criticism into practice in hundreds of essays during half a century. Despite his preoccupation with Yiddish literature, he did not disparage the striving of the Hebrew writers who were reviving the ancient tongue. He was the principal advisor of the Louis LaMed Foundation for the Advancement of Hebrew and Yiddish Literature. In 1941, he published under its auspices a study, *Bilingualism in the History of Jewish Literature*. He pointed out that bilingualism was a Jewish tradition since biblical days. Parts of the Books of Ezra and Daniel were composed in Aramaic, while the other biblical books were in Hebrew.

During the Golden Age of Sephardic literature, writers and readers used both Hebrew and Arabic. In more recent centuries, Hebrew and Yiddish were used in ethical tracts, in devotional prayers, and by bilingual authors. Although some opposition to bilingualism arose from time to time, the fact remained that Jews were more often bilingual than monolingual. Both Hebrew and Yiddish were pillars that sustained the Jewish structure. Hence, the creative energies of Hebraists and Yiddishists should not be frittered away in mutual recriminations but should be utilized for the enrichment of a common Jewish culture.

Niger's contribution to Yiddish culture was best summarized by the poet H. Leivick at the critic's funeral in 1955: "Niger experienced in his lifetime all the sorrows of a Jew nowadays. More than once he shared our Jewish destiny, peering into the depths of the abyss; more than once he stood beneath the raised fist and the gun of death-dealing evil. He saw the hand of the murderer; he felt the pain of the victim; and there arose in him the clarity of great understanding, the purity of a humanistic view of the world. He learned to judge the world not according to the severity of law but according to that loftiest reason which embraces compassion, as he penetrated into the essence of tragedy, human and Jewish. To Yiddish literature, initially of small dimensions, he brought the light of reason and of genuine, sorrow-crowned humanism; the light of the restrained smile and of considerate love for our people's destiny; and then, as the power of Yiddish grew and flourished, he helped to convert it into a great tabernacle."

5

The Hegemony of Kiev

JEWISH LITERARY CREATIVITY in revolutionary and post-revolutionary Russia was largely centered in the three cities of Kiev, intellectual capital of the Ukraine, Minsk, capital of White Russia, and Moscow, into which Jews began to stream once the Czarist restrictions were lifted.

Intoxication gripped Jewish youth when the hour of emancipation from centuries-old disabilities came in 1917. A galaxy of radiant and courageous poets, whose creative energy was released after the war years of enforced silence, trumpeted forth their joy at the new order which promised them guarantees of freedom and equality. They were ready to embrace the whole world in a universal dance of fraternity. Their holiday mood was, however, short-lived. The incursion of pogrom hordes, led by Denikin, Petlura, Machno and other counter-revolutionists into the provinces of the Pale inhabited by most Jews brought death and tragedy to hundreds of thousands.

The Yiddish poets then took up sword and pen to preserve the newly gained and once more imperiled freedom. Two of them, Osher Shvartzman and Beinish Shteinman, fell at the front in their twenties before their lyric talent had a chance to ripen. When victory finally came after a hard struggle that decimated dozens of Jewish townlets, hunger set in throughout the devastated provinces. The severe and probably necessary restrictions of military communism were supplanted by the New Economic Policy, which gave greater leeway to individual initiative not only in business and industry but also in literature and journalism.

During the years of the N.E.P., Kiev exercised hegemony over Yiddish literature in Russia, since the Warsaw and Vilna centers had been severed from Soviet territory; Moscow and Minsk were not yet sufficiently articulate to offer a serious challenge; and the Wise Men of Odessa, who had used Hebrew far more than Yiddish as their literary medium, were either silent or had emigrated to New York, Berlin and Palestine.

Three alternatives faced Russian Jews during the first post-revolutionary decade. After the Balfour Declaration of 1917, they could answer the call of Zion, leave legally or, more often, illegally for the promised Jewish homeland. There they could continue their Hassidic or rabbinic traditions, immerse themselves in biblical learning, or as secularists develop a neo-Hebrew culture. Thousands chose this path, joined kibbutzim, buttressed Jewish national and religious institutions, and paved the way for the establishment of an independent Jewish state.

Another alternative, once freedom of movement was vouchsafed to Jews, was to leave the cramped towns and townlets of the Pale for the cities and provinces of the vast Soviet realm, especially for the great metropolitan centers of Moscow and Leningrad. There they could slough their ghetto characteristics, intermarry, and assimilate into the Slavic majority. Hundreds of thousands chose this path.

A third alternative favored not Jewish disappearance, whether through emigration or assimilation, but rather an intensification of Jewish belongingness and the reconstruction of the Jewish nationality on Soviet soil, either in their existing communities or in new concentrations in Crimea or some other autonomous Jewish region. This was the alternative chosen by millions and at first supported by the government. For these millions, Yiddish was the chief unifying factor.

Religion was on the decline, since Marxists had dubbed it opium for the masses and good Communists were expected to espouse atheism. Zionism was looked at askance as a form of alien nationalism and its leaders were imprisoned or exiled. The dense concentration of Jews in Ukrainian towns was especially favorable for the growth of Yiddish cultural institutions and the Communist regime generously subsidized schools, libraries, press, scholarly and literary groups. The Kiev Group then forged to the van. The mentors of this group were David Bergelson and Der Nister, talented writers whose reputation was already well established before the Revolution.

Bergelson, who was born in 1884 at Sarne, a small town in the province of Kiev, first attracted attention in 1909 with his novelette *Railroad Station (Arum Vokzal)*. His earliest long novel *After All (Nokh Alemen)* was hailed in 1913 as the tenderest masterpiece of impressionistic writing. Thereafter he continued to enrich Yiddish literature with plays and narratives of enduring value.

From the work of this post-classical writer more than from the blatant noises of partisan propagandists one can gain a good insight into the transformations that swept over the millions of Jews between the Dnieper and the Dniester, the Baltic and the Black Seas, during the first half of the twentieth century. Their spiritual distress and their unflagging idealism, their decadent moods and their unrealized hopes for a Messianic morrow live on in his prose epics and dramas.

Two literary strains commingle and merge in this novelist of Ukrainian Jewry. His Russian lineage goes back to Goncharov, Turgenev and Chekhov. His Jewishness owes more to the folklore of the Pale and to the Yiddish revival launched by Mendele and Peretz than to the Bible and the sages of the Talmud.

Bergelson is not of the giants of the pen and his voice does not ring out in stentorian tones demanding attention and allegiance. His is the almost inaudible voice of the way-farer on the abandoned by-paths and forgotten lanes of dying towns. Silence hovers about his characters, silence and lone-liness, loneliness and melancholy. Though young in years, his heroes and heroines are old in their moods. Their faces are pale and colorless. Their eyes are deep sunken. They are prematurely tired. They resemble tender autumnal flow-ers that are nipped by the first frost and that can never regain the energy to blossom in full glowing October. They lower their heads in mild resignation and wait patiently for their dreary end.

Mirel Hurwitz, the heroine of Bergelson's finest novel, *After All,* and his most carefully drawn character, best illus-trates his pre-Soviet types. As the only child of a well-to-do and highly respected merchant, she lives in daydreams and indulges in vague longing for some indefinable arena of ac-tion larger than the few streets of her little town. At seven-teen she drifts into an engagement with a nice young man of the neighborhood, a young man acceptable to her parents, her relatives and public opinion in general. But when she gets to the provincial capital on a visit and when she sees wider horizons than she has hitherto known, she becomes utterly dissatisfied with her narrow circle and its traditional, intolerant views. She breaks off her engagement and resumes her passive reveling in nebulous visions of freedom, in misty dreams of vast panoramas. Day follows day with unvarying routine, with activities that are not too meaningful. Months come and go. They unite to years and the years meander on lazily.

Mirel's melancholy smile turns ironic. Her tiredness turns to utter indifference to the few joys or sorrows that might fall into her lap. She drifts into a practical marriage with-out any real desire and without much resistance. The eter-nal sameness saps what remains of her youth and rebellious-ness. Her mind and her feelings become dulled. From a kindhearted, hard-working, slow-witted husband who bores her, she seeks relief by returning to her parents. But there everything is as petty and as empty as before. The same people are still engaged in the same talk as in all the preced-

ing years. The best of her acquaintances are still dissatisfied
with life, but not a single one of them does anything concrete to overcome this dissatisfaction. They get together at
each other's homes and over a cup of tea they lament the
passing of time and the barrenness of their world. Then each
of them goes back to his own hearth and resumes his monot-
onous activities and undeviating habits. Their today does
not really differ from their yesterday or yesteryear, nor will
their tomorrow be any different because of their exertions.
They will continue to vegetate on and on, unless an unexpected catastrophe intervenes. And yet, they are all the time
conscious that somehow, somewhere, storms must be brewing
and that the almost universal urge for a dramatic change
must be materializing into action.

Young Bergelson is aware of the teeming activity of the
large metropolitan centers in which slumber the forces of the
future. But in his pre-revolutionary tales, he is primarily the
chronicler of the little towns whose past, though never too
bright or too glorious, was incomparably better than their
hopeless present: "I am sitting so long at the gate of the
town into which nobody enters and which no one leaves. All
that I once knew, I have long ago forgotten and only a
single thought remains in my mind, the thought that all,
all have died and that I alone have survived. Hence, I am
really no longer waiting for anybody. And when I look about
me again and when I feel the energy and the power that
slumber in me, I do not even sigh any more. I merely think
that I am the guardian of a dead town."

Bergelson is an Impressionist. He describes not events
themselves but rather the echo of events in the souls of
human beings. He is a painter of twilight moods, of late
autumn landscapes, of withering hopes, of chronic unhappi-
ness, of ineffectual yearning for the unexpected and the
dramatic.

The Revolution of 1917 galvanized the lethargic villages
and towns of the Ukraine. The Jewish middle class, whose
dying had been the main theme of Bergelson, was, however,
beyond recovery. Catastrophe followed catastrophe. During
the years of civil strife and of military communism, the for-

mer respected burghers of hundreds of communities between the Dnieper and the Dniester were, on the one hand, hounded and massacred because of their Jewishness by the followers of Petlura and Denikin and, on the other hand, despoiled and degraded because of their bourgeois origin by the Bolshevik conquerors. The slight alleviation of their fundamentally hopeless status during the period of the N.E.P. did not long endure. Starvation and exile, economic decay and migration to the interior provinces of Russia decimated their ranks throughout the 1930's, and the Nazi avalanche of the early 1940's annihilated the survivors and engulfed whatever remained of their cultural institutions and their traditional way of life.

Bergelson had early voiced his faith in the new Russia that was arising out of the ruins of Czardom, feudalism and foreign exploitation. He participated in the Yiddish publications and cultural activities of revolutionary Kiev from 1917 to 1919. His few years in Berlin during the period of the N.E.P. and his trip to the United States in 1929 merely confirmed him in his preference for Soviet society. In the short stories of *Biro-Bidjaner* (1934) and in his long novels of the 1930's, *Penek* and *Dnieper,* he depicted the painful transition to the new order. Despite his affirmation of the dominant Communist regime, there is, however, even in these works, unmistakable nostalgia for a world that is no more, the world of his childhood, its unhurried pace, its shabby respectability, its wasteful aimlessness. There is also the recognition that, in the Communist state even as in the capitalist state, assimilation of Jewish culture to the cultural patterns of non-Jewish neighbors is still a long way off.

During the Second World War, Bergelson enriched Soviet Jewry with finely chiseled short stories, of which the best is *Between Mountains (Zvishen Berg).* His last novel, *Two Worlds (Zvei Veltn)* was being published in Moscow in 1948, when all news of him ceased. Throughout the next decade, every question about him addressed to Soviet authorities and to Soviet writers was answered with silence. After the death of Stalin, this silence was broken and his liquidation on August 12, 1952 was confirmed as a miscarriage of justice.

The same purge to which Bergelson fell a victim also removed from the literary scene the finest of the symbolist novelists and poets, Der Nister, pseudonymn of Pinchas Kahanovitch, who was born in 1884 in the city of Berditchev and who perished in a Soviet prison a few years before the firing squad blotted out the lives of his Kiev associates.

This Yiddish-Hebrew pseudonym, which may be translated as the Hidden One or the Occult Person, well characterizes him as the outstanding representative of Neoromanticism among the Yiddish writers of the Ukraine.

Der Nister began in 1907 with prose poems, dream images, in which Jewish, Christian and Olympian supernatural creatures were intermingled. He continued in 1912 and 1918 with songs, odes, versified prayers, allegories of God and Satan, mystic visions that spanned heaven and earth and dissolved in nebulous melancholy, ballads which were meant to delight children but which also hinted at meanings beyond their grasp. Thus, the tree that resists the peasant's axe and is as reluctant to die as the horse pursued by the bear, the white goat that lulls the infant to sleep, the sprites that dwell in abandoned ruins, the gnome that bestows wealth, the cat that feeds its playmate the mouse, the rooster that is the sole companion and nurse of the sick grandmother —all have traits and feelings not unlike those of human beings and yet they are at the same time symbols of abstractions and qualities. What Marc Chagall sought to express in color, Der Nister attempted in verse and poetic prose.

As the translator into Yiddish of Hans Christian Anderson's fairy tales and as a student of cabalistic lore, Der Nister succeeded in combining European and Hebraic elements in his tales. He also felt strongly the influence of Rabbi Nachman Bratslaver, the most talented of the Hassidic weavers of stories. Forests alternate with deserts, enchanters and witches with angels, demons and Nazarites, bears of the north with lions of the south. Amidst the whirl of events that traverse earth and moon and starry constellations, the loneliness of the individual peers through as he roams far and wide in search of holiness and ultimate wisdom. Unhappy with his own age and powerless to change it, such a person attempts to break out of it. He wanders on and on beyond any specific time or clearly defined realm. Now and then he encounters a hermit or a graybeard who is even further removed from normal pleasures and mundane pursuits and therefore closer to the source of essential insight. They help him to overcome demonic temptations. They find for him a track through seemingly trackless wastes. They accompany him for a while through the darkest mazes of forests. They weave their tales into his tales.

Der Nister's reputation as a leading member of the Kiev Group was already well established when the Russian Revolution broke out. As a non-political writer, he felt ever more and more isolated amidst the contending ideological coteries and left for Berlin. There he published two volumes of *Contemplations* (*Gedakht,* 1922), stories that followed the model of Nachman Bratslaver. In one story, he made a beggar the savior of kings. In others, he introduced magic stones, a healing mirror, a wolf that traveled faster than the wind. Transported on the back of the wolf, the hero of the *Bovo-Maisse* could quickly reach the remote land where his betrothed, a paralyzed princess, was awaiting his coming and he her recovery from a baneful spell.

After returning to the Ukraine, Der Nister was silent for several years and, when he resumed publication in 1929, his volume *From My Treasures* (*Fun Meine Giter*) betrayed a pessimism not evident earlier. The opening narrative was put in the mouth of a madman in a madhouse. This madman related his experiences in converting mud to gold until he became the supreme lord of the land and arrogant beyond all mortals. Then Der Nister sketched the downfall and degradation of this plutocrat, who in his final extremity, after exhausting all other means of feeding ten hungry bears, had to offer them his own ten fingers and his heart to gnaw at. Beyond the apparent meaning of these changes of fortune, the reader senses the author's hints of intense anguish and spiritual distress, but hints so deeply veiled that their true import still defies clarification. Perhaps such labyrinthean mystification was necessary if the romantic writer wished to remain true to his inner self and yet to survive at a time when anti-Romanticism and Socialist Realism were the prescribed slogans for literature.

A decade later, however, the pressure upon Der Nister was too great to be successfully resisted. In his major work *Family Mashber,* the first volume of which appeared in 1939, he adopted the realistic style of writing demanded of all Soviet novelists. However, he applied it not to contemporary life but to an era which was already historic and to a social order of which only vestiges remained: Berdichev of the 1870's.

Caught between his sympathy for his tradition-rooted characters and the necessity of following the anti-religious Communist party line, he added an apologetic preface. In it, he explained that he deemed it artistically more desirable not to pronounce the doom of his characters in advance but rather to portray them proceeding slowly and inevitably to their historic destiny, the abyss. He wanted to let them unfold their glamorous traits no less than their ugly ones and then to show how the logic of their further inner development would drive them unalterably to decay and damnation. He promised that, together with the still uncompleted later volumes, his work would put the finishing touches to an old generation which was steeped in medievalism and would also trace the tragic beginning of a more enlightened way of life which would gradually ripen into revolutionary activities and sweep away the accumulated rot of centuries.

The city depicted by Der Nister developed in the form of three concentric circles. The innermost circle, the market district, was the heart of all business activities. The second circle embraced the residential area, in which were concentrated religious and cultural activities of the Jewish community. The third circle, suburbia, was inhabited by the poorest of the poor, criminals, cranks, prostitutes, the subversive and revolutionary elements that would later topple the entire social edifice.

The Mashbers belong to the patricians of the city. Luzi, the oldest brother, faces a spiritual crisis when the Hassidic rabbi in whom he found sustenance and guidance passes away. Ultimately he discovers the genuineness he seeks: he joins the despised, poor, ardent Bratslaver Hassidim. Among them, he comes to understand and to appreciate the true humanity in the town's third circle.

Moshe Mashber, the second brother, puts his faith solely in business and lives primarily in order to accumulate wealth. By experiencing a business crisis and a decline of fortune, he is humbled in his pride and is saved from despair by a saintly pseudo-beggar, a *Lamedvovnik*.

Alter Mashber, the youngest brother, has to overcome pain and illness. When his clouded mind recovers, he accepts the equality of all human beings and is happy to marry the maid of the Mashber household. The stratified social structure, as exemplified by this well-to-do family, begins to show fissures and its ultimate collapse can be predicted.

This collapse occurs in the second volume, which was published in 1948 in the United States but not in Russia: in that year all Yiddish publications ceased in the Soviet Union, not to be resumed until after Stalin's death. Moshe Mashber's wealth disintegrates, he is forced into bankruptcy, he is imprisoned for fraud, and on his release he dies a broken man. Meanwhile, Luzi Mashber continues his quiet acts of kindness and love in behalf of the despised and oppressed members of the Jewish community, as befits an adherent of Bratslav Hassidism. He is joined by Sruli, a saint in tatters, and by Michel Bukier, whose eternal questioning leads to excessive skepticism and, as a result, to unmerited persecution on the part of the town's religious fanatics. In these three characters, but especially in Luzi Mashber, the author depicts himself and his kind, silent, self-effacing approach.

Only once does Luzi break out in eloquence. Then he expresses his undying hope and unshakeable faith in his Jewish people. His words spring from the heart of the author, who otherwise had to masquerade his feelings: "Israel is beloved. Neither the pains of *Galut* nor his expulsion from his father's table stops him from feeling himself to be God's child, chosen to reign in the future. Let not the nations of the earth rejoice in the rich portion allotted to them now and let them not look down upon Israel, which is now black as are the tents of Kedar. Israel is indeed divided and left at the mercy of many swords which hang above his head and compel him to beg for life's sustenance of all the cruel murderers in this world. Let not the nations rejoice and mock Israel, who appears strange, disunited, an outcast stepchild among them. The curse upon Israel is only temporary, no matter how long it lasts. His lot, to be an unhappy beggar on accursed roads, will ultimately end. He will be the light and salvation predicted and promised by the Prophets. Yet even now and in all generations when catastrophes overwhelm Israel, saints arise who fathom the meaning of Israel's destiny, who accompany him on his thorny road with love and compassion, and who gladly receive the arrows meant for him. They and their followers are fortunate enough to feel Israel's sublime pain, the pain of the insulted, injured and tortured heart of the world. Israel is God's beloved, an example to mankind of the fortitude and dignity with which one bears suffering even when the knife is at one's throat. Beloved is Israel, who even in darkest moments still retains a shimmer of hope in salvation, salvation not alone for himself but for all mankind, for whom he is the blessed victim and also herald of the Messianic promise of a time when all tears will be wiped away from all faces. Yes, a time will come when to the Holy Mountain there will troop, as to a wedding, sages and crowned light-bearing saints, with the Anointed One in their midst and the whole world following them—man, woman and child, not only of the human species but also of beasts and cattle and birds—all of whom will be lifted up and filled with knowledge of that day of universal rejoicing, every sage with his admirers, every prophet with his followers, every saint with his disciples, everyone who guarded the Holy Flame amidst storms and prevented its extinction. My brothers, guard this Flame bequeated to you, guard it until the Messianic era when all knees will bend before the Savior and all heads of all living creatures in which there is a living soul will ask His blessing. Guard the Flame, my brothers!"

Luzi's ardent words of hope and comfort were rudely

interrupted by a stone hurled at him through a window. Even so was this valedictory of Der Nister, upon which he worked for more than a decade, rudely interrupted by the Soviet secret police who came to arrest him. His first words on that occasion are reported to have been: "Thank God, you came at last. I have waited for you so long." Thereafter silence engulfed him, and death in prison on June 4, 1950.

Premonitions of his end filled the second volume of Der Nister's masterpiece, upon which he continued to work while one after another of his friends, colleagues and followers were vanishing from the public eye and terror stalked the survivors. The final chapters, therefore, overemphasized scenes of dying and bared the long hidden suffering of a tortured soul.

The author was expected to revile a people and a tradition which he loved so fervently in his heart of hearts and he had no way of knowing whether this love, concealed beneath an outer veneer of apparent dislike and locked up in not easily decipherable symbolic language, would ever penetrate to readers in later years or be intelligible to them. In the morass in which he was forced to move in his last years, he remained a hidden saint, the noblest personality among the Soviet Yiddish writers.

The most talented disciple of Der Nister was Leib Kvitko (1890–1952), who together with David Hofstein and Peretz Markish formed the lyric triumvirate of the Kiev Group. These poets came to the fore during the period of revolution and military communism, 1917 to 1921. They were tragically stirred by the Ukrainian pogroms which followed the initial wave of liberation. They left the communities that were drenched in Jewish blood. They found a temporary asylum in Berlin of the early Weimar Republic. They returned to Kiev during the thaw of the New Economic Policy in the mid-1920's. There, as well as in Kharkov and Moscow, they devoted the next two decades to directing literary, educational and cultural activities in the Yiddish tongue and to hymning the glory of Soviet achievements in war and peace. Despite their patriotic submission to every aspect of Soviet policy, all three were imprisoned in 1948 during Stalin's purge of Jewish intellectuals and, after four years of interrogation, torture, suspense, perished in 1952.

Kvitko stemmed from an impoverished rabbinical family of Podolia and was orphaned at an early age. Wandering from town to town, he barely eked out a living at various trades. When the Revolution broke out, he welcomed it as ushering in an era of justice and equality.

In a lyric of 1917, he bade farewell to the old, joyless, flowerless, songless world. After the gun and the sword will have destroyed the yoke of ages, he was certain that peace would sprout and a healthy youth, with fiery blood in its veins, would march on and on, free and strong.

In another lyric, Kvitko described Red Youth, radiant and intoxicated with the new freedom, streaming and storming onward, while parents stood on the sidelines and looked on horrified. The rift between the generation of mice and the generation of wrath was unbridgeable. "Though my father dies of hunger and calls me to his couch, I try not to hear. I must belong to the storm of destruction, to the hammers that build a new structure. I become more young, more free. Our East is afire at dawn and a new day begins."

During the following two years, however, Kvitko experienced Petlura's reign of terror in Ukrainian Jewish communities. He then composed lyrics full of hatred toward a foe who smashed cradles and hanged infants and full of love for his long suffering Jewish people. In an unforgettable lyric in the volume *1919*, he depicted Jesus, the Jewish child worshiped by the perpetrators of pogroms, as going about from place to place, bloodstained and crucified, with Jewish pain in his eyes and Jewish patience in his veins. As Jesus passed houses where Jewish children once frolicked, he dared not look into them. He paused on roads where his image was displayed, tore it down, and bowed his head in shame. Stopping before every priest's home, he scratched on the walls in embittered silence deep black crosses of shame.

In another lyric, Kvitko saw his ancestors pleading with him not to curse the murderers but to forgive them. "Was not every murderer once a child? Does not every murderer laugh and smile at his own child? Forgive, forgive!" But young blood seethed in the poet's veins and, viewing the aftermath of slaughtered communities, he rather prayed for the strength to hate, strength which, as a Jew, he did not possess.

In the lyric anthology *Youth* (*Yugend*), which appeared early in 1922, after the defeat of the counter-revolutionary forces, Kvitko reverted to his earlier enthusiastic mood, glorying in Soviet achievements, in the war of youth against parental authority, in the burning of the old rags of the defunct order. "I am as young as the dawn and as fresh as the dew. I'll build a new temple in the sun-blest day. Go away, you oldsters, depart with the day. Your heart is an old fiddle whose song is long ended. We are the blood-and-fire youngsters who paint with clear colors a new life and a bright panorama."

Kvitko's lyrics *Green Grass*, which appeared in 1922, after his arrival in Berlin, reprinted the poems of his earlier volume *Steps* (*Tritt*, 1919) and added others full of joy in his youthful exuberance, radiant in dreams, treasuring memories, delighting in hopes. After his return to the Ukraine in 1925, he resumed writing tales for children of Yiddish elementary classes and lyrics to be sung in nursery schools and kindergartens. Some of these emphasized social responsibility, Communist reconstruction, the need for agricultural pioneering; but most spoke joyously to the heart of children about ponies and calves, fishermen's dancing skiffs, fiddles that enchanted birds and bees and hens. Kvitko was undoubtedly Soviet Russia's greatest master of the juvenile lyric.

Kvitko's tales, on the other hand, lack originality. They follow faithfully the approved formula for Soviet narrators. They feature Soviet heroes who engage in underground activities, unmask traitors, and succeed in conspiratorial work abroad. Such a hero is Presber in the novel *Rio Grande Furs* (*Riogrander Fel*, 1928). Presber aids Hamburg's proletarian rebels in 1923. He participates in the capture of a ship after it leaves the German harbor for the high seas and in the diversion of its cargo to revolutionary China. Despite a smashed hand and the loss of an ear, he is back in

Hamburg from the Far East within a year and helps to lure a traitorous Soviet agent back to Russia for proper punishment.

Kvitko's *Selected Works* (*Geklibene Verk,* 1937) were dedicated to Stalin and abounded in flattery to him. Stalin was clothed with the divine attributes of omniscience and omnipotence, in a lullaby sung by a child to its mother. The child dreamed that it went to a forest to cut tree trunks to build a ship which would float over seas and catch golden fish. The child was able to frighten off an intruding hare and to ward off a fox, but then there came a pack of wolves that wanted to tear it to pieces. Stalin heard what was going on and he sent a tank to the rescue. The tank shot up the wolves and brought the child back to its mother. In another dream, the child sailed on the ship. Rains came and a great wind which capsized the ship. Stalin heard the cries of the child as it was being swallowed by the waves and he sent a hydroplane which scattered the storm and brought the child back to the Kremlin. In a third dream, the child heard the door open. Someone entered, picked it up and talked to it like a loving father. "Well, guess who it was. Surely you know!" The same volume also included tributes to Voroshilov, Marshal Budenny, war heroes of the Red Army, and sailors of the Red Fleet, all of whom were absolutely fearless and were furthering the victory of the proletariat and the liberation of the world.

Kvitko's last volume, *Songs of My Moods* (*Gesang Fun Mein Gemiet,* 1947), contained the poems he composed after the Nazi attacks upon Russia in 1941. They abounded in invective against German barbarism and in praise of Soviet heroism and self-sacrifice. They also made mention of Jewish fighters and Jewish fliers who avenged German misdeeds. A little over a year after the appearance of this patriotic poetic collection, Kvitko was imprisoned on charges trumped up by the secret police upon Stalin's urging. Together with other Jewish poets and novelists, he was shot on August 12, 1952. Two years later, he was rehabilitated as another innocent victim of miscarried justice and hailed as the great poet who united in his art the destinies of the Jewish, Russian and Ukrainian cultural groups.

David Hofstein (1889–1952) was only a year older than Kvitko, but he began to write much earlier. He grew up in a Volynian village at the edge of a forest as the oldest of eleven children and his first lyrics reflected his intimate contact with nature in its various aspects. They were united into poetic cycles entitled "Fields," "Mountains," "Forest." These idyllic songs of nature, begun in 1911, continued until his cycle "Snow" in 1919. They breathe the freshness of youth and the joy of early love. He speaks of himself as a young branch of an old tree, as gathering young strength from the old trunk. He sings of young brows, young knees, young days, young hearts, young joy. He is ecstatic with wild joy, pristine joy, sun-joy, hot joy, new joy.

Meanwhile, the Revolution of 1917 broke in upon his gentle moods and stirred him to rapturous acceptance of the new socialist reality. Ten years earlier he had been refused admission to the University of Kiev because of the restricted quota for Jewish students. He then had to acquire his higher education by himself without the guidance of teachers. Now he was elevated to the position of a lecturer in Moscow and he could head the Yiddish Cultural League in Kiev. He felt himself to be at last a free individual, the equal of all proletarians within the Soviet realm. His verses welcomed the dawned day of revolution, the glories of October and May, the rainbow colors that flooded the world, the brotherhood of peoples. He was happy to take his place in the vanguard of advancing mankind, marching proudly in step with millions of toilers. He called himself a bit of resounding copper that wakened the tired and drowned out the feeble-hearted, so that the procession under the Red Flag should not falter or retreat. His songs hailing the achievements of the Revolution established his popularity not only in his own land but also in radical Jewish circles beyond its borders.

Hofstein's elegies, in which he mourned for the Ukrainian Jewish communities devastated by Petlura, Denikin and counter-revolutionary hordes, appeared in 1922, with illustrations by Marc Chagall. Passing through ruined towns, Hofstein wondered whether anything could compensate for a single drop of a child's innocent blood. He noted that for generations the Ukrainian marketplaces had echoed with the drunken songs and the boots of bandits, and that the shadow of shame was still lingering on Ukrainian highways.

Brave in the exercise of his new freedom, Hofstein protested against the dominant sector of the Jewish Communist movement, the *Yevsektsie,* for its endorsing the banning of Hebrew and the persecution of Hebrew writers. He then discovered that he too was suspect and subject to persecution for daring to speak up. He thereupon left Russia in 1923. For a time he lived in Leipzig and in Berlin. Then he moved on to Palestine. In the Jewish homeland he contributed Hebrew songs, chiefly to periodicals of the Labor Zionists. Seeking inspiration in the Bible and in Jewish legends, he completed a dramatic poem, *Saul,* in 1924, and an Expressionistic spectacle, *Messianic Times (Moshiakhs Tsaiten),* in 1925.

The former work depicted the first king of Israel at the beginning and at the end of his troubled reign. The real hero, however, was the populace rather than this tragic ruler. In the first scene, the people of Israel are faced with the aggression of their Ammonite neighbors. They realize that the corrupt sons of the Prophet Samuel are incompetent, unable to protect them, and they therefore demand a strong monarch to lead them. Despite Samuel's warning not to accept the yoke of a monarchy, they proceed to acclaim Saul as king.

The second scene then shows the aftermath of this unwise decision: Saul in his last moments at Gilboa. Wielding absolute power, his character has deteriorated. Moody, depressed, consorting with witches, he has become unpopular with his subjects. When these again find themselves harassed by enemies on all sides, they rise up in revolt against the capricious ruler. After his children are slain and the trapped monarch falls upon his sword, there is general acclamation: "The King is dead, long live the People!" Free once more, the masses live on, fight, create, eternally strong, forever rejuvenated.

Parallels between the dramatized events and contemporary Russian events were not difficult to discover and afforded an insight into the poet's thinking while abroad.

When restrictions upon individual initiative were temporarily loosened during the period of the N.E.P., writers began to feel a thawing also of oppressive measures imposed upon literary expression and publishing during the earlier period of military communism. After Kvitko and Markish returned to Kiev, Hofstein too was overcome by longing for Russia, especially for his children who had remained there. Confessing his heresies and promising atonement, he was permitted to resume his lecturing, editing, writing and translating.

In the preface to his *Songs* (*Lieder*, 1935), he referred to the labyrinthian road on which he traveled before he became a militant Marxist. He recalled his early religious upbringing, the idyllic delusions of his childhood, his contentment with admiring phenomena as a mere onlooker, his gradual questioning of essences, until his final abandonment of his position on the sidelines and his becoming a participant in the struggle for a better world.

After his return to Russia in 1926, Hofstein had to follow faithfully prescribed patterns of thinking, creating and the various gyrations of the party line. He had to sing optimistically of a freedom he no longer saw about him and of a future he no longer believed in unreservedly. As a result, the quality of his poems declined while the quantity kept on increasing. The subdued idyllic tone of his genuinely beautiful early poems gave way to a raucous overidealization of Soviet achievements in all fields. He even sang of "dear Soviet writing paper." In 1930, he wrote a hymn to the tractor as the tender-limbed steel horse of the free earth. In 1931, he hailed the construction of a dam along the Dnieper. In 1932, he was supposedly inspired by the launching of an Arctic icebreaker. In 1935, he eulogized aluminum as the Socialist metal. In 1936, he sang out again and again and again his gratitude to Stalin as the leader and friend of all free peoples. In 1937, he put into verse his worship of the Hammer and the Sickle. He glorified the restoration of Kiev as the Ukrainian capital. He saw Birobidjan as the promised home for the Jewish proletariat of all lands. Not in the desolate wastes of Palestine but in the seething steppes and primeval forests of the Jewish autonomous region in Siberia would Jewish genius flourish and great deeds be done.

Never again did Hofstein treat a biblical theme or refer to Jewish historic events. In a poem on woman as the alluring wonder in the ethereal world, he did mention that naive grandfathers related that woman first ate of the sweet fruit of knowledge. He hesitated, however, to betray the fact that his true source was the Book of Genesis. Nevertheless, now and then an ambiguous verse for a moment revealed like a lightning flash a corner of his soul inaccessible to casual readers. Thus, he prophesied a deluge of pitch and sulphur which would descend upon all lands. He hinted that, though eyes looked up through tears of blood to cruel gods of destruction, everyone must still continue to execute on the edge of a sword a fervent dance of supreme joy. He compared conscience to a dog torn from its leash. He felt that it was good to be bitten suddenly by its sharp teeth in the midst of too much servility and constantly calculating steps. Conscience enabled a person, after a thousand years, to utter at least a single bitter growl of nay.

After years of pretended prescribed joy, a moment of true joyous enthusiasm broke forth from him in 1948 when the new State of Israel came into existence with the blessing of Russia. He could then hail the young Jewish democracy without fear of retribution: "May the joy hidden in me reach out to all of you. I stand at my window and tell the world Good Morning." He gave assurance that the thin thread which linked him to his beginning had not torn.

Before the year was over, Hofstein was made to realize that he had revealed too loudly and too soon his joy at Israel's rebirth. The Soviet attitude toward Israel was changing, and what had been permitted at the beginning of the year was condemned as heretical before the end of the year. Hofstein was seized along with the other Jewish intellectuals of the Kiev Group. He was transported to Moscow for more severe interrogation of his purported deviationism, then condemned to a tortured existence in remote Siberian Tomsk, and finally shot on August 12, 1952, together with his prison mate David Bergelson. He also was later rehabilitated as a victim of the so-called personality cult.

Peretz Markish (1895–1952), the youngest of the Kiev triumvirate, published his first lyrics in 1917 and participated in the anthology *Eigens* of the following year, a combined venture of the Kiev Group, which then included not only Kvitko and Hofstein but also Bergelson, Der Nister, Yekheskel Dobrushin, Nachman Maisel and Kadia Molodowsky. This anthology gave expression to the general enthusiasm at the fall of Czarism and the liberation of the Jewish people along with the Ukrainian and Russian masses.

Markish's first volume, *Thresholds* (*Shveln*), appeared in 1919, the same year as Kvitko's first volume, *Steps* (*Trit*), and Hofstein's, *Along Roads* (*Bei Vegn*). Revolutionary romanticism gripped him no less than others of his circle. The past was over and gone. The future was veiled. The present was exciting and heroic. Lyrics burst from the heart of young Markish like an avalanche and were gathered in eight collections between 1919 and 1922. The best of these, *The Mound* (*Die Kupe,* 1922), has been compared to Chaim Nachman Bialik's powerful elegies following the Kishinev pogrom of 1903, especially in the vigorous protest against God, a God who permitted the massacre of his faithful people.

During the following years, Markish lived in Warsaw and was the recognized leader of a group of young Expressionist poets whom Hillel Zeitlin, editor of the influential Warsaw daily *Moment,* attacked as "The Gang"—*Khaliastre*—and who then adopted this name as a badge of honor and used it as the title of two anthologies. The first of these appeared in Warsaw in 1922 under the editorship of Markish and I. J. Singer. The second appeared in Paris two years later under the editorship of Markish and Oizer Varshavsky, with illustrations by Marc Chagall.

As the idol of Yiddish avant-garde writers, Markish was triumphantly received in London, Berlin and Paris. His extraordinarily handsome features, his melodious voice and his powerful gestures added to the effectiveness of his poems, which he recited and chanted to large, applauding audiences. Maturer critics, however, voiced the hope that the poet's feverish fermentation and Expressionistic hysteria would subside with greater maturity and would be replaced by more disciplined artistry. S. Niger characterized him in 1922 as a firebrand hurled forth from the revolutionary flame and as Pegasus on the run whirling around in a chaotic tornado, without goal or direction.

Throughout his entire odyssey, which led him as far as Jerusalem, Markish never slackened in his enthusiasm for the achievements of the Communist revolution. He defended the new Yiddish poets of Kiev as superior to the Yiddish lyricists of other lands. In his view, a spring torrent had descended upon the Jewish Pale and had swept away the idyllic, sweet, Sabbath melancholy which had characterized the entire inter-revolutionary period between 1905 and 1917. A world had been destroyed and a new one had been created. Yiddish poetry should, therefore, no longer be nostalgic and funereal but forward-looking and joyous. It should mirror the storm and stress of the new Soviet reality. Markish saw no contradiction between being a good Communist and a good Jew.

When he returned to Russia in 1926, he had no deviationary past to regret or to atone for. He was accepted in Kiev and in Moscow as the literary spokesman for revolutionary youth. In his hymn *My Generation* (*Mein Dor*, 1927), he eulogized the red dawn spreading from Russia, rousing, kindling, dazzling, liberating the remaining five-sixths of the globe that were not yet communistic. His marching song for May Day, 1928, roared and boomed and thundered and called for a united effort to break the workers' chains in all lands.

Markish's first novel, *Generation Follows Generation* (*Dor Ein, Dor Ois,* 1929), presented in two volumes the liberation of the multi-racial Ukraine from reactionary forces. The hero of the first volume was Mendel, the representative of the older, tradition-bound Jewish generation. The hero of the second volume was his son Ezra, who was caught up in Bolshevist enthusiasm and eager to build a better order. Both father and son sacrificed their lives for their fellow men but each did so for a different objective and in a different way. The Orthodox father sought to insure the survival of the Jewish community by bending before the havoc-wreaking, incited pogromists and hoping to minimize the damage. His was a passive martyrdom because any other form of resistance by a minority group, which had been denied weapons for self-defense, was unthinkable. The Communist son could plan and execute active resistance because the Revolution liberated Ukraine's Jews and enabled them to participate on equal terms with others in fighting political and social injustice.

Markish's second novel, *One Plus One* (*Eins Oif Eins*, 1934), presented as its central figure a Jewish bricklayer who left America after twenty-eight years of toil in order to lay bricks for Socialism in the Soviet state and who gradually came to understand that, despite certain hardships and an apparent lack of efficiency, Russian ways of working, creating, living were, on the whole, superior to American ways.

Markish's overlong poem in thirty cantos, *Brothers* (*Brieder*, 1929), concentrated once more on the theme of revolution. It chronicled the heroism of young Jewish proletarians, two brothers in a Ukrainian townlet, who sacrificed their lives for the triumph of their Communist ideal.

The poet's adoration of the dominant regime reached its climax in his epic *On Stalin* (*Poeme Vegn Stalinen*, 1940). In bombastic rhetoric, he sang of the great Stalin to whom all persons stretched out their hands in gratitude, Stalin from whose eyes lightning flashed and at whose feet thunders prostrated themselves, Stalin who covered Russia with light and clothed it with a coat of steel so that it could become the foremost fortress of this planet, the foremost homeland of thought. It is doubtful whether these hollow phrases, devoid of any lyric felicity, sprang from the heart of the poet. They probably had to be penned because all Yiddish poets, who had been at the forefront of the struggle against the Nazi philosophy in the 1930's, were suspected of not being too enthusiastic about the Molotov-Ribbentrop Pact which in 1939 pointed to an alliance between Stalin's Russia and Hitler's Germany.

Then came Hitler's betrayal of Stalin and the Nazi invasion of Russia. Markish then began his last and greatest poem, *War* (*Milkhome*), an epic in 162 cantos, upon which he worked throughout the war and post-war years and which was published in 1948, shortly before he was forever silenced by prison entombment. The poem covers the events that followed the invasion. Its main emphasis is on the suffering and heroism of Jewish individuals.

Unforgettable is the figure of Gur-Arye, the sole survivor of a slaughtered community. In a magnificent scene, he arises at night from the pit of the murdered Jews, feels himself miraculously still alive, escapes to a forest, and ultimately gets to a peasant's hut. As he collapses on the threshold, he sees an image of Jesus on the wall. In a visionary trance he then talks to Jesus as one crucified Jew to another, asking him whether he also came from the pit and whether he would now be going again to the suffering Jews still surviving in ghettos, to be with them at another crucifixion. Would Jesus now still preach non-resistance? Would he let widows and orphans be handed over to the Nazi murderers? Foxes, smelling recently living limbs around the pits, have already left their forest lairs in anticipation of a promising feast. "Go, Jesus! Let those at the ghetto gates know that nobody ascended to heaven from the Cross, that you too are hiding in a peasant's hut. You have served the hangsmen far more than the liberators by turning your other cheek. Throw away your crown of thorns, step on it, pulverize it! Go to the ghetto! There you will meet innumerable crucified children who are holier and purer than you, the Nazarene."

Despite Markish's faithful services to the Soviet regime, he did not escape four years of torture in a Moscow prison on the usual trumped up charges and a firing squad on August 12, 1952. He was, however, rehabilitated soon after the death of his adored Stalin. In 1957, his poems reappeared, but in a Russian rendering prepared by forty-two different translators. This attested to the fact that he had at least forty-two literary admirers with a thorough mastery of Yiddish, and yet the official explanation for the non-appearance of his works in Yiddish was that there no longer seemed to be any interest in Yiddish. In 1959, his uncompleted poetic epic, *Heritage (Yerusha)*, was published in Buenos Aires in the original Yiddish but not in Moscow or Kiev, where Yiddish continued to be frowned on. In 1964, his prose epic, *Generation Follows Generation,* was reprinted abroad but not in Russia, the land he loved and for which he agonized.

The apex of the literary creativity concentrated in post-revolutionary Kiev was reached in the second anthology of *Eigens,* in 1920. Here were included major tales of Bergelson and Der Nister and poems by all three of the lyric triumvirate. Symbolist abstractions and universal moods still dominated and proletarian tones were muted. Beinish Shteinman (1897–1919) and Osher Shvartzman (1890–1919), two young poets who met their end a few months earlier while fighting with the Red Army in the Ukraine, were represented by works only remotely connected with their heroic deeds.

Shteinman, in his dramatic poem *Messiah ben Yosef,* depicted a gloomy world over which Lilith, Queen of the Night, had ruled for a thousand years. When Messiah ben Yosef appeared amidst thunder, lightning and a reemerging sun, the enslaved populace hailed him as the long-yearned-for redeemer. Lilith, seeing her reign threatened, tried to calm her subjects and to lure the Messiah into her arms. When he disdained her overtures, she then tried her last stratagem. She pretended to join in the universal enthusiasm at the coming of the radiant Messiah who, as she explained, would bring happiness to innumerable later generations but not to the generation of transition. The present night-born generation was destined to fertilize with its blood the millennium to be. The disappointed populace then turned angrily upon the Messiah and stoned him. Again Lilith had triumphed, but her Dominion of Night would not endure forever. While the chorus joined in her outcry: "Messiah will not arise, he will not come," three little stars, fading away in the gathering gloom, sang tremulously: "Yet will he come, yet will he come," thus hinting that the premature, inadequate Messiah, son of Joseph, would be followed in the fullness of time by the true Messiah, son of David, who would usher in the genuine Messianic Age.

Osher Shvartzman's songs in *Eigens,* though written at the front lines from 1914 on, dealt with twilight moods when the sun poured its last yellow upon quiet fields and with summer evenings when the cattle returned to recline on the dewy grass. In a lyric prayer from the battlefield, he begged God not to delay any longer his mercy to those upon whom he poured out wrath but to bring back to dark, hungry townlets lit windows and abundant bread from plowed fields.

Shvartzman left as his legacy hardly more than sixty lyrics, but these sufficed to put him in the foremost rank of the Kiev Group. From 1911 on, he had served in the Russian cavalry, had experienced humiliations because of his Jewish origin, and was demobilized only after the Bolsheviks seized power. Then he returned to Kiev and participated in the publications of the Yiddish Communists. He felt closest to his cousin David Hofstein, who later edited his poems.

Despite the influence of Heine's *Weltschmerz,* Lermontov's Russian melancholy, and Bialik's tragic pathos, Shvartzman retained a sunny outlook and sang enthusiastic hymns to love and nature, freedom and joy, friendship and youth. Life in barracks from 1911 to 1914 and at the front from 1914 to 1917 was not easy for a sensitive poet and often he fled from drunken, carousing comrades to commune with himself and to record his feelings in verse. Most of his preserved songs, however, were composed in his last two years. When Kiev fell into the hands of Petlura and Ukrainian bands, he joined the Communist underground and, when pogroms on a large scale were perpetrated in town after town, he enlisted in the Red Army to avenge the innocent blood of his kinsmen and to safeguard the fruits of the Revolution. In one of his last poems, he wrote: "I shall not return to the land until I shall hear the full word of redemption." He did not return. His heroic death in battle, however, lent an aura to his personality and gave rise to lyric tributes by Hofstein, Kvitko, Itzik Fefer, Aaron Kushnirov, Ezra Fininberg, Aaron Vergelis, Moshe Khashtchevatsky and many other poets. His deeds were recounted and his poems studied

in Soviet Yiddish schools until the last school was closed and
the Kiev Group was liquidated.

Moshe Khashtchevatsky (1897–1943), who wrote Shvartzman's biography and who idealized him ever since their first
meeting in 1917, also died a hero's death in the Red Army,
fighting in a later war to save Moscow from the Nazis, but
by then Yiddish poets could no longer be held up as models
for Soviet youth, Jewish or non-Jewish. A pall of silence
descended upon him and not a single one of his many volumes of verse and prose has been reprinted since his death.

Khashtchevatsky's best lyrics were the early ones of his
Kiev period, when the N.E.P. still permitted considerable
freedom of expression. David Hofstein then compared him
to the Russian Symbolist Fedor Sologub. In an introduction
to Khashtchevatsky's first volume of verse, *Thirst* (*Durst*,
1922), he characterized the young poet as the cheerful por-
traitist of life's heaviness and his poems as sweet magic,
pure joy hovering over foaming poisons, red sunrays above
the green mold of swamps.

Though caught up in the fast-moving events, Khashtchevatsky could not easily dissociate himself from the old ways
of the Ukrainian townlet. His symbolic name for the Jewish
townlet was "The Swamp." The twenty-year-old poet set
out to search for the lost days of his youth and found that
these had retreated to the swamp, where they sat brooding
in an ever aging circle. He wanted to forget gray, gloomy
yesterdays and to turn his face to the morrow. But he could
not. Byronic tones infiltrated his lyric cries. "My cries go
up to heaven but heaven is covered with clouds. Or perhaps
there is no heaven and all my efforts are vain. I am lost
in the world even as Hagar in the parched desert. No miracle
is in sight, no water to fill my pitcher. I am destined to feel
my way blindly in the dark wilderness."

Khashtchevatsky compared his songs to raindrops that
came too late and to letters sent to friends who were already
dead. He longed for tranquility, for a roof above his head,
for a haven of peace within his four walls.

With the ending of the N.E.P., he had to stop singing
of his own sorrows and joys. He then followed the prescribed

party line. He rhapsodized Lenin, Stalin, industrial enterprises, Birobidjan, the Red Army and the Black Sea fleet. His poetic epic *Lenin* (1937) consisted of seven cantos. It began with Lenin's birth. It recorded the various stages of his revolutionary career. It ended with a requiem upon his death and with Stalin taking up Lenin's heritage: to guard the achievements of Communism. During the Second World War, however, Khashtchevatsky's last poems, *Once and Now* (*Amol un Haint*, 1943), reverted to biblical imagery. He stressed the Jewish aspects of the conflict no less than the Russian. He saw the Jewish struggle against Hitler as a continuation of David's struggle against Goliath, Samson's against the Philistines, and the Maccabeans against the Syrians. When the war ended and such sentiments were punished as evidences of Jewish nationalism, the poet was no longer among the living.

The decade from the Revolution to the end of the N.E.P. was the most productive decade of Soviet Yiddish literature and the Kiev Group harbored the greatest concentration of Yiddish literary talent. Despite the increasingly harsh restrictions of the following decades, the Kiev writers were able to maintain themselves as a viable group until they were decimated by war and imprisonment and their leaders executed by the firing squad on August 12, 1952.

6

The Challenge of Minsk

THE HEGEMONY OF KIEV was supported by the significant Yiddish literary center of Kharkov, the capital of the Ukraine after the Revolution, but was challenged by the large White Russian center of Minsk and, above all, by the ever growing Jewish center in the Soviet capital, Moscow. The literary critics of the latter two aspiring Yiddish centers scented heresies in the Kiev Group and contrasted the proletarian realism and Communist patriotism of their own writers with the decadent symbolism and apparent lack of Communist fervor among the Ukrainian Yiddish writers, with the single exception of Itzig Fefer. The attacks increased as the comparative freedom of the N.E.P. gave way to the stricter party control introduced in the early 1930's.

The Minsk critics were especially vehement in their denunciation. They flaunted their own superpatriotism and their own unflinching adherence to the party line, yet their end came earlier and the liquidation of their center was more thorough.

In the Czarist Empire, Minsk had been unable to rival its neighbors, Vilna and Warsaw, and after the Revolution it vainly sought to equal the achievements of Kiev and Moscow. The worker-poets, who came to the fore in its newly founded periodicals during the period of military Communism, were rich in optimism but poor in talent, full of enthusiasm for the new freedom but unable to embody this enthusiasm in works of distinction. They vociferously called upon the Jewish masses to battle for eternal peace and universal justice. They appealed to Jewish youth to destroy the traditional religious values and institutions and to forge a brighter future for all peoples in an earthly paradise. But their versified calls and dramatized appeals had far more propagandistic than artistic worth.

When the civil war ended and greater economic and political stability was established during the N.E.P. years, higher literary standards were demanded of writers. With the founding of the Yiddish organ *Shtern* in 1925, the Minsk Group became more significant. In its columns, essayists of distinction laid down rules for Yiddish proletarian literature and meted out stern rebukes to all who dared to deviate from these rules. Considerable authority was wielded by Ber Orshansky (1883–1945), who headed a Yiddish section in the Institute for White Russian Culture, by Yashe Bronshtein (1906–1937), who despite his youth pontificated as professor of Yiddish literature until he was liquidated as an enemy of the people, and by Khatzkl Dunietz, who as editor of the Yiddish daily *Oktiaber* faithfully interpreted the party line in literature as well as in politics until his arrest in 1935 by the secret police and his liquidation as a counter-revolutionary Trotskyite soon thereafter.

In 1928, Moshe Kulbak (1896–1940), who had lived in Vilna and Berlin, joined the Minsk Group. He was followed in 1929 by Max Erik (1898–1937), who directed Yiddish literary research both in Minsk and in Kiev until his arrest and death in a prison camp.

Of the Minsk poets, only Selig Axelrod (1904–1941) and Izzie Charik (1898–1937) commanded attention far beyond the borders of White Russia—until the former was shot for the crime of Jewish nationalism and the latter tortured to death in Russian prisons for as yet unrevealed heresies.

Axelrod had spent his youth in a Yeshiva and was deeply immersed in Jewish tradition when the Revolution broke out. In the five volumes of his lyrics, published between 1922 and 1938, he combined acceptance of the new revolutionary regime with nostalgic sadness at the disintegration of the warm hearth of his father and grandfather. In his lyric cycle "Old Home," he described the hopeless, emaciated faces of his graying parents, who remained behind in their lonely, decaying rooms while their three sons scattered in diverse directions, each occupied with his own destiny.

Axelrod confessed that he could not soar beyond his own individual emotions, that preoccupation with himself often made him forget the common weal. His subjectivity, his melancholy, his alternating between fear and hope made him suspect at a time when objectivity, optimism and unquestioning obedience to party programs were prescribed. He was accused of overemphasizing the bourgeois "I" and failing to stress the proletarian "we," of brooding Hamlet-like over the meaning of existence while profoundly dramatic events surged all about him, of following the decadent example of Sergei Yessenin, the Russian peasant-poet who proved incapable of adjusting to the Soviet reality and who committed suicide in 1925. Despite Axelrod's efforts to rehabilitate himself with songs of the glory of the Red Army, he was adjudged to be too Jewish-minded in his general outlook and was executed on June 26, 1941, two days before the German invaders entered Minsk.

The story of Axelrod's execution was revealed by a fellow prisoner, the Yiddish writer Herschel Weinrauch, author of *Blood On the Sun* (*Blit Uf Der Zun*, 1950). Before the Germans approached the White Russian capital, bombs from their planes set fire to the prison. When the prisoners clamored to be let out, the guards and secret police opened the bars and asked the prisoners to arrange themselves in rows, the political prisoners on one side and the criminals on the other. Since the records were destroyed in the conflagration, some political prisoners, including Weinrauch, preferred to take their chances with the thieves and murderers. Axelrod, truthful to the end, joined the column of political offenders.

These were marched off to a nearby forest clearing and shot without further ado. The hardened criminals were set free when their guards, fearful for their own lives, disappeared as the Germans came ever nearer. Weinrauch, who soon found himself behind the front, joined a partisan group, succeeded in finding his way to a Russian outpost, was evacuated to Samarkand, enlisted in the Soviet army, fought bravely against the Nazis, won officer's rank, was wounded in battle, and finally, after perilous adventures and utmost disillusionment with Soviet ideals, escaped to Palestine.

Izzie Charik rose like a meteor, flared brightly for a decade and a half on the literary horizon, and disappeared into the silence of an unknown grave at the age of thirty-nine.

As the son of a cobbler, Charik experienced early privations, joined the Red Army in 1919 as a young revolutionist, and was accepted into the Communist Party as a most devoted member. When his first lyrics appeared in 1920, his talent was immediately recognized and he was sent to Moscow to study literature and art. His lyric volume *On the Earth* (*Uf der Erd,* 1926) earned him the title of "singer of the muds of Minsk." As editor of the literary periodical *Shtern,* he became the most influential member of the Minsk Group. In 1935 he was honored by a book of eulogies, in which noted critics paid tribute to his poetic genius and to his political reliability. Nevertheless, two years later while at the height of his fame, he too fell a victim to a Stalinist purge.

As though he had a premonition of his early death, he expressed his eagerness to drain life of its experiences quickly and in the raw. "I care not if I am unknown to posterity and if nobody preserves my footsteps; now, now, when hearts are afire, I arrive with fists in my song." He longed for storm-filled days and restless nights. "My restlessness whirls like the wings of a windmill." His main subject matter was the galvanization of the dormant Jewish townlet, the transformation of bearded idlers to creative tillers of the good earth. He felt that there was no need for Jews to tarry any longer amidst the muds of Minsk at a time when the Urals and the

Crimea beckoned and the vast spaces of all European and Asiatic Russia were open to them. The attachment to parents must be severed. "Pass away, pass away, you melancholy sires with frightened, snow-braided beards. From the last tragic collapse, you remained as the last witnesses. Pass away, pass away, you melancholy sires." Lenin's dictum that Soviet power plus electricity equals Communism was illustrated by Charik in a poetic narrative in which a simple, obedient Jewish worker participated in the building of an electric station and by his vigilance helped to thwart attempted sabotage. After three years of colossal exertion, electric blood finally streamed from city to city and Communism had scored another magnificent victory.

Charik included in this narrative a hymn of adoration to the G.P.U., the secret police that stood on guard everywhere and that came at midnight to shatter the nests of the dissident. One midnight in 1937, the police came for the adoring poet and he was silenced forever. Two decades after his disappearance he was rehabilitated as an innocent victim of Stalin's personality cult and his poems were published in translation.

Moshe Kulbak's literary career spanned two decades, of which the first was spent in Kovno, Vilna and Berlin, and the second in Minsk. He began to write poems in 1916 in the neo-romantic tradition, some of them in Hebrew under the influence of Ahad-Haam. Typical of his early period was the Symbolist poem "Lamed-Vov" (1920). Its hero was the chimney sweep Shmuel Itze, the eternally wandering Jew, who swept the ashes from a thousand chimneys but who could not clean out the ashes from his own soul. Mired in pain and darkness, he yearned for light and holiness, even as did Samael, the pain-filled, infernal counterpart of the Lord of Heaven. Only after he faced, understood and overcame the chaotic, negative, ugly force of Samael did Shmuel Itze attain to salvation.

Kulbak resided in Berlin from 1920 to 1923, when German Expressionism was at its height. The influence of this literary movement interpenetrated the grotesque episodes of his prose narratives *Messiah Ben Ephraim* (1924) and *Monday* (*Montag*, 1926). These rambling tales alternated

between the realm of reality and a metaphysical world beyond reality, a world where *Lamedvovniks* roamed and where
man, escaping from self, became one with the bird of the
forest, the cow on the meadow, and the loam of the earth.

Kulbak's Expressionistic lyrics were full of the joy of
life. His earlier tired receptivity gave way to an active grasp-
ing of sensations. He wanted to embrace the entire earth,
to dissolve into song, to be drunk with laughter and ecstasy.
He saw in Soviet Russia the radiant sun of renewal, the
splendid realm of social justice, a giant bearing golden tablets
of universal liberation. He hailed Russia's bronze youths
who responded to the ringing of the bells of freedom, who
left the feeble-hearted oldsters behind them and marched
forth to a more vigorous future.

Kulbak's Expressionistic period ended in 1928, when he
cast in his lot with the Minsk Group. He found that Expressionism was condemned by the Soviet literary spokesmen as
heretical and that he would have to confine himself to write
in accordance with the requirements of Socialist Realism.
He did so in his novel *Zelmenianer* (I, 1931, II, 1935).

In the two volumes of this novel Kulbak portrayed a
Jewish family whose members had vegetated for seventy years
in a decaying district and who discovered, after the Bolshevist Revolution, that their material and cultural structure
was built on a rotting foundation. Despite their Oblomov-
ism, inertia, resistance to progress, they had to accept electri-
fication of their district and the erection of new, bright, tall
buildings in place of their antiquated, spider-encrusted, loam
houses. Kulbak's crotchety characters, steeped in Jewish traditional behavior, were the heirs of Mendele's and Sholom
Aleichem's *Luftmenschen*. But even his young Bolshevik innovators did not entirely slough their family characteristics.
Their creator could not avoid smiling at them once in a
while. Because of his mildly ironic approach, he fell afoul
of the grimly serious Soviet critics. These critics could not
tolerate his laughter and his apparent unwillingness to depict
the representatives of the post-revolutionary youth as flaw-
lessly heroic. They were somewhat mollified a few years
later by his *Disner Childe Harold* (1933), a satirical epic
based on his Berlin experiences during the early years of

the Weimar Republic. There his humor was directed against the degenerate German bourgeoisie, a welcome target in the year of Hitler's ascent to power. While the title was reminiscent of Byron, the influence of Heine's comic epic *Germany, A Winter's Tale* was even more obvious.

In 1937, at the height of Kulbak's success, while his poems were being sung, his *Zelmenianer* widely read, and his last play performed in Moscow to the accompaniment of good reviews, the secret police swooped down upon him, forbade further performances of his plays, and banned all mention of his books. After his transportation to a Siberian prison camp, silence enveloped him. He dragged on a slave laborer's existence until 1940. Sixteen years after he perished, he was rehabilitated as an innocent victim of Stalin's personality cult.

After the liquidation of the Minsk writers in 1936 and 1937, only the Moscow center continued to function as the rival of Kiev. Before long, the rigid discipline and strict uniformity imposed by the Stalin dictatorship effaced any distinction between the literary centers. Writers became party functionaries and literature a useful tool of the state in molding a Soviet type of being. The Yiddish language was still tolerated but the content was restricted to non-Jewish themes insofar as possible. The proclaimed slogan was: "Soviet in content, Yiddish in form." But content and form could not always be easily wrenched apart, since words and phrases, especially those derived from the Hebrew, were laden with Jewish historic associations. Writers, therefore, had to exercise extreme caution in their use of language, avoiding Hebraisms and biblical expressions whenever possible. Because they often faltered and stumbled, they exposed themselves to Communist heresy hunting and political inquisitions. They were repeatedly forced to repent unpremeditated sins and lived in a constant state of insecurity. Besides, the constantly shifting party line resulted in works that were hailed as Soviet literary achievements at one time being labeled subversive at a later time. With writers distraught and confused, the quality of their publications declined even before all Yiddish writing was suppressed during Stalin's last years.

7

The Dominance
of Moscow

THE MAIN ORGAN of the Yiddish Communists from
1918 was *Emes*, published in Moscow. Its editor, Moshe
Litvakov (1875–1937) was the chief spokesman for the Soviet
party line in literature until his liquidation. In his young
years he had been a leader of the Labor Zionists and had
written in Russian, Hebrew and Yiddish on social and literary problems. Upon the outbreak of the Revolution, he
became active in the Kiev Group and participated in its
journals and anthologies. In 1921 he left for Moscow and
the following year he entered upon his career as editor of
Emes.

Thereupon, this scion of a religious family, who until
his seventeenth year had himself been immersed in Talmudic
studies and who until his fortieth year had preached Zionism,
undertook a vigorous campaign to uproot Jewish religious
observances and Jewish national aspirations. He flaunted his
godlessness and raged against Jewish petrifaction and Zionist
chauvinism. In his critical articles and as Professor of Yiddish
Literature and History, however, he often could not avoid
touching on the Jewish past. Indeed, the two volumes which

contained his best literary essays, *Amidst Unrest* (*In Umruh*, 1918, 1926), called attention to the cultural heritage which proletarian writers inherited from Morris Rosenfeld, Abraham Reisen, Sholom Aleichem and Peretz.

When the American Yiddish poet H. Leivick visited Moscow in 1925 and rebuked its Jewish men of letters for their isolationism and their complete break with the past, Litvakov, in an essay "Heritage and Hegemony," replied that Soviet writers were prepared to accept some aspects of the Jewish cultural heritage, aspects which contained desirable values for the working masses, but that they must insist on the hegemony of Soviet Yiddish literature in the contemporary world.

Litvakov pointed out that, unlike Russian literature which was revolutionary throughout the century since Pushkin, Yiddish literature was chiefly rooted in religious tradition and mirrored reactionary, nationalistic aspirations. Created by bourgeois intellectuals, it was more at home in the house of prayer, the kitchen or the business office than amidst political demonstrations, strikes or riots. Except for the Kiev Group of poets, it was caught unprepared for a society and a culture based on the dictatorship of the proletariat. A new beginning had to be made and was being made by poets such as Lipe Resnik, Itzik Fefer, Ezra Fininberg, Aaron Kushnirov, Shmuel Halkin and Izzie Charik. While these poets were revolutionizing Yiddish vocabulary and filling Yiddish literature with new content, Yiddish writers in America, Poland and elsewhere were sinking into the slough of decadence, nationalist clericalism and Zionist chauvinism. They could only hope to emerge from esthetic fogginess to the bright sun of revolutionary creativity by following the example of the Russian Yiddish writers and by recognizing the superiority of the planned Soviet literature. Only Moscow could teach them to curb their capricious intuition and to create according to well-defined proletarian regulations. They could then become the vanguard and trumpeters of the coming social revolutions in their lands. The choice was between orientation toward Jerusalem, symbol of a decayed past, or orientation toward Moscow, symbol of a sunlit future. "When Yiddish literature abroad will proceed on the road to Moscow and attain to momentous results, we shall rejoice with it and, if it be worthy, we shall not contend with it for hegemony. But until then hegemony belongs to us, to Moscow."

Despite Litvakov's militant assertion of Soviet superiority in literature as well as in all other fields of endeavor, he was not spared attacks by even more fanatical followers of Stalin. These professed to see in his essays fragmentary remnants of Jewish nationalism and separatism. By counterattacking his opponents, he was able to outmaneuver efforts to purge him in 1931 and 1932. He continued his antireligious campaign and his editing of *Emes* until 1937. In the major purge of that year, he too was arrested as an enemy of the people and perished in prison within a few weeks.

The power Litvakov had wielded, then passed into younger hands. In the decade after Litvakov's fall from grace, Itzik Fefer (1900–1952) dominated the literary scene. His rise can be ascribed to three factors: his proletarian orthodoxy, his power of invective, his lyric talent.

As a youth of nineteen, Fefer fought with the Bolsheviks against Denikin. When Kiev was captured by Denikin, he remained in the city and engaged in underground activities. He was caught and imprisoned. When his mother learned that her son was in danger of being shot, she set out from her townlet of Shpole for Kiev. Though Denikin's underlings threw her out of the train when they discovered that she was a Jewess, she continued on foot. The typhus epidemic then raging in the devastated city chained both mother and son to hospital beds. Fefer recovered and was liberated by the Red army shortly thereafter but she, who came to comfort him, was borne to her grave. Twenty years later, Fefer paid moving tribute to her in a poem which stressed both the loving care with which she surrounded him and her courage in sending him forth to fight against the foes of the Revolution.

Fefer's finest songs dealt with the civil war, his leaving Shpole, his participating in battles, the storming of Kiev, pogroms, hunger, and, despite all, joy atop ruins. His emphasis was not on the cruel events themselves but rather on his emotional reaction to them, the moods they evoked, above all, the mood of exhilaration. "When the blood is fresh and young, then the road is fresh and young."

Fefer trod the narrow road of strict party conformity. His power of invective helped him to down opponents and to rise ever higher in the Soviet literary hierarchy. His study on *Yiddish Literature in the Capitalist Lands,* published in Kiev in 1933, displayed his mastery of the vocabulary of literary derogation. For him, Bialik was an agent provocateur and propagandist, Aaron Zeitlin a Fascist, I. J. Singer a rabbinical pornographer, Aaron Glanz-Leyeles a nonsensical reactionary, Leivick an ape-romanticist who dreamed of returning to the savage era of the orangutan, Shimon Dubnow a clerical chauvinist who committed the crime of accusing the Ukrainians of organizing pogroms. "Calm down, worthy historian, Mr. Dubnow! We know who organized the pogroms. We remember well your comrade and Jabotinsky's comrade: the pogromist Simon Petlura, as well as his predecessors of all the three hundred years about which you babble."

Fefer derided Asch, Zhitlowsky, Bialik, Einhorn, Leshtchinsky, Abraham Cahan, Max Weinreich and Old Dubnow as incompetent assistants of the ailing bourgeoisie. He called them literary physicians who were themselves sick and unable to stop the march of the Revolution to world ascendancy. He held out hope only for a few fellow-traveling petit-bourgeois writers who had become confused because of the economic depression in the land of prosperity, America, and who were jumping from the Fascist swamp onto the bandwagon of Socialist reconstruction.

During the Second World War, Fefer rose to the rank of lieutenant colonel and in 1943 he was sent to the United States and Canada together with the Soviet's best Yiddish actor, Shlomo Michoels (1890–1948), in order to win Jewish support for the Soviet struggle against the Nazis. It was then that he penned his proud lyric affirming his joy in belonging to the Jewish group, to the people of Samson, the Maccabeans, Spinoza, Marx and Heine.

This affirmation was soon to cost him dearly. Despite his many services to the Soviet cause, this feared spokesman for the party line in Yiddish literature also fell a victim to Stalin's axe. Arrested in 1948, he too was tortured for four years and finally shot on the tragic August 12, 1952, together with his friends and foes.

Aaron Kushnirov (1890–1949) was one of Fefer's earliest and staunchest supporters. In a lyric "Epistle to Fefer," he hailed the latter in 1930 as a comrade-in-arms in the struggle against Symbolism and Romanticism and for Socialist Realism. Kushnirov too was glad to load his own lyrics with gunpowder and to encase them in steel. According to him, the times were calling for metallic hammering and not for the filigree work of jeweled images. Every esthetic cat could file and polish. Veiled hints, abstractions, impartial objectivity must be replaced by clarity, concreteness, party-mindedness.

Fefer, in his reply, welcomed Kushnirov into the marching shock brigade of poets. En route to electric days, the tempo must be forced and whosoever tarried must be shoved aside. Poetry was not a tickling of rhymes but a weapon in the class struggle. It must pierce with the spear of satire and be as vitriolic as a pasquil. Poets must be prepared to fight with both song and shrapnel when the country called them.

Kushnirov had begun in 1921 with a volume of lyrics, *Walls (Vent)*, to which David Hofstein had written a glowing introduction. The title poem was a stirring outcry of the Walls. These had been condemned for thousands of years to listen but not to speak out. At last, relief from their enforced silence was granted them. The echo of iron steps was penetrating to them. Revolutionary power was compelling even the haughty granite to bend and kneel before it. Plastered with placards and posters, the Walls recovered their voices. They too could blare forth: "We hear the firm, heavy, triumphant marching."

Moving to Moscow in 1922, Kushnirov immediately be-

came involved in the literary projects of the Yiddish section
of the Moscow Association of Proletarian Writers. His short
stories *Children of the People* (*Kinder fun Folk,* 1928) were
welcomed as models of good Soviet prose. He was invited in
1928 to co-edit the Minsk Yiddish organ *Shtern,* but soon
returned to Moscow, where his plays were to be staged and
where the star of his friend Fefer was in the ascendancy. He
thus escaped the bloody purge which overwhelmed the Minsk
Group a few years later.

When the Germans invaded Russia, Kushnirov, at the
age of fifty-four, volunteered for the front. He fought like
a hero, won medals and distinctions as an officer, and published battle lyrics. The most moving of these lyrics was
"Father-Commander," composed in 1944. He described himself peering at night into the tired faces of the eighteen-
year-old soldiers under his command, the fledglings who had
just learned to take wing. Before dawn he might have to
send these young eagles into battle. Many would fall, perhaps he himself. But, if he should manage to escape bullet
or shrapnel, he would have difficulty after the battle in recalling the smiles or the names of the missing—even as
other officers were unable to recall his own eighteen-year-old
son, who had also been sent into battle and was never heard
from again.

Despite Kushnirov's services to his Soviet fatherland, he
too did not survive Stalin's dictatorship. During the war,
which called for a maximum effort of all nationalities, he
too found the courage, as did Fefer, to proclaim his love
for his bleeding but unbowed Jewish people, which had
survived the ravages of four thousand years. The poem
"Through This World" contained the stanza: "With my
face, with my fate, I belong to my people, eternally trodden
under foot but never crushed, eternally threshed but never
annihilated."

Kushnirov's last public appearance took place in October
1948, soon after the Moscow Anti-Fascist Committee had
been liquidated as a nest of traitors. By that time Shlomo
Michoels had been mysteriously murdered and almost all
the other leading members were under arrest. The Moscow

organization of Soviet writers called a special meeting to discuss the problem of Yiddish literature, obviously a subversive literature, as proved by the fact that its outstanding representatives had been imprisoned. Kushnirov was delegated to speak at this meeting and as a faithful party member to vilify Yiddish literature, whose fate had already been sealed by the highest authorities. The gathering was to give expression to public indignation. The guilt of the accused was taken for granted, since in a Soviet state innocent persons would not have been hailed away and kept under arrest. As a good Communist, Kushnirov was chosen to castigate the writers who had fallen from grace. He was at his seat waiting for the chairman to call him to mount the platform. At this moment, one of his friends walked up to him quietly and whispered in his ear that during the preceding night the aged, ailing literary critic Yekheskel Dobrushin, to whom he had dedicated a poem from the battlefront, had been arrested. He then heard his own name called as the next speaker. Trembling and glassy-eyed, he arose, walked onto the platform, tried to speak, but could not utter a sound. His lips moved, his body was distorted in pain. Minutes passed. An uncomfortable silence spread among the audience, then he was helped from the hall. Another Communist stalwart substituted for him with the prescribed vituperation. There then followed the arrest of the Yiddish writers of Kiev, Minsk, Odessa, Kishinev, Czernovitz, and other cities.

Kushnirov did not recover from this experience. Illness chained him to his bed and he passed away in his own home six months later.

Another poet whose liquidation was averted by illness was Shmuel Halkin (1897–1960). Stemming from a large family rooted in traditional Jewishness, he never lost his love for the Jewish people, even though he was forced to sublimate this love during the Stalin era. His early religious training had taught him that the purpose of human existence was moral perfection, that every individual was a microcosm which bore responsibility for the macrocosm, and that every evil deed increased the evil content of the world.

Halkin long vacillated between painting and literature.

The decision was made for him when he came to Kiev in 1921 and Peretz Markish accepted for publication his first short lyric. Its eight lines contained Halkin's basic theme: the striving to retain the Sabbath mood and to bring the holiday tone to weekdays.

In 1922, he left for Moscow. There David Hofstein helped him to publish his first lyric booklet. Nevertheless, though living in the Soviet capital, he still contemplated settling in Palestine and until 1924 he even belonged to a Zionist circle. A Hebrew song, *"Shir Hachalutza,"* written at this time, gave expression to his Zionist longing. It was not published until after his death and then it appeared only in Israel. A Yiddish poem entitled "Russia" lamented that every one in Russia who had a bit of land could plant a tree on it and wait for the fruit; only "we," after so many years of horror, must still seek a new earth. Halkin, in his autobiographic sketch, listed among the poets who influenced him most throughout his life the medieval Sephardic poets Yehuda Halevi and Solomon ibn Gabirol.

No wonder, therefore, that Halkin's poems of the 1920's were attacked by critics as voicing nostalgic despair and falling outside of the new requirements for proletarian art. In 1932, he was compelled to confess his errors and to repudiate his Jewish nationalistic heresies. He promised to "give Soviet literature at least one book worthy of the time." However, *Shulamis,* a dramatic poem based on Goldfaden's musical drama, hardly fulfilled this promise. *Bar Kochba,* another verse drama, did so only partly. Both were produced in Yiddish theaters. Halkin preferred to devote his lyric gift to the non-controversial task of translating into Yiddish foreign classics such as Shakespeare, Longfellow, Kipling, and older Russian classics such as Pushkin and Tyutchev. During the Second World War he wrote a dramatic poem on the Warsaw ghetto uprising. It was to have been staged by the Moscow Yiddish Theater, but when the liquidation of Yiddish culture set in, the theater was shut down, and Halkin was arrested. When his health broke down in prison, he spent a year and a half in the prison hospital and was then released because of his impaired heart. He survived longer than most of his Jewish literary colleagues, long enough to experience rehabilitation in 1958. After his death in 1960, his birthplace, Rogatchov, in White Russia, named a street after him, a rare honor for a Soviet Jewish poet.

Rehabilitation also came to Shmuel Persov (1890–1952), the talented Moscow novelist, five years after his liquidation. A rebel against Czarist authority in his boyhood, Persov escaped to America at the age of sixteen, when the Revolution of 1905 ended in disaster, but returned to Russia in 1917, filled with enthusiasm for the Communist regime. As an official in a Moscow cooperative, he wrote on economics for Russian journals, but his original sketches and short stories appeared in Yiddish organs from 1918. He was a founder and pillar of the *Yevsektsie,* the Yiddish Section of the Moscow Association of Proletarian Writers.

Persov's short story *Derelicts* (*Sherblekh,* 1922) anticipated the method of Socialist Realism and was enthusiastically received by his Moscow literary colleagues. It described the broken remnants of social groups which had been formerly dominant: a Greek Orthodox priest, a tubercular Czarist officer, a Jewish merchant. These derelicts are huddled together in a prison cell, alternating between fear of liquidation by the Bolshevik masters of the town and hope of liberation by counter-revolutionary peasant hordes. This story was later incorporated in the volume *Corn Bread* (*Kornbroit,* 1928), narratives of the bitter struggle between adherents and saboteurs of the revolutionary order.

Persov avoided the black-and-white technique of less talented Communist storytellers and propagandists. He peered into the tortured souls of former petty Jewish tradesmen and he laid bare the psychological difficulties which they faced in adjusting to a new way of life. He had sympathetic understanding for the declassed storekeepers whose windowless, doorless trading booths looked out upon the marketplace like open mouths from which the teeth had been drawn. He realized that such impoverished Jews were not enemies of society but rather bewildered persons whose standard of values had been too suddenly upset and who could not yet grasp the greater desirability of productive

toil as peasants or as factory workers. In the final story of
Corn Bread, Persov mirrored himself in the figure of the
government agent who set out to collect overdue taxes from
Jews still clinging to their decaying homes, dram shops,
market hovels, and who did not have the heart to attach
their last possessions as payment.

In the tales of *Day and Night* (*Tog un Nakht,* 1933),
Persov again documented his love for Jews as Jews. He had
a leading character of the title story inveigh against sending
the declassed Jews of a deteriorating townlet to work in
the factories and mines in the heart of Russia because these
Jews in their loneliness and uprootedness would quickly lose
their precious Jewish uniqueness and would assimilate to
the overwhelming majority of non-Jewish fellow workers.
He preferred to see them settled in Birobidjan, Crimea and
other agricultural colonies that were predominantly Jewish,
so that they could retain their own language and cultural
associations because "The Russian Bolsheviks know that
the Jewish people is an homogeneous people." Such sentiments, tolerated in the young years of the Communist regime, were later denounced as Jewish nationalist deviationism and their author had to pay with his life for having
voiced them.

When the Germans invaded Russia, Persov wrote a series
of stories about Jewish heroes of the Red Army and the role
of Jewish partisans behind the various fronts. His pride in
specifically Jewish patriotism and in the contributions of
Jews to the victory of the Soviet forces found expression in
his book *Your Name Is People* (*Dein Nomen is Folk,* 1944).
This book was regarded as additional confirmation of the
accusation leveled against him that he was espousing Jewish
separatism. He was arrested together with the other Jewish
proletarian writers of Moscow and shot in 1952. Five years
later he was rehabilitated as another innocent victim of the
Stalin cult. A selection of his works appeared in 1957 in a
Russian translation. Not until a decade after his liquidation
did a fragment of his unpublished prose appear in Russia's
only Yiddish periodical, *Sovetish Heimland.*

The literary beginnings of Ezra Fininberg (1899–1946)

go back to the revolutionary year. In his early poems, though written under the Communist regime, he cannot tear himself away from the Jewish past. In a poem on his grandfather's "Wednesday," he sees this past, with its worm rot and cancerous petrifaction, continuing into the new era and attaching its prongs into his soul. High above his grandfather's "Wednesday," the Milky Way leads to a marble home, where trees of purest gold spread their giant foliage. He, however, still feels the crippling effect of the decaying townlets and the hoary traditions which link him to his Jewish ancestors.

Finenberg's muse does not shout. It pleads for more mildness, less anger, more tolerance, less coldness. In the 1920's he sings of personal aches and joys, tender love and childhood innocence. In the 1930's, his verses are less genuine. They lose freshness and picturesqueness. Jewish themes and references disappear and expressions that might arouse religious reminiscences are excised. He has to sublimate whatever love he may have for the Jewish people.

The Jewish tone reappears, however, in the songs *From the Battlefield (Fun Shlakhtfeld,* 1943). After two years at the front, facing death daily, defending the Soviet fatherland against the Nazi invaders, he returns on furlough to Moscow and finds poisoned glances directed upon him by his own countrymen. In the lyric, "My Report" *(Main Barikht),* he proudly retorts to those Moscovites who look upon him, the Jewish defender of Moscow, as an alien. He tells them that he is indeed Semitic in his features, in his gait, in his heart, but nevertheless no more of a stranger than the Russian, the Ukrainian, the Soviet warriors of other ethnic origins. He invokes the spirit of the Yiddish writers, his comrades, who died at the front during the preceding two years. There was Buzi Olievsky (1908–1941) who composed Yiddish songs for children, lyrics of Soviet prowess in the air, tales of Birobidjan. There was Meir Viner (1893–1941), the Galician philosopher and critic, who gave up a promising career in Berlin and freely cast in his lot with the Soviets in 1926. Viner enriched literary history with valuable studies on folklore, Axenfeld, Mendele, and Sholom Aleichem. But when Russia was in danger, he exchanged the pen for the gun and fell in defense of the city of Vyazma in the early months of the conflict.

There was Fininberg's best friend, Aaron Gurshtein (1895–1941), who collaborated with Viner on problems of literary criticism, who taught literature at the University of Moscow and at pedagogical institutes of Kiev and Odessa, and whose career was cut short when he fell resisting the Nazi foe.

There was Shmuel Nissan Godiner (1893–1942), a skilled narrator who followed in the footsteps of David Bergelson and Der Nister. His most popular novel was *The Man with the Gun* (*Der Mensh Mit Der Biks,* 1928). In the very first month of the German invasion, he left Moscow in order to fight with the partisans in the occupied region and died a hero's death a year later.

There was Yashe Zeldin (1901–1941), the first Yiddish poet to write songs of the Russian fleet, songs based upon his own experiences in the Soviet navy from 1923. He translated Vladimir Mayakovsky and Lermontov into Yiddish and collaborated with Godiner and Kushnirov in dramatic playlets. He too volunteered for military action and lost his life in battle.

There was Shmuel Rossin (1890–1941), poet, narrator, dramatist, who was among the first casualties of the war. Finenberg himself would soon be returning to the flaming front, where he would be battling for Jewish honor as well as for the Soviet fatherland. "My people, my Jewish people, you it was that gave me the glow, the pain, the radiance, the deep courage. . . . You accompanied me, the soldier, every night. You stood at my side every morn. You are not impure, my people. Your foe is filth and impurity. You are pure, my Jewish people, and holy is your blood."

When Fininberg in his last poems mentions his people, he means the Jewish people. He no longer eschews biblical imagery. Marching westward with the advancing troops to liberate Ukrainian towns formerly inhabited mainly by Jews, he laments that no familiar Jewish tones greet him and that no Jewish breath is visible anywhere. Slaughtered are the millions, buried in swamps and ditches, and he himself is bereft of his Jewish friends and relatives. But the blood of the Jewish martyrs calls for retribution and his martial stanzas in his beloved Yiddish tongue will echo the call.

Fininberg's last collection of lyrics, *In Gigantic Fire* (*In Rizikn Feier,* 1946), includes hymns of triumph. Berlin has fallen, the insolent city that sought to rule over all lands. The guns are silent. The blood-encrusted fields are turning green. The poet can again dream of children that will be born on a peaceful earth under a milder sky.

Shmuel Rossin, whom Finenberg included among the Jewish heroes who fell in battle, was a gentle-voiced poet who found it difficult to join the optimistic chorus that hailed as a stupendous achievement every event that occurred in Soviet Russia. During the stormy revolutionary period, he was content to versify fairy tales for children. His *Grandmother Tales* (*Bobe Meises,* 1919) were specifically Jewish in atmosphere and imagery. The savior, for example, who helped the blind Mirele to escape death and who restored her sight was not Lenin but the Prophet Elijah.

In Moscow, Rossin felt lonely and estranged from his neighbors. He longed for the warm Jewish atmosphere of his youth. He was certain that, if he could be united with his own ethnic kinsmen and share his songs with them, then he would attain to heights of inspiration now beyond his reach. Fresh streams rushing up from the depths of his being would hurl him upward to ever loftier peaks. Apparently, however, the past was over and gone. He had been wrenched from it. He had been severed from his roots. "I feel, I feel that here my head, my heart, my hands are superfluous."

To those who asked him to turn his face to the future and to sing joyously of reconstruction, he replied, as early as 1924, that it was not easy to silence one's woes. Perhaps sadness and longing were not desirable subjects for the poet in the new era but one could not compel the heart to march in step like a soldier. A heart sometimes cried out in pain, even though it should know that this was no time for individual sorrow. But a heart was only a heart and the joy encompassing all others could not shield it from its own woe.

Rossin continued, therefore, in his lyric booklets of the

1920's, to sing of love's longing and fulfillment, of tears and kisses, of the blossoming of lips in spring and the pain of parting in autumn. Such love lyrics were rare among the Yiddish poets of Moscow. Even in his translations, Rossin chose not lyrics of social protest or of proletarian heroes but rather such love lyrics as Heinrich Heine's "Asra" and Richard Wagner's "Song to the Evening Star" from *Tannhäuser*.

Shortly before the Second World War, Rossin's last booklet appeared, *Songs About My Father (Lieder Vegn Taten*, 1939). His father, whom he had lost at thirteen, became for him the symbol of all Jewish fathers. He remembered him as restless, joyless, careworn, wandering from village to village with pack on back, trying to eke out a bare living for his family.

Rossin's pure, melancholy lyrics could not be used to advance any party cause and were allowed to lapse into oblivion after their author's death.

The war against the Nazis exacted a proportionately larger toll of the Jewish population than of any other ethnic group in Russia because extermination of Jews was proclaimed as official German policy—the so-called Final Solution—and was carried out ruthlessly in all the temporarily occupied provinces. The toll of Jewish writers was also proportionately larger. Twenty years after the Soviet victory, *Sovetish Heimland* paid tribute to forty Yiddish writers—twenty-one talented in verse and nineteen in prose—who perished while battling the foe.

To these great losses must be added the still greater casualties which followed in the post-war years when Stalin undertook to root out Yiddish literature and its creators. With the closing of the last Yiddish theaters, the Yiddish press, the Yiddish schools, the Yiddish publishing plants, and with the imprisonment and execution of the anti-Fascist Yiddish literary elite on trumped-up charges, for which Beria, the head of Stalin's secret police was afterwards blamed, a pall of silence descended upon all Yiddish activities.

By the mid-century, Yiddish literature in Russia seemed

doomed to extinction. Nevertheless, soon after the death of Stalin in 1953, a revulsion set in against the cultural genocide directed against the Jews by the supreme Communist hierarchy. This revulsion compelled the Soviet authorities to rehabilitate many of the innocent victims of Stalin's purges and to loosen somewhat the imposed strictures against Yiddish culture.

When permission was granted in 1962 for the publication of the first and only post-Stalin literary periodical in Yiddish, the bi-monthly *Sovetish Heimland,* it was discovered that a considerable number of Yiddish writers had survived the bloody terror of Nazism and Stalinism. Within the limitations imposed by Communist doctrine, these writers resumed literary expression in Yiddish. Though they were restricted to but a single organ, by 1966 they were able to effect the expansion of the bi-monthly to a monthly. They also succeeded in prying ajar somewhat the ban upon the publication of Yiddish books. Half a century after the Communist Revolution, Yiddish literature was showing signs of unexpected vitality and its often proclaimed death had not set in.

8

Galician Neoromanticism

THE YEARS 1904 to 1909 were the birth years of Yiddish
Neoromanticism in Galicia. The central figure of this movement was Shmuel Jacob Imber (1889–1942), son of the minor
Hebrew writer Shmarya Imber (1868–1950) and nephew of
the Hebrew minstrel Naftali Herz Imber (1856–1909), author of *Hatikvah*, the hymn of the Zionist movement and
of the State of Israel.

In 1904, Gershom Bader (1868–1953) founded the first
Yiddish daily in Galicia, the *Lemberg Tageblatt*. In the same
year Melech Chmelnitzky (1885–1946) made his debut in
Yiddish, abandoning Polish completely. Soon thereafter he
became the literary editor of the *Tageblatt* and opened its
columns to aspiring young writers. It was in this daily that
Jacob Mestel (1884–1958), who later was famed on three continents as actor, theatrical manager and innovator, published
his first, dream-drenched lyrics. But it was not until Imber
appeared upon the Lemberg literary scene in 1909 and was
joined by his youthful disciple Melech Ravitch (b. 1893)
that Lemberg forged ahead as an important center of Yiddish
Neoromanticism.

Lemberg had always looked to Vienna for its inspiration, and in Vienna anti-Naturalistic trends were dominant since the turn of the century. *Jungwien,* allied to the Symbolist movement, claimed the allegiance of Jewish writers in the German tongue far more than of non-Jewish writers. The former included Arthur Schnitzler (1862–1931), a physician specializing in psychotherapy, who delved into subconscious strata of the soul and in his literary works unlocked infinite possibilities dormant within each person; Richard Beer-Hofmann (1866–1945), whose dignified affirmation of Jewishness found expression in biblical plays, classics of German literature and landmarks in the Jewish cultural renascence; Peter Altenberg (1859–1919), author of witty, impressionistic sketches and melancholy aphorisms; Felix Salten (1869–1945), feuilletonist of the influential daily *Neue Freie Presse,* author of humorous, satiric, erotic novels and plays, later best remembered for *Bambi,* a children's classic; Karl Kraus (1874–1936), essayist and dramatist who broke away early from the group and founded his own satiric, critical periodical, *Die Fackel* (1899–1936), as an influential weapon in the struggle against intellectual hypocrisy and social corruption; and, youngest of the group, Stefan Zweig (1881–1942), who excelled in poetry, drama, short stories, essays, biographies, who strove to be a Good European and to effect a synthesis of Germanic and Hebraic culture, and who ended as a refugee in Brazil and a suicide.

The Yiddish poets of Lemberg were magnetically drawn to Vienna and, when the First World War broke out, most of them found their way to the Hapsburg capital. Included in this group were Imber, David Königsberg and Melech Ravitch.

Imber was a gentle poet who reached out toward lyric perfection but could not attain it. He sang in simple, melodious quatrains and traditional stanzaic forms about uncomplicated emotions, timid longings, the pain of unfulfilled love, attachment to Palestine's holy soil, romantic nature far removed from his urban abode. Often he imitated Heine, whom he translated but whose complex personality was beyond his grasp. His lyrics abounded in echoes of Heine's doves and nightingales, reluctant damsels and gallant, love-lorn knights. Like young Heine, he opened his bleeding heart to the world, he flirted with death and the grave, he dissolved in tears at the slightest pretext, but the profundity of the martyr of Montmartre eluded him.

In the poetic romance *Estherke* (1911), Imber retold with lachrymose sentimentalism a fourteenth-century legend which the folklore of Polish Jewry still retained: the love of Esther, the beautiful daughter of a Jewish blacksmith, and Kasimir, the chivalrous King of Poland. Imber depicted the Jew of the centuries of exile as a powerless giant, preserved by God but scorned by man. This giant would regain pristine strength only by returning to Zion.

Imber visited the Holy Land in 1912 and wrote many songs of Zion. These were translated into Russian by the Hebrew-Russian poetess Elisheva in 1916, but they were, unfortunately, never set to music as was the case with the *Hatikvah* of his uncle. They stemmed from the longing of his heart for Jewish resurgence in Palestine far more than from his actual observations there. Though he looked upon real scenes and met real pioneers, he saw them with eyes of wonder and through a colorful veil of traditional folklore, even as Eliakum Zunser and Abraham Mapu envisaged them half a century earlier without stepping upon the sacred land.

There was a song of the Matriarch Rachel who could not be comforted after the exile of her children. Every night she arose from her grave and wandered forth in search of them. But now her tears of sorrow were giving way to tears of joy as she saw them beginning to stream homeward to her. Another lyric voiced Imber's renewed faith in a divine purpose, ever since he came in contact with the toiling pioneers on the God-kissed earth. He called on his contemporaries who were still waiting on the sidelines to join in the blessed labor of redemption, to dig up the parched, long-neglected soil, to bring into blossom the desolate banks of the Jordan. The sweat of Jewish exertion would wash away the accumulated stains of millennia. He thanked God for having brought him into this world in the generation of his people's glorious rebirth rather than in the preceding generations of decay, and for letting him witness the dawn of the splendor that would in later years envelop his entire people.

Not long after the publication of his poems of a Jewish homeland, Imber was drafted into the army to fight for the Austro-Hungarian homeland. In the midst of war, however, he continued to write poems in which he sought to tie the golden threads of an idyllic Jewish life of the past to the innocent life of an idealized Jewish future.

These poems were included in the volume *Inter Arma* (1918), which he edited and which also contained contributions by his former Lemberg associates Uri Zvi Greenberg, Jacob Mestel, David Königsberg and Melech Ravitch, all of whom were then involved in the war effort. These poets also participated in the literary monthly *Nayland* (1918–1919), which Imber founded immediately after the war. In this periodical, his predilection for Neoromantic and Impressionistic literary trends came to the fore in the foreign authors whom he introduced to Yiddish readers. These included Rabindranath Tagore, Selma Lagerlöf, Oscar Wilde and Knut Hamsun. His own associates, however, were gradually being weaned away from Impressionism toward the Expressionism of Franz Werfel, Elsa Lasker-Schüler and other stormy disciples. Uri Zvi Greenberg and Melech Ravitch left for Warsaw. Jacob Mestel left for America. Imber himself also left for the United States in 1921 but he was not happy there. Five years later he returned to Lemberg, where he felt most at home. There he continued to write his Neoromantic ballads, songs and critical articles, until he was murdered by his Ukrainian neighbors during a purge of Galician Jews in 1942.

David Königsberg (1889–1942) once referred to Imber as the head of "Young Galicia" and to himself as its heart. He is one of the ablest sonneteers in the Yiddish tongue. Although his translation of Heine's *Book of Songs* (*Buch der Lieder*) was never published, the influence of this German poet upon him was no less enduring than upon Imber. This influence was most strongly felt in Königsberg's first volume, simply entitled *Songs* (*Lieder*, 1912). In this volume, the only one in which quatrains and not sonnets predominate, he sings of his preference for silent joys, far from the excitement of raging competitiveness. He compares himself to a bird that builds itself a nest on a tall tree and pours out its heart in melodies that seep down to other hearts. He does not delude himself that his gentle tones of a culture which is being wafted away by the winds of change can affect the course of people's lives, but he hopes that these tones can bring a bit of delight to leisure hours. Let others sow and reap and harvest ripe corn for daily bread; he is content to meander among the many-colored flowers that grow in his fields, even if these flowers cannot be put to practical use. Let others follow the guidance of reason, but not he, the lover of dreams. In his eyes, reason is a sharp sword which cuts through the beautiful threads of golden days. As a romantic poet, he would rather dispense with it, indulge in sweet sorrows, recapture fading memories, garland himself with lyric pearls, and hearken to night's deep mysteries.

Königsberg's love sonnets were composed after he left Lemberg and came under Viennese influence. His language became encrusted with Germanisms. His sonnets abounded in antiquated imagery of damsels, knights and nightingales. He no longer gave frank, intimate expression to his feelings but rather compressed them into artificial molds. The young Galician poet lost his naiveté during years of fighting in the Austro-Hungarian army for a cause he did not believe in and during his sojourn in Vienna, recovering from a wound he received at the front. He toyed with *Weltschmerz,* serenaded imaginary maidens, flirted with death, but he failed to reflect genuinely his own experiences in the mud of the trenches and in the daily struggle to ward off starvation. Only when he touched national Jewish chords did he rise above mediocrity. Then he called upon the Supreme Judge to pour out righteous wrath upon those who seared the sons of Israel with pogroms. Then he portrayed Jews as exiled princes who never lost their aristocratic bearing in all their harried wanderings and who still dreamed royal dreams of a homecoming to their historic land and heritage.

After the Balfour Declaration of 1917, Königsberg felt that the hour had struck for the end of the *Galut,* the horn of redemption had sounded and all the sleepers among his people must now arise to welcome the Messiah who came to lead them forth from millennial woe. As for himself, he was content to be a bridge over which others could cross into the Promised Land. He never did get beyond Lemberg's horizon in his later years. He lived in a village in its vicinity and perished at the hands of the Nazis in the Janow extermination camp.

Melech Chmelnitzky (1885–1946) came to Galicia from Kiev at the age of twelve and grew up in Lemberg. He then went on to study at the University of Vienna and remained in this city as a practicing physician until the Nazi occupation compelled him to flee to the United States in 1939.

In his youth, under the influence of the decadent, satanic Polish novelist Stanislaw Przybyszewski (1868–1927), he wrote in Polish and translated Yiddish poetry into Polish, but with the founding of the *Lemberger Tageblatt* in 1904, he turned to Yiddish and translated Polish and German poets into Yiddish. Although he was widely known as a writer of popular articles on medical subjects for more than a third of a century, his most original work was contained in three lyric booklets filled with sad, tired, decadent moods and nostalgic recollections of childhood years. Sitting at the bedside of patients, cooling their feverish brows and comforting them, he often obtained insight into hidden recesses of their souls, and became ever gentler, ever sadder, ever more resigned, ever more aware of the dream life that consciousness suppressed. He became the singer of night, of the ripples made by subterranean forces that rose to the surface in unguarded moments. His best verses, those of his Viennese period, were melodic, abounding in assonances, undulating with gentle rhythms at a time when Expressionistic, explosive, jagged outcries were more fashionable in Austrian and Yiddish circles. He had to reconcile himself to being little read, and his lyric productivity therefore dwindled after the early 1920's.

Galician Neoromanticism in the Imber mood was continued by Mendl Neugröschel (1903–1965), the biographer of Melech Chmelnitsky. In the lyrics of Neugröschel's *Tents*

(*Gezelten,* 1930), a sweet tiredness pervaded existence as in the Viennese poems of young Hofmannsthal. The elegiac mood of autumn, the constant awareness of the transitoriness of youth and love, the emphasis upon the pain of existence and upon the holiness of dying, all pointed to an oversensitive, non-viable generation that was heading toward a final debacle. Neugröschel, a lawyer by profession, experienced the death throes of the Danubian republic and Nazi brutality in Dachau and Buchenwald, but was able to get to Brazil before World War II and later on to the United States.

In New York, he felt forlorn and desolate, especially after the war. In one of his saddest lyrics, he described himself walking along Norfolk Street and Henry Street, in the heart of the Jewish East Side, as if he were walking among exotic tribes of Haiti. "Is this my people? My destiny? My language? O, gray words, long withered!" He wondered for whom he was still penning his verses and reasoned that perhaps, when he would be laid to rest in the poet's corner of a Brooklyn Jewish cemetery near his fellow Romanticists Mani-Leib and Moshe Leib Halpern, he would there help to guard the last bastion of the Yiddish word.

Ber Schnaper (1903–1943) was no less pessimistic in his outlook upon life than was Neugröschel. The son of a cobbler, he grew up on the outskirts of Lemberg. In a poem dedicated to Neugröschel, he characterized himself and his entire group of Galician poets as singers of pale, melancholy, unobtrusive songs, as lyric birds who fly and fly without knowing whither. His entire literary career spanned but a single decade. His first book of verse, *Scum (Upshoym),* appeared in 1927 and his last one, *Blue Words (Bloe Verter),* in 1937. In these, the mood of decay predominates. His milieu is the little townlet or the poor district on the edge of the big city. His Jews know only hunger and need. They lead useless lives in their old, crumbling houses. These houses are so dark and filthy that, if an erring ray of light were to find its way into their interior through the tear-stained windows, it would blush for shame at what it saw. The women he describes know neither joy nor plenitude. They are worked to exhaustion during the day and are bitten and flayed at night by savage husbands. They are constantly pregnant and angry at the world. They wait for the redeeming hour when they will hear the quiet footsteps of Death the Reaper who will come to claim them. Their anemic children sleep on rags in cellar nooks in which spiders walk about as lords. The hands of these children are like dry branches and they rummage for bits of moldy bread which the teeming mice may have left over.

Life is for Schnaper a puss-filled wound. His typical characters are the old prostitute, the street urchin, the blind beggar, the lonely spinster. He is weary of his human lot, since human beings are handicapped by their structure as reasoning creatures. He would prefer an existence which is all feeling and all instinct, an existence like that of a bug or a bee.

Nevertheless, when Schnaper finally succeeded in exchanging his Galician townlet for the metropolises of Vienna and Warsaw, he was even more unhappy. He then glanced back upon the wretched townlet, which in his childhood was still mired in medieval petrifaction, as a grandmother might look back upon her dream-filled past. He described this townlet in the lyrics of *My Town* (*Mayn Shtot*, 1932) as peaceful, pious, modest, gilded with sunlight and silvered with moonlight. Its Jews were engaged in discussions with God, who might otherwise have felt very lonely amongst the stars. God's countenance was mirrored in their faces and God's kindness in their hearts.

The poet lamented that the transformation which war and industrialization brought to the Jewish townlet banished beauty and poetry from its streets. The crooked houses were straightened and now stood on parade in long rows like soldiers at attention. Each settlement was naked, exposed, devoid of individuality, and he, the Yiddish poet, walked about among the dull, renovated lanes like an unburied corpse waiting for the final rites.

In contrast to Ber Schnaper, Ber Horowitz (1895–1942) entered upon the Yiddish scene full of the joy of life, overflowing with health and energy. Born in a Galician village in the Carpathian Mountains, he had barely completed a

Polish Gymnasium in Stanislaw when he was called to serve in the Austrian army. His early lyric "Galicia 1914" recorded the mood of the multi-national recruits among whom he was thrown. While the Poles of Galicia went to battle singing of the coming redemption of Poland and the Ukrainians of the liberation of the Ukraine, the Jewish soldiers sang songs that dripped tears of futility, not understanding why they were required to kill or be killed.

Horowitz saw war not as a glorious field for heroism but as a senseless slaughter of God's creatures. He depicted war through the tired eyes of the one-armed, one-legged invalid in the hospital who watched the rhythmic march of the battalions that were leaving Vienna for the front. On the drill field with three hundred companions who were practicing sharpshooting, the young poet wandered in imagination to the Caucasus and to Naples, distant places where mothers were at the same time bidding farewell to sons who would ere long fall as victims to the more accurately fired bullets of the three hundred so-called enemies or patriots. He depicted mothers as the principal sufferers and their sons as helpless pawns of a military machine.

In his post-war lyrics, Horowitz glorified the Jewish villagers of the Carpathian Range. His Jewish peasants could catch a bull by the horns and wrestle it down. His village children intoned Hebrew and Yiddish tunes and their games simulated jousts between Turks and Palestinian *shomrim,* or watchmen. Idyllic poems conveyed the shudder experienced by the lonely wanderer in the forest at night, the melodious magic of the birds who disported themselves in their free realm between the green treetops and the blue sky.

Horowitz's prose tales were designed not only to entertain but to convey a moral. They often centered about the Baal Shem, founder of Hassidism. In one of them, a Carpathian Robin Hood came under the influence of the Baal Shem, who had retired to a forest in the mountains in order to meditate on God's wonders. In another story, the Baal Shem exorcized an evil spirit that had found entry into a young man's body at birth. He then substituted the righteous soul which properly belonged there but that had until then not been able to enter the occupied body. In Horowitz's best narrative, "The Legend of the Madonna," he intermingled Jewish and Christian folklore. He had the Madonna descend from her pedestal in a forest chapel and hand over the jewels with which she was bedecked to a poor, aged widow as dowry for a marriageable daughter.

Horowitz's first volume of verse, *From My Home in the Mountains (Fun Mayn Heym in die Berg,* 1919), was followed by his only other original book of poems, *Smell of Earth (Reyekh Fun Erd,* 1930), in which he continued his joyous hymns to life, his sensuous grasp of nature and love. In contrast to the uprooted, melancholy, Neoromantic poets who yearned for the big cities, he returned from a temporary sojourn in Vienna to his native Galician village like a sick bird to its old nest. There he recuperated from sophistication and rationalization; there he sang lullabies to his child, Piniele with the golden hair; there his verses proclaimed how lovely was this earth and how good it was to be a human being on it.

In 1938, Horowitz published a volume of translations of Jewish poems by non-Jewish Polish poets. These were to document his faith in the possibility of a peaceful coexistence of Jews and non-Jews on the soil of Poland. Four years later his life was cut short when the Nazis, unhindered, if not actually assisted by his Polish and Ukrainian neighbors, massacred nine thousand Jews of Stanislaw in a single day.

Though Horowitz's robust, joyous affirmation of life distinguished him from most Galician Neoromanticists, he was nevertheless closely connected with this group, which centered about Imber. It was Imber who first discovered Horowitz as a poet and printed his lyrics in *Nayland,* the literary monthly he edited in Lemberg. When most members of this group found their way to Vienna, *Nayland* was succeeded in February 1920 by the more militant quarterly *Kritik,* which fought against the rising tide of Expressionism.

The editor of this organ was Moshe Zilburg (1884–1942?), who had been compelled to leave his native Vilna because of revolutionary activities and who had settled in Lemberg before the First World War and in Vienna at its conclusion.

He took over the leadership of the Galician group when Imber left for the United States. He succeeded in winning the allegiance to his quarterly of Melech Ravitch, Melech Chmelnitzky, Moshe Gross-Zimmermann, Ber Horowitz, David Königsberg, Mendel Singer, A. M. Fuchs, and others.

In an opening manifesto, the declaration was made that *Kritik* was to serve the youth of Lemberg, Warsaw, New York and Vilna. It was to be the link binding all Jews who recognized that without the living Yiddish word Jewish life could not flourish. A series of articles by Zilburg attacked Martin Buber, Max Brod, Simon Bernfeld, and all Zionist and communal leaders who wrote in German or Polish. Zilburg accused them of undermining Jewish existence by their arrogance toward the East European Jews. These writers had become estranged from the townlets in which the Jewish masses dwelt. They had acquired so-called higher education in the large centers of Central and Western Europe, but, having experienced rejection by the outsiders whom they courted, they had returned to elevate their benighted brethren with the superior alien wisdom imbibed from strangers. Zilburg expressed ironically his gratitude for the praise that these rediscoverers of the Eastern Jews bestowed upon them. There was Max Brod, an admirer of the half-assimilated Jewish girls, who grafted intellectualism upon a religious base. There was Hermann Cohen who tried to convince Eastern Jews that they were close relatives of Kaiser Wilhelm's subjects. There was young Nahum Goldmann, whose Lithuanian soul had experienced transmutation to a Western one. All of them were seeking to erase the true features of the Jewish face so that it would become as pale and expressionless as their own. They were flooding the orphaned Yiddish youth with German-Jewish periodicals such as *Jüdische Rundschau* and *Der Jude*. One of them was even Germanizing the Bible with a new translation reminiscent of his reforming predecessor Moses Mendelssohn.

With biting satire, Zilburg castigated the neo-intellectuals who professed to believe in religion but did not practice it, who espoused Zionism but continued to live in Berlin and Warsaw, who sympathized with Socialism but did not work for it, who endorsed Jewish nationalism but sank ever deeper in the slough of assimilationism. As the antithesis to these neo-intellectuals, Zilburg hailed the genuine ghetto Jew, relatively healthy in body and soul, normal in his Jewish reactions, rooted in the language and folkways of Jewish traditions. He, therefore, advocated the slogan "Back to the Ghetto!"—not the medieval ghetto with its yellow badge but the ghetto type of cultural autonomy, the retention of Jewish uniqueness in speech and habits of thought, the transformation of outside influences and spiritual forces into Jewish forms.

Zilburg was followed by Moshe Gross-Zimmermann with articles on "Problems of Form in Yiddish Literature." The latter attacked Expressionism as a formless, chaotic movement, and defended the Galician group's Impressionism as aiming at perfection of form. Moshe Livshitz (1894–1940) countered with a defense of Expressionism, especially as practiced by Moshe Broderzon, a newly risen star over the Yiddish horizon. Livshitz's approach foreshadowed the gradual disintegration of the unity which had bound the young writers of Vienna under the aegis of Imber, who did not return from America until 1925. Expressionism was luring away strong pillars of the original Neoromantic group, including Melech Ravitch and Uri Zvi Greenberg.

Melech Ravitch (b. 1893) is primarily a poet, even though his travel sketches, critical essays, philosophical discourses, and autobiographic volumes far exceed his lyrics in quantity.

Stemming from a family long rooted in eastern Galicia, his has been a life of uprootedness spanning five continents. His wandering began at fourteen when he left his native townlet, Redom, for the larger town of Stanislau and two years later for the still larger town of Lemberg. His twenties were spent in the capital of the Austro-Hungarian dual monarchy as a bank clerk and at various fronts during World War I. His thirties were spent in the capital of the new Poland as secretary of the Yiddish Authors' League. Then followed still longer odysseys, which swept the restless poet on to Australia, South America, Canada and Israel. Not until the end of his sixties did he reconcile himself to a stable domicile in Montreal.

Peretz, passing through Stanislau in 1908 after the conclusion of the Czernovitz Yiddish Conference, made an indelible impress upon the fifteen-year-old lad who was being trained in a commercial academy for a business career. Despite a better mastery of Polish and German, Ravitch then decided to become a Yiddish poet. His earliest lyrics, composed between his sixteenth and his nineteenth year, appeared in 1912 and were followed by twelve more volumes of verse during the next four decades. In 1954, Ravitch made a selection of his best poems under the title *The Songs of My Songs (Die Lieder Fun Maine Lieder)*. From these poems, as well as from the autobiographic volumes *The Story of My Life (Dos Maaseh-Bukh Fun Main Leben*, I, 1962; II, 1964) and the essays of the volume *Jewish Thought in the Twentieth Century (Einems Yiedishe Makhshoves in 20. Yorhundert*, 1949), the literary personality of Ravitch can be reconstructed.

The first literary circle in which Ravitch found a congenial atmosphere and encouragement for his creative striving was the Lemberg Group, which in 1910 included not only the poets S. M. Imber and David Königsberg but also the realistic novelist A. M. Fuchs (b. 1890), the Zionist editor Berl Locker (b. 1887), the Hebrew poets Gershon Schofman (b. 1880) and Uri Zvi Greenberg (b. 1894), and the Yiddish actor Ludwig Satz (1891–1944). Ravitch and S. J. Imber roomed together, hungered together, and in Imber, Ravitch found a severe critic who stimulated him to his utmost efforts and who collaborated with him in the search for lyric perfection.

Ravitch's youthful verses *At the Threshold (Oyf der Shvel*, 1912) betray the influence of S. M. Imber and of Heinrich Heine, Imber's master. They are full of *Weltschmerz*, sweet melancholy, and overflow with sentimental love for all mankind. Ravitch sings of dawning dreams, tender friendships, regret at the loss of childhood innocence, and wonder at the blossoming of his heart in first love.

The poems of Ravitch's Vienna decade, which followed

the Galician period, are more cheerful, even though they were composed in the midst of war and the crash of the Hapsburg Empire. During free hours in military barracks, between 1916 and 1918, Ravitch completed his cycle *Spinoza,* a lyric tribute to the lonely philosopher in whom he found the embodiment of absolute truth and goodness. In this cycle there was already revealed the poet's inclination to versify ideological questions, to concretize thoughts, emotions, intuitions in vivid images. He depicted the life and death of Spinoza as anchored in calmness and devoid of sadness, despite persecution and excommunication. He showed Death curtseying before the sage, offering him the bread and salt of hospitality, the keys to the City Beyond Life, and begging him to enter. "And the sage assented with a smile and with a gallant bow, and took the hand of Death." Spinoza's system of thought remained a principal inspiration for Ravitch's own thinking throughout all later years. Indeed, he ranked Spinoza with Moses and Jesus.

In Vienna, Ravitch came into contact not only with the Yiddish poets who had fled from his native Galicia when it was overrun by the Russian army but also with poets whose medium was German. He was especially drawn to Stefan Zweig and to Uriel Birnbaum (1894–1956), the younger son of the Zionist pioneer Nathan Birnbaum (1864–1937). He joined in the prevailing admiration for early Expressionists such as Else Lasker-Schüler (1869–1945) and Franz Werfel (1890–1945). He was invited by Albert Ehrenstein (1886–1950) to translate into Yiddish the poetry of the New Germany. Soon his fame spread to New York, where the Yiddish writers of "Die Yunge" commended his verses. Reuben Iceland called him a great luminary on the poetic horizon and David Ignatoff welcomed him as a comrade-in-arms.

With the appearance of *Naked Songs* (*Nakte Lieder,* 1921), Ravitch forsook rhyme, regular metric lines and stanzas, and followed the Expressionistic tide in subject matter and in rebellious exhilaration. He now saw the poet's mission as the conscience of the world, as comforter amidst adversity, as the voice of the silent, suffering creatures, man, woman, child, beast and plant. His elegy "Mother Earth," written under the impact of his older brother's suicide, ascended from outbursts of pain to a pantheistic acceptance of human destiny in its mysterious passage from the womb of the individual mother to the womb of the universal mother, Mother Earth.

In 1921, Ravitch gave up his comfortable position in a bank and his stable existence in the cosmopolitan capital of the Austrian Republic in order to escape from the assimilationist conflagration which he saw raging there among Jews. As an antidote to the poison of decay which he felt was eroding Viennese Jewish intellectual circles, he developed a love for Polish, Lithuanian and Ukrainian Jewry. Though he himself had moved far from religious orthodoxy, he still viewed religiously oriented Eastern European Jewry as basically sound and healthy. He was, however, even more impressed by the Yiddish revival. Warsaw beckoned to him as the main Yiddish literary center. A brief visit there convinced him that he should make his home in this city, which then contained the greatest concentration of Yiddish writers.

Soon after his arrival, Ravitch found himself in the midst of increasing activity as editor, as poet, as a key figure in various artistic projects, and as General Secretary of the Jewish Writers' Association, which had a membership of 250 authors. From 1921 to 1923, he was associated with Peretz Markish and Uri Zvi Greenberg in the struggle against realism in art. The triumvirate adapted the innovations of German Expressionism and Russian Futurism. They succeeded in outraging public opinion and were branded as the *Khaliastre* or "Gang." They accepted this designation as a badge of honor and termed their literary anthologies *Khaliastre*. They succeeded in attracting as contributors David Hofstein, I. Kipnis, Moshe Khashchevatsky, Israel Stern, I. J. Singer, and Oizer Varshavsky. Not all of these writers were in sympathy with the striving of the *Khaliastre*, but they were impressed by the vitality of the triumvirate.

Ravitch's *Naked Songs* had already anticipated Uri Zvi Greenberg's call for the free, naked human expression, for the chaotic outcry of the blood. Ravitch's "Song to the Human Body," 1922, called for the dethronement of mind and proclaimed the autonomous sovereignty of every limb in the confederation of the human frame. His "Song to the Sun," 1923, was an ecstatic, rhythmic yell to the radiant source out of which arose the earth and all life. Rocks, plants, whales, elephants, eagles, apes and humans were characterized as but torn bits of sun, eternally whirling in orbits, dancing around the solar God.

Ravitch no longer wished to fixate momentary impressions as in his earlier poems. He rather sought to discover essences, absolutes. He wanted to ascend from personal moods to universal moods, to become the lyric spokesman of a super-individual collective. In his "Song of Hate and Love for the Jewish People," 1924, he spoke out as the voice of the pogromized, post-war generation. He pleaded with Jehovah to wrap the *tallit* of chosenness about another people, since the Jewish people had already paid with enough blood for the many centuries of chosenness. In the world of today, he held, there was no longer any need for the moral, intellectual people of Moses, Jesus, and Spinoza. "Lord of Being and non-Being, we give you back our eternal existence. Give us eternal non-existence."

The climax of the *Khaliastre's* striving was reached in the issues of *Albatross,* edited by Greenberg in 1922. This periodical of the New Poetry proclaimed itself as the organ of convulsive individualism. It preached exaltation, renovation, revolution of the spirit. It saw its cruel, chaotic songs as the honest expression of the naked, disheveled, uprooted, blood-drenched generation, a generation in transition between the twilight of one world and the dawn of another.

The Yiddish Expressionists of the *Khaliastre* set out to fragmentize the language of Peretz and Mendele and to rebuild it anew, even as Vladimir Mayakovsky was then attempting with the Russian language. They preferred rhythmic tautness and explosiveness to the rounded, melodious verse. Greenberg compared the Yiddish of the time with its exhausted clichés to a street harlot with whom everybody had slept and who has become ripe for death. Ravitch referred to the new poetry of himself and his colleagues as naked poetry pulsating between the two poles of love and death and appealing to the instincts rather than to the mind. "Poetry communicates from nerve to nerve, from heart to heart, from sex to sex, from sadness to sadness, from laughter to laughter. It is an elemental outcry in which are commingled water and fire, earth and gold, word and blood." Greenberg's verse epic *Mephisto*, 1922, presented the spirit of negation which reigned over our world. Of the forces that stirred throughout the universe, nine-tenths paid allegiance to Mephisto and only one-tenth remained faithful to God. As for our specific mortal realm, the Deity did not bother with what went on there, while Mephisto was eternally awake and exercising his suzerainty.

The revolutionary excitement of the *Khaliastre* was short-lived. The poetic triumvirate scattered in three widely divergent directions, physically and ideologically. Markish stormed into the Soviet capital singing hymns to Communism. Greenberg abandoned Yiddish for Hebrew and became in Israel an extreme exponent of Zionist Revisionism. Ravitch migrated to Australia and continued to wrestle with ethical questions and with the meaning of Diaspora existence.

Ravitch's moods and experiences of restless years until his settling in Melbourne in 1936 were reflected in the songs and ballads of the volume *Continents and Oceans (Kontinenten un Okeanen, 1937)*. With greater maturity, he gave up efforts to shock readers. Turning from Expressionism, he aimed at maximum clarity and intelligibility. Walt Whitman, the bard of pure humanity, became his ideal. He proclaimed himself to be a citizen of the world, an a-national poet. Yet, though his themes ranged over all continents, his treatment of these themes was always unmistakably Jewish. Poems of Harbin, Peking and Singapore alternated with dramatic ballads of Johannesburg, Moscow and New York. His Whitmanesque hymns to New York visualized the restless, light-flooded American metropolis as reaching up to cosmic heights, as the crucible of races, cultures, tongues, as the womb of the new man of coming millennia. The poet paid lyric tribute to this generous city which offered freedom and hospitality to two million of his pale, frightened, despairing

Jewish brothers and sisters, when these were forced to flee
from modern Pharaonic oppression.

In 1937, Ravitch left Australia and resumed his wandering over the face of the globe. He sojourned a year in Buenos
Aires and two years in New York. In 1941, he finally decided
to make Montreal the center of his activities, a center from
which he set out for other lands whenever the lure of wandering overcame him but to which he always returned. Not
even Israel, which he visited in 1950 and where he stayed
from 1954 to 1956, could wean him away from the Canadian
metropolis. There he succeeded in unfolding rich activities
as educator, literary mentor and publicist. From this vantage
point, he could survey and react to the ever-changing Jewish scene and record his impressions in four additional volumes of verse. His book of essays, *Jewish Thought in the
Twentieth Century,* 1949, created a considerable stir in the
Jewish press. It voiced his faith in the unity of the Jewish
people as a world people and his wish that the post-biblical
thinking, feeling, prophetic vision and historical creativity
of this people be canonized in a volume comparable to the
Bible. A similar suggestion had been made by Abraham
Coralnik in 1928 without arousing much attention. Ravitch's
passionate espousal of the idea after the Nazi holocaust and
during the birth struggles of the Jewish homeland was better timed. Like Coralnik, he wrote not from a partisan viewpoint but as an eclecticist who respected all shades of com-
mitments from extreme Zionism to extreme Communism.
Affirming Jewish unity in space and time, he urged that the
wisdom of all groups, all generations and all languages should
form the basis for careful winnowing by the best minds before inclusion in such a definitive volume.

Ravitch saw the original Book of Books, in all its kaleidoscopic variety of subjects, styles and moods, revolving
about a single idea, the idea of the oneness of God. He believed that the new, additional Book of Books should revolve
about the oneness of Man—an idea which first dawned among
the ancient Prophets as a longing for an individual redeemer
of all mankind, the Messiah, and which then developed into

the concept of a people of redeemers, the Jewish people as the bearers of Messianism.

Ravitch's later writings culminated in his autobiographic volumes *The Tale of My Life* (*Dos Maase-Bukh Fun Main Leben*, I, 1962; II, 1964), in which the cultural life of Galicia since the closing of the nineteenth century was vividly depicted and in which the writers of his generation, friends and foes, were delineated sympathetically, generously, picturesquely. In these volumes as well as in the three volumes of *My Encyclopedia* (*Main Leksikon*, I, 1945; II, 1947; III, 1958), Ravitch, the impressionistic chronicler, performed a service for Yiddish literature of no less value than his earlier services as lyricist and as catalyst of the Galician and Warsaw poets.

Lemberg as the center of Galician Yiddish resurgence exerted a strong influence upon other thriving Jewish communities. Among these the town of Kolomea felt the pull of both Lemberg and Czernovitz. It was in Kolomea that Naftoli Gross (1897–1956) was born and Shlome Bickel (1896–1969) grew up.

Although Gross left his east Galician birthplace at the age of sixteen and spent his entire adult life in New York, he never really freed himself from the spell of Kolomea and of the surrounding Carpathian foothills. In his father's house at the edge of a forest, he heard folk tales of long, long ago, and they brought a flush of joy to him. He was especially fascinated by the legendary deeds of Dobush, the Robin Hood of the Carpathians, and by the humble saintliness of the Baal Shem, who also roamed this mountain range. In this he was following the precedent set by Ber Horowitz.

In the poems composed on American soil, Gross romanticized old Jews of Kolomea, who studied Torah and walked in God's ways, and young Jews, whose laughter and tears streamed from a genuine, uncorrupted heart. Though the weekdays of such Jews might be full of restless toil, their Sabbaths were blessed with holiness and contentment. It was this Sabbath mood that Gross sought to recapture in verse.

Picturesque characters of Galicia and not of New York

predominated in his verses. There was the *maggid,* whose comforting oratory brought near to every listener patriarchs and prophets of a distant past, mystics and hidden saints of more recent days, and Messiah, who was expected to come riding into town and to put an end to all troubles. There was the cabalist who had renounced all worldly pleasures and was eagerly awaiting the blessed hour of mankind's final redemption. There was the town rabbi, who never smiled because he bore upon his shoulders the burdens of the entire religious community as its respected spokesman to the reigning duke in the silent castle. There was the pious Jew, who sought to execute God's will in every act and thought, no matter how trivial. There was the merchant, who was no less tempestuous than was the Sambation River until Friday noon; just as this fabled river ceased its raging and whirling on the eve of the Sabbath, so too did the harried tradesman relax then in the midst of his family and intone sweet melodies of the Song of Songs.

Gross called his Galician Jews "a people of pure dreamers and poets." In their dreams they sated themselves with what they lacked in real life: their poor huts became palaces and their humble turrets golden minarets. The girl of marriageable age likened herself to Rachel waiting at the well for her Jacob and to Shulamith soon to be wooed by King Solomon, her beloved. The red-bearded, silent, fearless drayman felt closer to stones and trees, cattle and wild beasts, than to mere mortals. The water carrier brought to poor and rich God's gift of water but he was most solicitous that men of learning be copiously supplied. Yossel Klezmer, to whom Gross devoted a dozen lyrics and ballads, entranced and uplifted as he fiddled away at the marketplace and at festive assemblies, assisted by his partner on the pipe, with Berl Blinder bimbamming on the bassviol and the Marshalik pouring out merry rhymes.

The first mature volume of lyrics, *Jews* (*Yiedn,* 1929), brought all of these types to the fore, especially in their gayer moods, and also heroes and heroines of biblical vintage, such as Samuel and Daniel, Yael and Bathsheba. The second volume, however, which appeared under the same title in

1938, reflected the harsher reality experienced by the poet during the decade of the Great Depression in America and the rise of Hitler in Europe. He then linked his own individual fate to that of the hungry, defiant masses. He lamented the waste of his life among asphalt pavements, grimy subways, and skies gray with smoke. He depicted the lean operator bent over a sewing machine hour after hour, day after day; the unemployed outcast, homeless save for a bench in Hester Street; the tens of thousands demonstrating at Union Square on May Day. He sang a ballad of Sacco and Vanzetti, two idealists who fought for their vision of freedom in the land of golden idols and whose death earned them a seat at the table of the immortal just. Old Kolomea of the poet's dream-filled youth, however, continued to break through his contemporary themes. Yossel Klezmer reappeared and so did Dobush and Elijah. Gross painted the joy of Jewish children on Passover night. He conjured up again the Purim that he had celebrated with masquerades and the exchange of sweets in the house of his father before he and his artist brother, Chaim Gross, departed for distant shores.

The poet's images and moods, usually so colorful and joyous, turned tragic and black when the Nazis wiped out the Jewish settlements of Galicia. The strings on Yossel Klezmer's fiddle snapped amidst the ruins and were silenced forever. The singer of Kolomea on America's soil became the mourner of Kolomea. Never did he curse the murderers who desecrated the human species with their vile deeds. He merely bewailed the end of a Jewish community that had flourished so long and to whose spirit he, the poet, could only give the inadequate tribute of his verses.

The Galician Neoromanticists did not include any titans of Yiddish literature but they did enrich it with lyrics of value; they did give expression, in talented Yiddish works, to their love of their cultural heritage; they did lessen the attractiveness of alien lures, German and Polish; they did help to maintain the quality of Jewish living during a period of war, revolutionary disturbances, and increasing anti-Jewish pressures.

9

Novelists of Poland

IN WARSAW, Peretz reigned supreme until his death in 1915. In the decade before World War I, his dominant position in Yiddish literature was almost unquestioned. From all of Eastern Europe, young men, talented and untalented, trekked to his home and brought him the first products of their pen. A word of encouragement from him opened the doors for them to publishers and editors. His first disciples, David Pinski, Sholem Asch, Peretz Hirshbein, expanded the range of Yiddish in directions in which he had pioneered. Their plays were produced on the stages of Europe and America and their narratives were translated into German, English, Russian and Polish. Only I. M. Weissenberg (1881–1938), the consistent exponent of pure Naturalism, still awaited recognition, comparable to theirs, which he felt was his due but which was being withheld from him.

The death of Peretz left an hiatus in Yiddish letters which was not easily filled. In the Polish capital, Weissenberg laid claim to the vacant throne and gathered about him a group of young novelists who followed in his Naturalistic footsteps. The most gifted among them were Oizer Varshav-

sky (1898–1944) and Shimon Horonchik (1889–1939). Weissenberg furthered their vogue during the early years of the
Polish Republic in the periodicals he edited and through
the publishing venture he founded. In the long run, however, the negative, analytical or purely descriptive creed of
Naturalism could not retain the allegiance of readers, since
it offered no guidance out of the impasse in which Polish
Jews found themselves in an ever deteriorating situation.
Only in the realm of the Soviets, where Socialist Realism
dominated during the Stalin Era, did the works of the
Polish Naturalists continue to find favor with critics and
educators.

Encouraged by Peretz, Weissenberg had begun with short
tales in 1904, but it was his novelette *A Townlet* (*A Shtetl,*
1906) which first attracted general interest. In contrast to
Sholem Asch's romantic idealization of small-town Jewish
life, Weissenberg painted this life as far from idyllic. As
early as the 1860's, Mendele Mocher Sforim had already uncovered the excrescences which had attached themselves to
the long dormant Jewish communities far from the mainstream of new ideas and revolutionary currents. But it was
Weissenberg, four decades later, who first stressed the impact
of the new revolutionary doctrines upon the townlets, rousing them from their lethargy and shattering their foundations.

Workers, in his stories, were becoming class conscious.
Emissaries of the Bund and of Polish Socialist parties were
infiltrating the townlets, fomenting strikes, organizing demonstrations against local and imperial authorities. Youths
rebelled against fathers and mothers, apprentices against
master craftsmen, the unbelievers who trusted the power of
pistols against the chanters of psalms who put their faith
in God. The restless spirit of 1905 permeated the political
scene. The harsh cry of the underprivileged resounded from
such narratives as *The Mad Village Lass* (*Die Meshuggene
In Dorf,* 1905), a pathetic tale of a young girl who desperately resisted her mother's efforts to compel her submission
to an imposed, unloved husband, or *One Generation Goes
and Another Comes* (*Dor Holekh Vdor Bo,* 1904), a short

story of an overworked, undernourished father who collapsed in a shoe establishment and of his eighteen-year-old
son who was expected to replace him immediately and to
continue to grind out profits for the boss.

In fighting fanatically and vitriolically for his ultra-
realistic approach, Weissenberg succeeded in raising up
many antagonists. These embittered his later years and gave
him a feeling of frustration and undeserved persecution.
His barbed polemics wounded many but they inflicted far
more harm upon himself by deflecting him from more posi-
tive, creative achievements. The promise of his early years
was not fulfilled. Nevertheless, he did stimulate believing
followers and he did bring excitement to the Warsaw literary scene.

Oizer Varshavsky's best novel, *Smugglers* (*Shmugler,*
1920), appeared under the aegis of Weissenberg and did not
deviate in the slightest from Weissenberg's Naturalistic
creed. Its theme was the demoralization of the Jewish townlet during the years of German occupation of Poland, 1915
to 1918. The young residents, healthy in body and mind,
had by then been conscripted to fight in the Czar's army.
Psychopaths, cripples, invalids, graybeards, underworld figures, and women were left and these somehow had to shift
for themselves. Smuggling became their principal occupation
and enabled them to survive. Fathers, in Varshavsky's novel,
gave their daughters as bribes to the German occupying
authorities. Pious patriarchs became informers for the sake
of a petty monetary reward. Husbands replaced their wives
with female smuggling assistants who could be useful as
decoys. In the synagogue, worshipers interrupted prayers
with mutual recriminations and brutal melees. Fists decided
disputes even in the presence of the rabbi and were more
effective than appeals to decency.

Varshavsky's novel had no central figure or main plot. It
offered a rich assortment of society's lower depths. His
thieves, prostitutes, liquor distillers, social outcasts, law-
breakers lived by their wits, courage and unscrupulousness.
Rarely did moments of tenderness break in upon harsh, cruel
days and only at the edge of the abyss. Such a moment came

to the smuggling team of Pantel and Mendel, father and son, after they had flayed each other in the cellar of a hunch-backed panderer. Another such moment came to Pantel after he kicked his pregnant wife and brought her near unto death. But the tenderest scenes took place between the dangerously ill Mendel and the prostitute Nache, who nursed him back to health. These scenes, in which pain purified him and pity renovated her, were reminiscent of Dostoevsky, Varshavsky's model.

The Jewish townlet emerged from World War I critically ill, according to Varshavsky, and without hope of convalescence. Uprooted from tradition, it had no ideals to fight for, no moral values to live by, no principles that could tame lust or avarice. The cynical novelist seemed to gloat at the passing of holiness from the dying Jewish communities and to mock at the rituals and folkways of pre-war vintage, outmoded in the post-war era.

The first significant novel of Shimon Horonchik, *Confused Ways* (*Farplonterte Vegn,* 1924), also appeared under the sponsorship of Weissenberg and also portrayed the physical and moral disintegration of the Polish-Jewish townlet during the years of German military occupation. This novel was followed by other Naturalistic narratives, such as *Whirr of Machines* (*Geroish Fun Mashinen,* 1928), which was based on the author's observations and experiences in a Polish lace factory, *1905* (1929), which depicted the struggle of Jewish workers during the year of the unsuccessful revolt against the Czarist regime, and *Swamp* (*Sump,* 1931), in which Horonchik's rich relatives served as models of hard-hearted exploiters.

The rise of factories during the first quarter of the century and the substitution of machine production for the individual handiwork of independent craftsmen resulted in a migration from villages and townlets to the larger cities and brought to the fore unscrupulous parvenus and class-conscious wage earners. Strikes, riots, fear of pogroms darkened the Jewish scene and were reflected in Horonchik's tales. Rarely did a gleam of sunlight break through his gloomy descriptions of Jewish life, probably because he

himself was constantly haunted by fear, poverty and loneliness.

When the German military authorities in 1915 occupied
the town of Kalish, which had been set afire by the retreat-
ing Russians, they corraled its male inhabitants, all of whom
were Jews, lined them up in rows, and shot every fifteenth
person. This was done to instill fear into the trapped community. Horonchik was the fourteenth in line. The shock
he was subjected to on that day reverberated in him as an
undefinable terror throughout his later years.

After his wife, who was his main support, left him, he
became ever more gloomy, more cynical, more restless. In
1934 he moved to Warsaw. There he witnessed the rising tide
of Polish anti-Semitism and sensed the gathering of even
more destructive forces against which Jews were powerless.
When the German army in 1939 again attacked Poland, he
fled from the Warsaw conflagration. But his will to live was
undermined. Arriving at the conclusion that the entire
world had become one vast swamp, he did not want to wait
to be engulfed in its mire. He gave up further flight, cut
his veins and let his life's blood ooze out.

Despite the keen observation of the Naturalistic writers
and their faithful reproduction of the fading of old traditions, the disintegration of long-established communal institutions, and the emergence of new, unhappy types and conflicts, they could not command popularity beyond the first
few years of their literary innovations: they offered no gleam
of cheer, no hope of a better tomorrow either on earth or in
the afterworld. They were therefore soon eclipsed by Neoromantic and mystical writers whose works could bring some
solace by conjuring up visions of a glorious Jewish past and
of a future redemption both on earth and in an imagined
heaven.

The Neoromantic, mystic drama *Dybbuk* by the folklorist
S. Anski (1863–1920), unperformed during his lifetime,
proved a phenomenal success at its first performance in
Warsaw on December 9, 1920, and held the stage for two
decades therafter.

The warm splendor of Hassidism shone through the

nostalgic tales of the Warsaw novelist Moshe Justman (1889–1942), who wrote under the pseudonym of B. Jeuschsohn. His articles in the Warsaw daily *Moment* until 1925 and his column in the rival Warsaw daily *Haint* from 1925 until his flight to Israel in 1939 won him a large following especially among troubled Hassidic youth, whch was then torn between traditionalism and the lure of modernism. His earliest novel, *At the Hassidic Court* (*Inm Rebbins Hoif,* 1911), stressed the joyous fervor prevailing in Hassidic circles. But it also depicted the infiltration of the doctrines of the *Maskilim* even among the children of the most stalwart Hassidim. The novelist loved the old order but recognized the inevitability of its further decline. For many years he immersed himself in the study of Jewish folklore and he retold tales of old with reverence and humor. His eight volumes *From Our Old Treasure* (*Fun Undzer Alten Oitzer,* 1932) were eagerly devoured by readers, both Orthodox and non-Orthodox.

Folklore material also supplied the basis for much of the best work of I. J. Trunk (1887–1961). Descended from rich patricians and famed rabbis, he enjoyed a carefree youth in his native village on the outskirts of Warsaw and then the finest secular and religious education under private tutors in the industrial city of Lodz. Coming under the influence of Peretz, he sought a synthesis of European rationalism and Jewish mysticism. Travels throughout Europe, Asia and Africa in his twenties gave him a background broad and deep, unsurpassed by any of his contemporaries at so early an age. On the eve of the First World War, he lived in Palestine and his early tales, *Fig Trees* (*Feigenboimer,* 1922), reflected his observations of its landscape and picturesque figures. The volume also included an artistic retelling of the Babylonian epic of Gilgamesh.

After spending the war years in Switzerland, Trunk returned to his native Poland, settled in a palatial home in Lodz and devoted himself to a life of study and contemplation. Admiring the Neoromanticism of Knut Hamsun, the iconoclasm of Friedrich Nietzsche and the estheticism of Oscar Wilde, he made these writers better known to Yiddish readers through meticulous essays and discerning critical comments. But he owed his greatest literary debt to the romanticism of the later Peretz. He saw in the realistic, satiric works of Peretz a temporary aberration and in the mystical Hassidic tales and dramas of Peretz a profound thinker's search for absolute truth transcending mere reason, flashes of ultimate insights, premonitions of spiritual values that emanated from the divine source of all knowledge. Despite his patrician background, his wealth and his leaning towards mysticism, Trunk became an adherent of the Bund and a supporter of its Socialist aspirations and its Diaspora nationalism.

His polemic essay *Yiddishism and Jewish History* (1930) was an extreme formulation of Shimon Dubnow's view that history and language were more important than territory in keeping Jews together as a distinct cultural group. History was not for him, however, pious ancestor worship but the heart of contemporary Jewish reality, the fountain from which the Jewish people drew the water of life, the national treasure from which Jews brought their unique contributions to mankind. To sever the Jews from the legacy of the past meant undermining their living roots. This past included Poland as well as Palestine, and Yiddish far more than Hebrew.

Negation of Yiddish, the tongue of the Jewish group personality in its densest concentration in Eastern Europe, meant reducing Jews to museum fossils, to epigones who survived merely as ruminating, rachitic descendants of a once vigorous historic entity. Jews must not let themselves be linguistically crippled, mummified, tied to the Procrustus bed of Hebrew. They should rather step out upon the world arena with their richly developed vernacular even as Dante had done when he composed his *Divine Comedy* in his Italian vernacular rather than in the sacred tongue of Catholicism. To seek a Jewish renaissance by means of two languages was, in Trunk's opinion, as absurd as a body trying to think with two heads or to feel with two hearts. In order to forestall national schizophrenia, he suggested retaining

Hebrew as the Latin of the Jews, as the medium for religious services, but to base Jewish nationalism on Yiddish.

By 1936, however, when Trunk reprinted his essay on Yiddishism in the volume *Near and Strange (Noent un Fremd)*, he was forced to acknowledge that the prospects for a Jewish Humanism based on Yiddish were growing ever dimmer. The Polish bastion of Yiddishism was crumbling. Three years later it collapsed. Trunk himself barely managed to escape via the Orient to the United States. The *grand seigneur* of Yiddish letters arrived in New York penniless. For the last two decades of his life he was engaged in a daily, difficult struggle for bread. Yet these proved to be his most creative years.

As Trunk looked back upon them during his final days, he saw them as the climax of his life-long search for the harmony of diversities, for unity amidst multiplicity, for Jewish integration in the cosmos. At first he had sought to find himself in nature, in the landscape of Poland, where he was born and reared. Then he had discovered that contemporary life was rooted in history, in the thoughts and deeds of the many preceding generations, and so he turned to write historical novels. His autobiographic, nostalgic prose epic in seven volumes *Poland (Poilen, 1944–1953)* occupied his main attention during his first years in America. It was a family chronicle but it also painted a warm, faithful portrait of Polish Jewry at the apex of its creative development and splendor. Then, in his final stage, he had freed himself from his infatuation with a Poland that was no longer the center of Jewishness and he sought in surviving myths, folklore, and folk tales the answers to the questions: how does the world look through Jewish eyes? how is it mirrored in the Jewish subconscious? how does Jewish history live in the imagination of the unsophisticated, unalienated Jew?

In his romance of a Jewish Don Quixote, *Simkhe Plakhte* (1951), Trunk combined two antithetical aspects of the Jewish soul. On the one hand, the inarticulate, Golem-like Simkhe reacted instinctively and unconsciously to the events happening around him. On the other hand, his Sancho

Panza, the Lithuanian rationalist Feivel, reacted with the subtle, refined irony of pure Jewish intellectualism. Simkhe, a water carrier of limited intelligence in a Polish townlet, found himself catapulted into ever higher social strata. Without being able to read or write, he ended up, against his own will, as a revered rabbi and as the chief advisor to the Polish nobility and even to the king himself. Feivke, the sharp-witted skeptic who was able to push the simpleton Simkhe up the ladder of worldly success, remained aware of the fickleness of fortune and stayed out of its clutches, content with a piece of bread, a bit of onion, and ever deepening insight into the follies of a transient world.

Trunk followed this comic romance with a narrative of the early adventures of Hershele Ostropoler, entitled *The World's Merriest Jew* (*Der Frehlekhster Yied In Der Velt,* 1953). The stories dealt with Hershele's years of apprenticeship. In this wag, Jewish folklore had created a figure who alternated between hope and disappointment and who finally reached the stage of laughing at the world and getting others to join in his laughter. According to Trunk, Jews could surmount the tragedies with which their past and present so richly endowed them because they possessed the gift of laughter. Instead of becoming the world's greatest pessimists, they managed to retain ineradicable faith in the ultimate triumph of goodness over evil. Their optimistic tales told of their waiting for the coming of Messiah and of the intervention meanwhile of his precursor Elijah and of one or another of the thirty-six *Lamedvovniks* or Hidden Saints to reverse direst ill fortune.

Undaunted by adversity, Trunk completed as his next romance *The World Is Full of Miracles* (*Die Velt Is Ful Mit Nissim,* 1955) and devoted his last year to composing tales about the founder of Hassidism, the Baal-Shem of Mezhbish, whom popular imagination had endowed with clairvoyance and the power of working miracles. Eleven of these tales were completed and were appended to his historical novel of the Messianic claimant Sabbatai Zvi, entitled *Messianic Storm* (*Moshiakh-Gevitter,* 1961).

Two other Polish novelists, I. J. Singer (1893–1944) and

his younger brother I. Bashevis Singer (b. 1904) were, like Trunk, offspring of Polish rabbinical families and deeply immersed in the folklore of Hassidism. The rise to fame of I. J. Singer beyond the boundaries of his native land must be ascribed in large measure to the dramatizations of his novels by Maurice Schwartz, who achieved phenomenal box-office successes with them, both in New York's Yiddish Art Theater and wherever he included them in his guest performances.

Yoshe Kalb (1932), a novel which Maurice Samuel translated into English under the title *The Sinner* (1933), presented a far less flattering picture of a prominent Hassidic Court than Trunk presented in his tales. Singer's Rabbi of Nyesheve is a powerful but temperamental and unascetic leader of thousands of Hassidim throughout Galicia and Russia. He is able to bully and cajole followers and opponents until he gets his way. After burying three wives, he is determined, in his sixties, to take young Malke as his fourth mate, but first he must marry off his youngest daughter, Serele. He succeeds in negotiating a match between Serele and the adolescent, God-seeking Nahum, despite the latter's resistance. When Nahum later catches sight of Malke, however, he is more attracted to her than to his own wife. In a moment of weakness he succumbs to her longing for him and thereafter he seeks to atone by a life of ascetic, penitent wandering. Always he strives for the purification of his soul. Nevertheless, he becomes involved in complicated situations. These reach a climax when he returns to Nyesheve after an absence of fifteen years and is put on trial by a Sanhedrin of seventy rabbis, who attempt to untangle the ramifications of his dual personality: saint and sinner, Yoshe Kalb the simpleton and Nahum the learned cabalist. The final court scene is tensely dramatic and accounts to a large extent for the success of the stage version of the novel.

Singer's finest prose epic is *The Brothers Ashkenazi* (1935), which an enthusiastic critic ranked with Tolstoy's great epics. It spans a century of Jewish life in Lodz, from the post-Napoleonic era to the Polish Republic of the 1920's. In three volumes, it depicts the rapid rise of Lodz from an insignificant village to a large metropolis, its efflorescence as a main textile center during the reign of the last Czars, and its decline when it was cut off from its hinterland, the vast Russian market, after the Revolution of 1917.

The German and Moravian master weavers and their followers, who brought this industry to the Polish settlement, encountered keen competition from Jewish importers, smugglers, peddlers and miscellaneous dealers who swarmed into the developing town. Soon Jews proved themselves to be indispensable as general agents also for the larger German firms. In the course of decades of patient, unremitting initiative, they were able to gain control of the industry.

Most successful was Max Ashkenazi, whose passion for hard work was inexhaustible. Despite repeated setbacks, he was able to amass wealth and to retain it. He became known as the King of Lodz. His principal rival was his twin brother, Jacob. Through the interlocking fate of the two brothers, their divergent characters, their feuds, their reconciliations, the author unfolded a rich panorama of flourishing Jewish activity in the midst of a hostile majority population of Poles, Russians and Germans. Jews managed to surmount ever changing varieties of discrimination and oppression, including Cossack pogroms, German occupation, revolutionary expropriation, Polish chauvinism. They participated in all liberal and radical movements, only to be thrust aside when these movements attained victory. They bled on all fronts and still somehow survived. In the virulently anti-Semitic New Poland, however, Lodz was doomed. It crumbled and putrefied. With the extinction of its last glimmer of industrial vitality, the Jew Max Ashkenazi, who had acquired the title of King of Lodz, also closed his eyes. Meanwhile, Zionist pioneers set out from the dying Polish city for Palestine and other Jews for America. They sought a new life and they left behind them the desolate and alien city where everything they built in the course of a century was built on shifting sand.

The basic theme underlying Singer's narratives is the loneliness of the individual who can never be understood in his uniqueness and who is fated to be trodden under the heel of the conformist masses. In *Chaver Nachman* (1938), translated by Maurice Samuel under the title *East of Eden* (1939), the novelist, who had himself experienced the harsh reality of Soviet Russia, voiced his disillusionment with the Communist panacea. In *Family Carnovsky* (1943), he let three centers of Jewish life pass in review—Poland, Germany, America—and arrived at pessimistic conclusions concerning all of them. Three generations were projected on a broad canvas. The earliest was that of the enlightened Polish Jew David Carnovsky. The second was that of his son, the successful German-Jewish physician Dr. Georg Carnovsky. The third was that of his grandson, the semi-Aryan Yego Carnovsky, who even on American soil was still infatuated with Nazi ideology and suffered from Jewish self-hatred. All three experience rejection by non-Jewish groups but none can find a way that might lead to salvation.

Singer himself concluded sadly, in an essay of October 1942, that efforts of Jews to live peacefully and happily among non-Jews constituted a two-thousand-year-old error, which should be rectified by the return of Jews to a territory of their own. Ever since Judea's defeat by the Romans, Jews sought to retain their group identity in lands of the Diaspora, and in almost every generation attempts to annihilate them were renewed. On the one hand, most Jews persisted in their refusal to submerge themselves in the dominant group. On the other hand, most non-Jews would not admit them to brotherhood save at the price of the obliteration of their group distinctiveness. The war between Rome and Jerusalem was still being waged, though under different slogans. Numerous explanations for this antagonism between Esau and Jacob were offered. These included religious fanaticism, economic rivalry, psychological incompatibility, racial, metaphysical and mystical theories. But the bitter fact remained that there was no peace between Jews and non-Jews crowded together on the same soil.

In Singer's view, the evidence of twenty centuries, culminating in Hitlerism, should suffice to convince the wildest optimists that a symbiosis of Jews and their non-Jewish compatriots was unattainable, that Jews could not live as a

people on other peoples' territories without arousing antagonism. Why then renew illusions which had always ended
in disappointment? "The people of Israel must again be
taken out of Egypt just like three thousand years ago. The
thornbush is burning in the fire and is calling to Moses,
the shepherd, who is busy feeding alien sheep in the desert."

I. J. Singer was the mentor of his younger brother, who
wrote under the name of "I. Bashevis." While the former
strove to veer from Neoromanticism to ever more transpar-
ent Realism, the latter preferred in his narratives to revel
in romantic visions that verged on the grotesque and to
move in the direction of the Expressionists and Surrealists.

The world of Bashevis abounds in evil, sickness, harshness, anger, beatings, tortures and horror. It is a strange
world in which wicked spirits tempt all creatures of flesh
and blood and in which demons wrestle with *Lamedvovniks*.
The weak among mortals succumb and end tragically. The
strong battle allurements, overcome temptations, seek atonement after initial missteps, and emerge as radiant personalities, a blessing to their fellows.

Bashevis cannot reconcile himself to the existence of
undeserved suffering, especially the undeserved suffering
which befell God's so-called chosen people. He is depressed
by the cruelties inflicted upon innocent children and saintly
graybeards at the hands of the most enlightened people in
the heart of contemporary Europe. The wounds of our century are, however, too vividly present and the catastrophe
too immense for him to be able to structure them within the
framework of an objective, artistic narrative. He, therefore,
prefers to go back in his imagination to tragedies on a more
manageable scale, those suffered by Polish Jewry in earlier
generations, from the massacres of Hetman Chmelnitzky's
hordes in the mid-seventeenth century to the pogroms perpetrated by the conquerors and the conquered of World
War I. Yet, even these tragedies, as narrated in chronicles
of survivors, are too horrible for him to describe directly
and he wisely limits himself to the after-effects of the crushing events. Thus, the novels *Satan in Goray* (1935), *The
Slave* (1962) and numerous short stories bring to life the

post-1648 era in grotesque images and mangled characters.

The former novel takes place in the townlet of Goray in 1665 and 1666. Although sixteen years have passed since Chmelnitzky's destructive raid, the community has not yet recovered. It lives in constant dread of another Cossack incursion. Its main hope is centered on the coming of Messiah, whose imminent appearance cabalists have predicted on the basis of mystic calculations. Bashevis reproduces the grim atmosphere of the terrorized, superstition-ridden Jews who are ripe for religious hysteria. When the satanic Gedalia arrives in Goray, he takes advantage of the community's longing to escape from despair and desolation. He announces that salvation is at hand: Messiah has already appeared on earth and has already revealed himself in distant Turkey in the figure of Sabbatai Zvi. He finds in the half-demented Rechele a prophetess whom he can mold to his purposes. Rechele, daughter of a patrician who was ruined in 1648, has been raised by a century-old deaf hag, her uncle's mother-in-law. This uncle, a slaughterer with black beard and red eyes, let the hag maltreat the sensitive child. Rechele was never allowed to leave her room to play outdoors. Her senile guardian hissed at her like a snake, cursed her with blood-curdling curses, tore out her hair, dunked her head in boiling water, beat her with bony hands, with a log, or with a moistened cat-o'-nine-tails. Psychological tortures included bedtime tales of dragons and wild beasts, dead souls that flew about incessantly, dybbuks that sought to enter into living bodies, murderers who lived in caves and consorted with witches, cannibals who roasted children on spits, a one-eyed savage on the lookout for a mate. As a result of such treatment, Rechele succumbed to fits of panic.

Gedalia, playing upon the willingness of Goray's Jews to believe in miracles, proclaims the girl's hysterical visions to be prophecies. As the new, self-appointed mentor of the inspired prophetess, he is able to manipulate himself into a position of dominance in the community. He has Rechele divorced from her ascetic husband so that he himself can marry her. He then institutes a reign of vice and moral degradation in the formerly pious townlet, on the theory that the world must be completely sunk in sin before the Messiah can arrive to purify it.

Bashevis delights in depicting Goray's sensual orgies, the wallowing of men and women in uncleanliness of spirit and flesh. He spares only a single character from the rampant degeneracy, Rabbi Beinish, but this aged, sympathetic communal leader is shown as helpless to stem the madness gripping all the inhabitants. Mortally ill, he begs to be taken to Lublin so as not to die in his native Goray, which has fallen under the domination of satanic forces.

A variation of *Satan in Goray,* Bashevis' earliest novel of mass hysteria, is the short story "The Ball," in which the arch-devil Samael himself takes a hand and debauches an entire town. He tempts its poor, pious Jews with the glitter of gold. He promises a chain of pearls and a thousand ducats to all unmarried persons who will marry before the crowing of the cock at dawn. This offer proves to be irresistible. Young and old are caught in the devil's net, participate in the black weddings, become mired in sensuality, and would have perished utterly in swamps of filth if not for the rabbi's vehement adjurations. The town's rabbi persists in calls to repentence and in quoting apt precepts of the Torah. Bit by bit, individuals emerge from the slough and find their way back to moral sobriety. Although many generations have passed since the night of orgy and black weddings, the memory of the devilish temptation lingers on and renders descendants immune to the lure of wealth and indecency.

The Slave is a novel dealing with a survivor of Chmelnitzky's massacres. Having fled from the Cossack murderers, Jacob was dragged away by Polish marauders and sold as a slave to a Polish landowner. Throughout lonely years among depraved peasants, enduring great hardships and in constant danger of being killed, he nevertheless retained his Jewish morals and religious observances. He even infected the Polish peasant girl Wanda with a longing for the Jewish faith. Ultimately, he was ransomed from his savage environment and escorted back to his native town. Wanda's image lived on in him, however, and he undertook to rescue her from her semi-pagan, semi-Christian village. During this period of upheaval and persecution, Jews were constantly on the move. The ex-slave Jacob found his way to a ravaged town which was being rebuilt by returning survivors. Wanda became an exemplary Jewish wife. But misfortune dogged the couple. After Wanda, renamed Sarah after her conversion, died in childbirth, Jacob fled with the infant to the Holy Land and raised his son to become a learned and pious son of Israel. He himself returned, after the Sabbatai Zvi debacle, to end his days and to be buried near his adored mate of alien stock.

Bashevis frequently breaks down the boundaries between the natural and the supernatural, between the living and the dead. In one tale, the beloved deceased wife of a rabbi enters the body of a young girl, lives there as Esther Kreindel the Second, remarries the widowed rabbi, and continues her interrupted earthly existence in the borrowed body. In another tale, a devil persuades a man and a woman to deviate ever more from the truth until they become so mired in falsehoods that he has them completely in his toils. They end on the gallows in this world and are directed to hell in the other world. A third tale, "The Mirror," is a monologue of a demon.

In "Taibele and Her Demon," a *badhen* overhears Taibele tell a story of a woman who was forced to consort with a demon. He thereupon impersonates this demon in the darkness of night and forces Taibele to submit to him, at first unwillingly and under horrible threats but before long most gladly.

In the gruesome tale "Blood," a woman and a *shohet* find their carnal ecstasy increased as the steaming blood of the butchered animals gurgles about them and as the death rattles supply tonal accompaniment. Ultimately, she becomes so ravenous and so passionately unrestrained that she prowls as a werewolf through the nights. Her escort, however, does at the end find a way to repent and atone.

Despite the infatuation of Bashevis with the horrible, he also composes now and then tender, idyllic tales in the tradition of Peretz. Such a narrative is *Short Friday,* the story of the simple tailor Shmul-Leibele and his good wife,

Shoshe. Their life of piety is symbolized by the holiness with which they usher in the Sabbath. Both pray that they might leave this world on the same day. Their prayer is grantd when they are asphyxiated by the fumes from the Sabbath stove and awaken to find themselves in their graves, side by side. The story ends with the author's concluding remarks: "Yes, the brief years of turmoil and temptation had come to an end. Shmul-Leibele and Shoshe had reached the true world. Man and wife grew silent. In the stillness they heard the flapping of wings, a quiet singing. An angel of God had come to guide Shmul-Leibele the tailor and his wife Shoshe into Paradise."

In *Gimpel the Fool* (1957), Bashevis portrays with kindness but also with gentle satire a pure simpleton who believes everything he is told. He assumes that all others are like himself, utterly without guile or malice. He is married off to a woman chosen for him by the community, lives with her for twenty years, and believes unquestioningly in her faithfulness. On her deathbed, she confesses to him that not a single one of their six children has been fathered by him. Yet, though everyone deceives him, he cannot bring himself to repay in like coin. This world may be a tissue of lies but beyond it is the world of truth toward which he heads by leading a blameless life. He hopes to reach that better world as soon as he passes the bourne of the grave.

The hero of the narrative *Spinoza of Market Street* (1961) is also a pure simpleton, despite a doctorate in philosophy and a life-long exposure to the wisdom of great thinkers. Dr. Nahum Fishelson, an abstemious scholar, lives alone in a Warsaw garret and devotes twenty-five years to the writing of a commentary on his idol Spinoza. Events pass him by as he thinks his solitary thoughts and communes with the pantheistic deity, the lord of logic and pure reason. Finally, however, the disturbances of the First World War also penetrate to the retreat of the Warsaw philosopher. A neighbor comes to nurse the sick man who has already reconciled himself to death. She manages to restore him to health. He marries her, and comes to understand that the cosmic forces which operate in the macrocosm also stream within him, that the whirl of universes in flux also embraces the emotional transformations to which he is being subjected. "Pardon me, Spinoza, I have become a fool!" he finally exclaims.

The Magician of Lublin (1959) is a novel of Jewish life in late nineteenth-century Poland. Its hero, the Jewish juggler and acrobatic performer Yasha Mazur, has become famous as the Magician of Lublin. In the course of journeying from place to place, he has sloughed his religious habits and has hurled himself into the pleasures of the flesh. These lead him to ever greater excesses and bring him to the verge of an abyss of crime. At the last moment, however, he retreats from evil and seeks self-purification. He realizes that there must be an accounting for every deed, every word, every thought, and that, in the final reckoning, good must triumph over evil. He concludes that each good act increases the goodness content of the universe and that each transgression delays the day of Messianic deliverance. Yasha the Magician thereupon becomes transformed into Reb Jacob the Penitent. He immures himself as a hermit in a small, doorless house, four cubits long and four cubits wide, with a tiny aperture through which he receives his daily food. He puts himself under this rigorous restraint, since otherwise he, the libertine with strong appetites, would be unable to resist the temptations of this world.

The most ambitious novel of Bashevis is *Family Moskat* (1950), a chronicle of the decline of a patrician family of Warsaw from its height in the first decade of the twentieth century to its final debacle in the Hitler period. The patriarch of the family, Reb Meshulam Moskat, combined Hassidic piety and shrewd business sense. In the course of fifty years, he accumulated considerable wealth. At eighty, he married a third wife and was still the chief support of his seven children, their mates, and many more grandchildren. After his death, the strong bonds uniting the various members of this large family were weakened. Religious observances fell into disuse. Traditional standards of conduct were discarded. Divorces increased. A few children drifted to apostasy, others embraced epicureanism, still others Zionism.

Most led unhappy lives, devoid of meaningful values. The First World War hastened the process of decay and, by the time the Second World War broke out, the surviving descendants were ripe for the end. Death took over. The final words were spoken while Warsaw was under Nazi bombardment and all routes of escape were cut off: "The Messiah will soon come . . . Death is the Messiah. That's the real truth."

If Meshulam Moskat stood out as the symbol of the stable, old order that was able to maintain itself until our century, Asa Heshel Bannet came to the fore as the symbol of the younger generation that set out in search of new wisdom and that was whirled about as driftwood by the storms that rocked Eastern European Jewish existence to its foundations. Coming to Warsaw at the age of nineteen, with a glowing letter of recommendation to the Moskats and with a copy of Spinoza's *Ethics*, this young prodigy of a distinguished rabbinical family sought to acquire knowledge of ultimate reality, to synthesize Torah and Enlightenment, but never got far in his studies. He became involved in emotional entanglements, married the wrong woman in a moment of despair, divorced her, then married the right woman only to make her unhappy also. Drafted into the Russian army to fight for the Czarist regime which persecuted Jews, he experienced revolutions and pogroms, and returned to Poland in time to be drafted into Pilsudski's army in which anti-Semitism also prevailed. Finally, he saw the rearisen Poland perish at the hands of Hitler's cohorts, while he, the symbolic contemporary Jew, continued to be the preferred victim of man's bestiality to man.

Bashevis abuses his literary talent by straining far too often for sensational effects, by indulging in exaggerations, by emphasizing sadistic aspects. Instead of a balanced view of Jewish life, he offers a distorted, demonic view. Though his fame in the 1960's exceeded that of any Jewish novelist since Sholem Asch, it was not likely to be as enduring as that of his older brother, I. J. Singer, whose novels presented a sounder insight into Polish-Jewish reality before its extinction.

10

Poets of Warsaw

LITTLE MORE THAN TWO DECADES elapsed between the liberation of Poland from the Czarist yoke and its partition between Nazi Germany and Communist Russia as a result of the Molotov-Ribbentrop Pact. These years did not bring about an abatement of anti-Semitism in the newly independent state. Nevertheless, Jewish energy was sufficiently released by the acquisition of certain rights guaranteed to ethnic and linguistic minorities so that an upsurge of creativeness could manifest itself in many fields, including literature.

Though Peretz, the chief inspirer of the Yiddish renascence, passed away in 1915, the seeds he had planted matured in the works of his many disciples both in Poland and across the Atlantic. Besides, other literary circles in the Polish capital continued to function until cut short by Hitler's invasion. The most influential of these was the circle centering about Hillel Zeitlin (1872–1943) and his two talented sons, Ahron (b. 1898) and Elchanan (1900–1943).

Even before Hillel Zeitlin came to Warsaw in 1908, his home in Homel and then in Vilna attracted publicists, poets and thinkers of different shades of opinion, who admired his religious sincerity and philosophical acumen. Frequent visitors included Z. I. Onochi (1878–1947), Zalman Shneour (1887–1959), Peretz Hirshbein (1880–1948), Yeshaihu Bershadski (1871–1908), and I. D. Berkovitch (1885–1967). In Warsaw the circle about this influential editor and sage expanded to include Mordecai Spector (1858–1925), Yone Rosenfeld (1880–1944), Yoel Mastboim (1884–1957), Jacob Steinberg (1887–1947), Yitzkhok Katzenelson (1886–1944), Jacob Fichman (1881–1958), Shlome Gilbert (1885–1942), Zysman Segalowitch (1884–1949), Menahem Boraisha (1888–1949), A. Almi (1892–1963), Moshe Teitch (1882–1935), Joseph Tunkel (1881–1949), Moshe Justman (1889–1942), A. Mukdoni (1878–1958), Baal Makhshoves (1873–1924), and Eliezer Shteinman (b. 1890).

Elchanan Zeitlin, in the first volume of his memoirs, *In A Literary House* (*In A Literarishe Shtub,* 1938), paints a broad panorama of the Vilna years but covers the Warsaw years only until 1914. A projected second volume never appeared, since the author died of hunger in the Warsaw Ghetto shortly after his father was shot by the Nazis. Fortunately, his brother Ahron survived, having been stranded in America while on a visit before the outbreak of hostilities.

Although Ahron Zeitlin stayed on in New York and was no less prolific during his three decades there as a journalist and poet than he had been during his earlier decades in Warsaw, his literary personality did not change appreciably throughout his American period. He merely added themes of the Holocaust and of the new Israel and refined the Symbolist technique and the mystic strain which characterized him since his first poetic epic, *Metatron,* was published in 1922.

Critics spoke of Zeitlin's lyrics as reasoned products, as ideas incorporated in images and rhythmic patterns. But he himself maintained that the original lyric impulse was somnambulistic and stemmed from the subconscious. This impulse produced the raw material upon which the poet's consciousness then acted and which he laboriously fashioned into an artistic whole. With greater maturity, a poet should therefore rework earlier versions until in time the poem approached perfection. He himself did not hesitate to revise lyrics even decades after their first appearance. The version of *Metatron* in the third volume of his *Complete Lyrics* (*Gezamelte Lieder,* 1957) was completely different from the one he composed thirty-six years earlier. Indeed, when this third volume appeared, ten years after the first two volumes, he reprinted several lyrics in a revised form and begged the reader to look upon earlier texts not as variants but as nonexistent. He preferred that his poems should be read and considered not chronologically as stages in his growth but rather thematically as expressions of his basic poetic configuration, as his life-long wrestling with God for an ultimate understanding of essences.

Zeitlin is a religious poet, deeply steeped in the Cabala and in Jewish mysticism. Devils, doubles, demons, dybbuks, ghosts, astral emanations, transmigrated souls, angels and archangels abound in his lyrics, ballads and dramas. The struggle between spirits of negation and pious followers of God is at times treated with delightful humor, as in the long poems *Jewish Demons* (*Yiedishe Shedim,* 1948) and *Shmuel Rosh Medina.* More often, however, there are serious encounters between personified forces of good and evil, between doubters and believers, between satanic emissaries and saintly personalities. In the end, goodness triumphs over evil, souls of sinners attain salvation, falsehood becomes manifest as but the shadow of truth, and death is revealed as a mere boundary between this life and a life hereafter. Even after Maidanek and the cruel end of his family, Zeitlin proclaims his trust in the God of his fathers, a God who destroys and recreates. To be a Jew means to be eternally running toward God, even if God is ultimately unreachable. It means waiting for the trumpet of the Messiah, even if the coming of the Messiah is so long delayed.

Zeitlin's Messiahs, true and false, range from Messiah Ben David, Messiah Ben Joseph, Menahem to Sabbatai Zvi and Jacob Frank. In addition, he brings to the fore many legendary figures who dream of bringing Messiah down from his heavenly abode to offer salvation to the suffering human race. Some of his legendary heroes ascend to upper realms of being and seek there to counteract the machinations of diabolical spirits. Such memorable, saintly, wonder-working Jews are the Baal Shem, Nachman Bratslaver, Leib Sores and Joseph della Rina.

The mystic mood and the Messianic visions which overhang so many of Zeitlin's lyrics also hover over his drama *Jacob Frank* (1929). This drama deals with two antithetical approaches to God, that of Frank, the most devoted disciple of Sabbatai Zvi, and that of the Baal Shem, Frank's contemporary and the exponent of a more spiritual doctrine. Frank, though a God-seeker, wades through the complexities of sin, lust, darkness, in the belief that only after the world is saturated with evil will the pendulum of the universe swing back toward spirit, purity, radiance. The Baal Shem, on the other hand, is the God-finder. He discerns God's presence everywhere. He sings hymns to all of God's creation. He lives simply, works hard and steers clear of overmuch questioning and brooding. Frank, with the aid of demonic powers, can create the body of a Golem, but only the Baal Shem, by invoking the Ineffable Name, can imbue it with life and feeling. In the end, the followers of Frank, the false Messiah, become confused and disillusioned. They grope in darkness and scatter in all directions. The Baal Shem, on the other hand, lights the way for a self-effacing, God-intoxicated, life-giving, religious movement, Hassidism.

Zeitlin's drama *Brenner* (1929) appeared in the same year as *Jacob Frank*. Its hero was Joseph Chaim Brenner, the Hebrew poet who had been killed in the Jaffa Pogrom of 1921. Brenner had, in his youth, come under the influence of the dramatist's father. He had then experienced imprisonment in Russia and had escaped to London, where he became active in Zionist circles. Under the impact of A. D. Gordon's "back to the soil" philosophy, he had worked as an agricultural laborer in Palestine until his violent death. Zeitlin, who had been in Palestine during the unrest of 1921, transferred to his dramatic hero much of his own stormy striving and pain-filled visions.

Brenner, as portrayed by Zeitlin, could not endure seeing

the Jewish people sleeping on its bundle of troubles or hiding in garrets while other peoples walked freely on their own soil under their own skies. He therefore sought to help his people by the power of his pen and by the example of his own physical labor, repeatedly exposing himself to danger and martyrdom. Through pain to salvation was his motto. Courageously adhering to his convictions, he neither fled from nor did he resist actively the incited, knife-wielding Arab who slew him. Brenner saw himself as the Jewish Abel who looked fearlessly into the eyes of the non-Jewish Cain. Thereafter the victim's blood cried out for atonement, not vengeance but atonement, and the fratricide recoiled branded and terror-ridden, pursued by his own awakened conscience.

Palestine was also the scene of Zeitlin's novel *Burning Earth* (*Brenendike Erd,* 1937). The theme of the novel was the Nili Affair of the First World War. "Nili" was the name of a small espionage group that centered about the Aaronson Family of Zichron Yaakov, and that hoped to gain Palestine for the Jews by helping the British win the war against the Turks. Zeitlin's was the first fictional treatment of the theme which Michael Blankfort later brought to wider attention through his novel *Behold the Fire* (1965) and especially through the motion picture based upon the novel.

Zysman Segalowitch (1884–1949) was only briefly associated with the Zeitlin circle. He stemmed from Bialystok, a center of the Jewish textile industry, but the pogrom of 1905 drove him forth from his native town. Despite a yearning for rootedness, he was constantly uprooted. Lodz, Warsaw, Odessa, Kiev, Moscow, Tel Aviv and New York were some of his way stations and each left its impress upon his restless personality.

Young Segalowitch was a romantic sentimentalist under the spell of Byronism and Heine's *Weltschmerz*. His poem *Kazmerzh* (1912) brought him early fame. It wove a tender web of colorful fantasy about an old townlet where piety and only slightly mellowing traditions prevailed. There the tired soul of the poet dreamed of forest nymphs and the great god Pan. There it longed for the freedom of the open spaces, the loveliness of dew-drunk flowers and the gaiety of singing, laughing Wanda, the Hassid's daughter. But girls like Wanda, full of the joy of life, run off with light-hearted Polish strangers, while Jewish young men, lacking the courage to defy religious taboos, remain with romantic daydreams, nebulous mirages, and the sadness of ages in exile.

Reisele, the *shokhet's* daughter and the heroine of Segalowitch's most popular ballad, also has a carefree, dancing, loving heart like Wanda. However, she lacks the wild courage to resist her angry father, who wants to mate her with a rabbi's son rather than with Motele, the sturdy, gay watchman with whom she shared happy hours. When her father learns of her enchantment with Motele, he cuts off the beautiful curls which make her so entrancing. She can then only muster the pathetic courage to drown herself in the cold waters of the Vistula.

Segalowitch's sentimental poems of love's ebb and flow, of joy seasoned with melancholy, of spring's white blossoms and autumn's golden charm, reach a climax in *Regina* (1915), the idyllic tale of the proud, elegant, mysterious woman, desired, found, lost, retrieved, and forever vanished, but leaving behind her evanescent fragrances and grateful memories. Such a woman arises out of a poet's dreams in the springtime of life, bubbles with overflowing vitality in the glow of summer, and dissolves with the snows of winter.

In the poetic drama *The Wall* (*Die Vant,* 1915), Segalowitch combines militancy with sentimentalism. He condemns the weeping and futile lamenting with which some Jews react to wrongs inflicted upon them. He advocates resistance no matter what the consequences. Though the Jewish hero of this drama dies, he does so sword in hand, thereby arousing the admiration of his aristocratic Polish adversary, who until then looked upon Jewish girls as free game and who despised Jewish men as cowards and money-grubbers.

The militant tone of Segalowitch, however, did not long endure. He remembered that the Revolution of 1905, in which he participated, ended in anti-Jewish outbreaks. Nor could he wax enthusiastic about the Communist Revolution. Unlike his younger brother Wolf-Hirsh Segalowitch (1890–1937), who cast in his lot with the Soviets, served them faithfully, and was shot by them when the Minsk Group of Jewish intellectuals was liquidated, the poet chose in 1919 to exchange Kiev and Moscow for Warsaw, where he survived for an additional three decades.

His years in the Polish capital were his happiest. There he continued to compose lucid, singable lyrics and sentimental stories. There he was idolized by Jewish youth and especially by women readers. There he presided over the Association of Yiddish Writers and Journalists.

In his book of memoirs *Tlomazke 13* (1946), he gave a moving, somewhat idealized portrait of the home of this Association, a center of Yiddish culture for more than two decades, before it was reduced to rubble by the Nazis and most of its members burnt to ashes at Maidanek and Treblinka. "Toward evening at a table, sat a group discussing philosophy, poetry, Cabala, and other matters—a little world severed from the great world outside . . . Often the discussions reached a very high level. Nobody wanted to budge from his seat or to be disturbed by the street's tumult. It might appear as though this were a consultation of conspirators, but actually these people were passive toward all conflicts. They lived in the world and felt the need of discussing everything that went on—everything. And though we ironically called one another idlers, the Association was for us a sort of university where we learned from each other. There was not a theme of contemporary or eternal problems which was not debated at our table."

The writer's club at Tlomazke 13 offered a forum and an audience not only for the Warsaw group but also for visitors from all lands, for poets, actors, sculptors, painters, composers. Non-Jewish writers were received at banquets and brought news of literary events abroad. They came from France and Norway, from Japan and India, from Communist and non-Communist lands.

The first product of Segalowitch's Warsaw period was the lyric cycle *Ripe Grapes* (*Tseitike Troiben*, 1920), in which he converted into melodious verses his delight in passionate love. In these verses there is no thought of yesterday and no fear of a tomorrow; there is only today, or rather tonight, for the enjoyment of the stars in heaven and the women on earth. The poet's ideal is to sing, to drink deep, to burn with love's intense flame until he is entirely consumed.

Within a few years, however, the poet was emptied of his dreams and his ecstasies. Sadness came with light wings and descended upon him with leaden heaviness. Youth and beauty were gone. The tabernacle he built for earthly divinities was empty. The moments he sought to sanctify through song were unblessed and unanointed. Nevertheless, he still preferred to meander along his own zigzag way, singing of the green earth in springtime and hating nobody, while others were carrying red banners and sharpening swords. At the same time, he feared that the harsh clash of steel would soon drown out his tender tunes. Like all who still lived with sentiments, he was becoming prematurely old, he was growing tired, he was only half awake.

Segalowitch's forebodings were realized in 1939, when the Germans descended upon Warsaw and he had to flee before their battalions. He fled from Warsaw to Lublin, from Lublin to Rovno, from Rovno to Vilna, from Vilna to Kovno. He experienced terror and hopelessness, cruelty and hard-heartedness, or at best indifference. Only fellow Jews, even while themselves in the shadow of death, shared with him their hearts, their blankets, their bits of bread, thus enabling him to survive his many ordeals and ultimately to make his way to Tel Aviv. Then he came to love his Jewish people with an ardor that no longer permitted satiric mocking of their failings. Then he grew to hate the efficient, cultured Teutonic barbarians with a hatred he never knew earlier.

Segalowitch's wanderings during the first years of the conflict until his coming to the land of his Jewish kinsmen were described by him in the volume *Burning Steps* (*Gebrente Trit*, 1947). But even in the comparative safety of Tel Aviv, he was haunted by the terror of the less fortunate Jews trapped in the Nazi cauldron. Visions of Treblinka pursued him by day and by night until he found emotional release in penning the heart-rending stanzas of the elegy *There*

(*Dorten*, 1944). By "there" he meant the hell in which his Jews were being burned, not figuratively but literally, burned by other human beings who were fashioned not in the image of God but in the image of devils.

The elegy is dedicated to Arthur Zigelbaum (1895–1943), the heroic Bundist leader who committed suicide in London in order to awaken the world's conscience to the Jewish tragedy in Poland.

In all the poetry of the Holocaust there is no poem, except "The Song of the Murdered Jewish People" by Yitzkhok Katzenelson (1886–1944), that can compare with Segalowitch's elegy in sheer power and intensity. The sentimental esthete is no longer sentimental and is sick of estheticism.

After the opening stanzas in which Jewish life before the Holocaust is nostalgically surveyed, there follow stanzas portraying the heroic three weeks when Warsaw's Jews fought with other Polish citizens to hold off the Nazi avalanche. With the fall of Warsaw, the Jews were at the mercy of gorillas in well-tailored suits, orangutans in uniforms, cravat-wearing tigers. Jews were caged in stifling ghettos, decimated by hunger and typhoid, yellow-badged and branded like cattle. Some fled but only to perish on icy roads, in swamps, at impassable borders, in compulsory labor camps, along the frozen taigas.

The poet poured searing curses upon all who sharpened knives for Jewish throats or who made life a hell for Jews because of a need for scapegoats. The time of apologies for Jewish mistakes was over. All languages and all dialects needed to be scanned for sufficient maledictions to hurl upon German hangsmen, the beasts in human shape who slaughtered their fellow men with the newest slaughter machines. The poet could not understand how stars still continued to shine in silent beauty upon such a world or why a deluge did not wipe out the entire unworthy human race. Talk of victory was in the air, but of what avail would victory be for the millions of Jews whose voices had been silenced forever? "I plead not to the robber for pity. I weep not before the cold murderer. But I still have a spark of faith and so I ask of a higher power: how can we cross the abyss? How can we forgive ourselves for living on? How can we still talk of humanity and of love? O, Lord of Mercy, have compassion upon us, the mourners. How can we, the lonely, the weak, mourn for so many victims, our brothers and sisters? Let our last prayer be: descend, O Lord, from on high and help us bury our dead, help us weep for them. By the dew of the living grass, by the light of pure dawns, we beg of you, O Lord of Mercy, don't have us say Kaddish for you!"

Segalowitch, in his last years, walked about as a silent skeleton, tall and emaciated, afflicted with tragic memories, having the will but lacking the strength to slap the world in the face. He saw yesterday's torturers attending picture galleries and listening to symphonic music, and he averted his eyes from them. He wished the entire human race to be annulled, because a race which did not avenge the millions innocently martyred, the children gassed with their mothers, did not deserve to survive. He himself was glad not to have to live much longer on this planet and was no doubt grateful when death came to him in 1949.

The unanswered cry of Segalowitch as to why such a catastrophic fate was meted out to Jews resounded in the Yiddish poems of martyrs and survivors. Kadia Molodowsky raised this question most poignantly in the introduction to her anthology *Songs of Destruction (Lieder Fun Khurban,* 1962). She, however, found refuge in faith. Above the abyss of pain and despite the incursion of critical reasoning, she continued to intone the words that comforted Jews even on their last walk to the gas chambers: *"Ani maamin,* I believe." Flames could not destroy this eternal faith. She was certain that Jews who had once arisen from the Valley of Dead Bones, as Ezekiel had foreseen, would also arise from the Valley of Ashes and reconstitute themselves, a free, viable, God-trusting people.

Kadia Molodowsky is generally regarded as the most talented Yiddish poetess. Although she has been creative in fiction, drama, criticism and as editor of the Yiddish literary quarterly *Sviva,* her main contribution has been to the treasure of Yiddish poetry. Her early lyrics and tales in verse were sung in Yiddish schools of Eastern Europe until these schools and their pupils ceased to be. They were sung in Yiddish classrooms in North and South America. They resounded in an excellent Hebrew rendering not only in Israel's kindergartens and elementary schools but also in Ulpanim where they delighted and rejuvenated oldsters. Her later lyrics probed deeper levels of lacerated Jewish hearts.

Born in 1894 in the Lithuanian townlet of Bereza-Kartuzka, the poetess received her first education from her father, who was a Hebrew teacher. She then went on to Warsaw and Odessa in order to prepare herself for a teaching career, which she then practiced for many years.

Her earliest lyrics, begun in 1920 and published in 1927 under the title *November Nights (Kheshvendike Teg)*, touched the hearts of women, for she sang of their sorrows and motherly tenderness, of cold rainy evenings when children offered comforting warmth, and of sleepless nights when tiny hands dispelled gloomy thoughts. Yet, while her women readers cradled infants and nourished them with full breasts, she herself cradled verses in lonely midnights and the children she nourished with her maternal love were the shouting, unruly pupils of her school. She tamed their savagery with the verses of her *Kindermaaselekh,* which were set to music when published in 1930 and which won her widest acclaim.

The uniqueness of these simple poetic tales, full of humor and apparent naiveté, lay in the vivid personification of objects. For her barefooted tots she penned a ballad of a pair of little shoes which a shoemaker hammered into life and sent out into the world to fetch him bread and salt and other necessities. One day the shoes stopped before a door, knocked and entered. There sat a child alone, barefoot, naked, unhappy. There the shoes remained, unwilling to proceed further, and the shoemaker is still waiting for them to return. For her coatless boys and girls, the poetess sang a ballad of a coat that was handed down from Shmulik to Yossel-Behr, to Beele, to Hindel, until it reached Pantel, the youngest child. Unlike his older brothers and sisters, who wore it three years, he proceeded to dismember it piece by piece within a few days. When only the holes were left, he pranced about, happy in his nakedness. For her emaciated pupils who had to assist parents with household chores, the lyricist intoned the merry ballad of Olke with the Parasolke, a six-year-old who was constantly called away from play in order to wash, scrub, peel, darn, and mind the baby, but who always managed to get back to imagined flights over radiant roads to far-off places.

Kadia Molodowsky animates the inanimate, as do most romantic poets. She gives a voice to things. Plates and pots and bottles talk, make demands upon each other, engage in quarrels, suffer casualties. The sun combs Berele's head with a golden comb. A letter journeys to various addresses by train and ship in response to a mother's request for news of her son. A washtub rolls up and down from floor to floor to offer laundering services to a different tenant each day. The poetess is always aware that no adult can fathom, as can a child, what a stone tells the listening sky above it or what the grass in springtime tries to communicate to its graying boss, the gardener.

In 1931, Kadia Molodowsky completed the maturer lyrics of *Dzike Gass,* a Warsaw street inhabited by the poor, the unemployed, the rebels against the social order, whose children she taught. She was torn between her conviction that she ought to join the march of the radical sansculottes and her longing for the carefree, joyous spirit of blossoming spring, moonlit fragrances and the green woods beyond the street's horizon. She tried to hide herself in an ivory tower. In vain! The call of her starving neighbors penetrated to her. She had to answer their call.

In the poems of *Fraidke* (1935) she depicted the proud, class-conscious laboring men and women of Warsaw, their strikes, their illegal activities, their enforced emigration from their native land. She herself left Poland in 1935. Her odyssey through European countries and on to the United States found poetic expression in the volume *My Native Land* (*In Land Fun Mein Gebein,* 1937). A mood of tiredness was beginning to creep into her exuberant personality as she was forced to learn ever new tongues and to face hate and woe. "There'll be so much to tell: how all the streams are bitter and how all, all yearn to be sweet."

Disappointment awaited her in New York. In the metropolis which had been through the Great Depression, she found sickening commercialism, exploitation and decadence similar to what she had left behind. Without a roof over her head and without a secure haven against hunger, she retreated to the rich fairyland of her dreams. In her verses drawn from the realm of memory, the suffering and cruelty of her Polish past were as effectively erased as are the sting and the poison of the bee in the final product of honey. Only beauty, kindness and the warmth of shared friendship remained.

This approach is reflected in her dramatic poem *All Windows to the Sun* (*Alle Fentzter Tzu der Zun*, 1938). The eleven scenes center about a child-hero, Boom, and his playmates. Their vivid imagination transformed little spools to immense railroad trains on which they could travel to romantic lands, far, far away. When Boom grew up, the same inventive talent let him construct a time machine in the form of a tower. This tower enabled its owner to relive historic happenings of earlier years. A demonstration before Sholom Aleichem's broker, Menachem Mendel, and the latter's multimillionaire client, Rothschildowitch, unlocked the injustices of the past. At one moment it showed Copernicus accused of rebellion against God's order by maintaining that the earth was not the stationary center and anchor of the universe. At another moment it showed Hirsh Lekert's execution in 1902 for his terrorist act in avenging the lashing of Jewish demonstrators in Vilna. Though Rothschildowitch refused to invest in this invention which talked to the conscience of man, salvation would come from other sources.

In 1942 the first novel of the famed lyricist appeared. Entitled *From Lublin to New York* (*Fun Lublin Biz New York*), it was ostensibly the diary of a refugee who had arrived in New York soon after the outbreak of World War II. It included many incidents and observations based upon the author's own privations during her early years of adjustment to the American scene. It was the weakest product of her pen and not until two decades later did she again experiment with the literary medium of the long novel. Her strength lay elsewhere.

The poems of *Only King David Remained* (*Der Melekh David Allein Is Gebliben,* 1946) were mostly written under the tragic impact of the war and the Holocaust. She often dreamed of her Sorolekh and Berelekh, the children trapped in the ghettos. She felt their searing tears. She heard their suppressed moaning. The ghosts of the slaughtered floated before her. In a moving psalm, she implored the God of Mercy to choose another people as victims of his blessings. The desolated House of Israel needed a respite. Every letter of the Ten Commandments had been paid for over and over again by the blood of infants and graybeards. It was time for others to be God's emissaries and for Jews to become simple shepherds, tanners, smiths.

With the founding of the Jewish state, the poetess left for Israel. Her play of 1949 bore the symbolic title *Toward the God of the Desert.* Its heroine was Donna Gracia Mendes, the sixteenth-century Marrano who found her way back to the faith of Israel and who, together with her nephew the Duke of Naxos, helped settle persecuted Jews of Italy in the Holy Land. At Tel Aviv she edited the periodical *Heim* (Home) from 1950 to 1952. Her songs of joy at the restoration of Zion appeared in 1952 under the title *Angels Come to Jerusalem* (*In Yerushalaim Kumen Malokhim*). Now that the dead bones of her people had taken on flesh again, she saw angels helping them lift the stones and drag the sand for the upbuilding of the new Jerusalem. Holy again was the abode of her forefathers, holy the gravel and the earth, the lamb and the goat. All life was blessed once more. The parched, starved, wounded mourners were feeling the sweetness of water, the fatness of corn, the renewed kindness of God.

Returning to the United States, she noted that Jewish children were growing up in a milieu no longer saturated with yearning for Zion, for whom ancestral glories were not alive during waking hours, and whose dreams were not infiltrated with Jewish aspirations for a unique future. She therefore undertook in her volume *On the Roads to Zion* (*Oif die Vegn Fun Zion,* 1957) to retell the tales of Jews who in all eras and from many lands tried to make their way to Israel. Her heroes ranged from Obadia of Bertinoro, who in 1488 set out from Italy, to David Ben Gurion, who arrived in 1906 to till the Palestinian soil and who later became Israel's first prime minister.

In 1957, the poetess collected her narratives, written during the preceding fifteen years, under the title *A House With Seven Windows* (*A Shtub Mit Zibn Fentzter*). These fifty-eight short stories may be grouped into tales of the old country, tales of immigrants in America, and tales that reach their climax in Israel. Those with an Eastern European background are filled with nostalgia for a vanished world: its devoutness, its integrity, its spirit of mutual help. The American narratives are more critical. They stress the substitution of superficial glamor for traditional values, the erosion of religious habits by materialistic concepts, the loosening of communal and family ties in the relentless drive for personal success. Nevertheless, even in America, the kindness of the Jewish heart reasserts itself. The residue of former, more pious generations dispels the spiritual indolence that darkens the lives of immigrants. A happy ending is generally effected. The author's disillusioned insight into human weakness is brightened by forgiveness and gentleness.

Kadia Molodowsky's ripe lyrics *Lights of the Thornbush* (*Licht fun Dornboim,* 1965) are characterized by brevity, simplicity and tender suggestiveness. They stir the imagination but calm the emotions. They breathe contentment with God and man. Even death holds no terror for her; she invokes it again and again as a welcome release from the burdens of existence that weigh so heavily. Since the Divine Potter created the human vessel and determined how much of life's foaming wine it may hold, of what avail are protests against one's lot? Let us accept with equal love roses and thorns, praise and blame. In her Jerusalem lyrics, the *Shechina* or Divine Presence spreads its light from the holy city over the entire earth; angels descend from heaven to awaken the dead and to teach children love of Torah; the very stones diffuse grace and light in all directions because they have been washed by tears and purified by suffering. These lyrics were often sung, recited and broadcast over Kol Israel radio, especially after the reunification of Jerusalem in 1967.

In her novel of life in Israel *At the Gate* (*Baym Toyer,* 1967), the poetess embodied her observations of the idealism and spirit of self-sacrifice which interpenetrated the simple activities of ordinary men and women.

In the 1960's a group of congenial writers and admirers gathered about her. Upon their urging she revived *Sviva,* the organ of prose and verse which she had originally founded in 1943. In its quarterly issues, poets of America and Israel, old masters and young beginners, found a common platform for the discussion of literary problems and for the publication of original literary products.

New York had replaced Warsaw as the center of Yiddish creativity.

II

American Epigones and Eclectics

THE YIDDISH WRITERS active on the American scene between the two world wars were almost all of Eastern European origin. Torn from their native roots and transplanted across the Atlantic, they still continued to reflect in their poems, dramas and novels the attitudes and ideologies of the Old World, even when they expanded their horizon to include subject matter based on their experiences in the New World.

Attempts begun by "Die Yunge" before the First World War and by the Insichists after this war to bring about indigenous American movements were not sustained by their successors who arrived during later decades. Indeed, after the 1920's there was not a single Yiddish group which could be properly designated as a literary movement with an original approach. There were only individual writers of greater or lesser talent who enriched the stream of Yiddish literature without modifying its direction. New poets could come to the attention of large audiences only through the medium of the daily press. This necessitated submission to the authority

187

of influential editors. Rebels against such authority faced years of frustration before they won a hearing.

It was to Abraham Cahan, editor of *Forverts,* that A. Lutzky (1894–1957) owed his early reputation as well as his pseudonym. He had arrived as Aaron Zucker from Lutzk in Volynia in 1914. Not until three years later were his first poems accepted by the New York dailies *Tageblatt* and *Tog.* When Abraham Cahan was then alerted to the rise of a new poetic talent who was beginning to appear in rival dailies, he immediately engaged him to write a weekly poem for his organ and changed the poet's name to A. Lutzky. After a year, Lutzky had to sail overseas to fight with the American forces in France. When he returned, after harrowing experiences in the trenches before Verdun, he astonished and perturbed readers with his strange new style.

Lutzky was a bizarre poet, adept at lyric acrobatics, a juggler of capricious word combinations which needed to be read aloud in order to be fully grasped. Animating the inanimate, he erased the distinction between immobile nature and mobile organisms. Water, rain, wind, fire, sunlight come to life, leap, dance and sing. A match rides on the back of a stream and thrills to the sight of ever new landscapes. A piece of paper, overwhelmed by the pain of existence, decides to commit suicide; it lies down on a railroad track, but when the locomotive nears, it regrets its hasty decision and flutters away, back to life. Another piece of paper is panic-stricken because rain threatens and it dreads becoming disintegrated by the wetness; but then the clouds pass away, the sun comes out, and the paper, relieved of fear, laughs a hearty laugh. Pennies meet in the pocket of a beggar and exchange stories of their past migrations. Waters run about the earth foaming with delight. A button weighs the merits of single loneliness versus marital unitedness. A pea and a bean, cooking in separate pots and facing their final moments before disintegration, still argue about their relative importance, until the pots begin to boil and then both are silenced and cease their individual existences.

Lutzky encircles his trembling woes with magic syllables until these woes are transformed into music and rhythmic movement. He is a humorist who smiles at the vanity of existence, a pessimist who cloaks with gaiety his disillusionment with the human merry-go-round. He acts the clown, though his heart bleeds because of the imperfections about him.

Lutzky's first volume, *Take It! It's Good for You!* (*Nemt Es! S'is Gut Far Aikh!*, 1927) begins with the lyric collections "Joyous and Vivacious" and "Songs and Dances" but merges into the collection "Somewhat Sad." In his second volume, entitled *The Beginning Is the Middle* (*Bereshis-Inmitten*, 1932), he finds relief from pessimism by atomizing time, space and other fundamental concepts. In his third volume, *Portraits* (*Portretn*, 1945), he attempts to sketch in words the silhouettes of Jewish contemporaries, writers, editors, trade-union leaders and public figures. His final volume, *A Book for Life* (*A Bukh Tsum Leben*, 1948) contains his most mature lyrics.

Lutzky heightened the effect of his verses by dramatic impersonations, acting out through facial expressions, gestures and bodily contortions what his words only hinted at. These impersonations have been imitated by leading actors and entertainers and have entered into the lasting Yiddish repertoire.

In contrast to Lutzky's explosive intensity and theatrical showmanship, Eliezer Greenberg (b. 1896) is restrained, contemplative, suggesting rather than expressing emotions. While Lutzky sublimates tears under a veneer of laughter, Greenberg transmutes even ecstasy into sadness. His imagination is tamed by censoring reason and his measured lines are of severe brevity.

Born in Lipkan, Bessarabia, Greenberg came in his youth under the influence of his literary townsmen Eliezer Steinbarg, Jacob Sternberg and Moshe Altman. Though he left for America in 1913 at the age of sixteen, he retained affectionate memories of this center of traditional Jewishness. However, his earliest songs already deal with New York's streets and avenues, houses and bridges. The Woolworth Tower symbolizes for him the vaulting ambition of twentieth-century man. Brooklyn Bridge's miracle of iron and steel testifies to the majestic victory of mind over matter. But New York also harbors crippled tenements where toilers suffer while laboring from dawn to dusk. The poet senses the travail of the workers, the monotony of their days when they are fully employed and their hunger when they are unemployed, as in the years of the Great Depression. The social tone then comes to the fore in his verses.

When tragedy strikes the Jewish people, however, the poet lays aside proletarian protests, individual sorrows and universal themes. He senses his kinsmen's danger. He sits by the waters of the Hudson, as his ancestors sat by the waters of Babylon; he weeps as he remembers the Jewish woe in the unfree lands and notes the indifference of the free lands to Jewish extermination. In a poetic monologue, he speaks through the voice of the dying Heine, who asks his ex-Jewish friend Karl Marx: "O Marx, how could we flee from our own stricken people and purchase our safety with baptismal water?" In another poem, Peretz meets Bontshe Schweig, the silent Jew, in the ruins of Warsaw's ghetto. As the sole survivor, after the Jews were set afire on all the world's scaffolds, he can no longer remain silent; he begs his creator, Peretz, to give him a tongue so that he can bear witness to the world's muteness, while the Jews, children and graybeards, poor and rich, were being exterminated. Elsewhere, the poet, grown rich in disillusionment, voices his refusal to march alongside of the triumphant democracies in the victory parades, for were not these democracies partners through their silence in the murder of his six million Jewish brothers?

In *Night Dialogue* (*Banakhtiker Dialog*, 1953), Greenberg communes with himself in silent hours of the night and reverts to his earlier, calmer, more meditative moods. He again drinks in with all his senses the loveliness of his limited world and forgoes the desire to roam beyond New York's horizon. He is at peace with himself, content to convert memories of man and tree and earth into lyric perfection.

Greenberg devoted critical studies to Moshe Leib Halpern, the poet of "Die Yunge," Jacob Glatstein, the poet of Insichism, and H. Leivick, the poet of Jewish Messianism.

He was influenced by these and other older contemporaries but did not follow in their footsteps. In the literary magazine *Gezelten,* which he co-edited with Elias Schulman from 1945 to 1949, he welcomed poets of every description. Eclectic in his own judgments, he encouraged them to follow their inner voice and not to give in to momentary lyric fashions.

Alongside of the works of major, long-recognized Yiddish writers such as Jacob Glatstein, David Ignatoff, Itzik Manger, Melech Ravitch, I. J. Trunk and Reuben Iceland, there appeared in the columns of *Gezelten* lyrics of many minor poets, some of whom were not welcomed in less eclectic organs. There was Jeremiah Hescheles, a virtuoso of the Yiddish language, whose verbal innovations were daring and original, whose imagery was rich and plastic, and whose themes, encased in sonnets, ranged from Talmud, Buddha and Socrates to Albert Einstein, entropy and the new biology. These sonnets were later published in book form as *Sonnets of Chaos* (*Soneten Fun Tohu Vavohu,* 1957). There was Herman Gold (1888–1953) who had begun to write in 1907, two years after his arrival in New York from Brisk in Lithuania, but who never attracted much attention. There was Alter Esselin (b. 1889), who maintained a lonely outpost of Yiddish culture in Milwaukee. There was Selik Heller (b. 1894), a Chicago poet who began in 1916 but whose chief contribution was the lyric volume *Sabbath* (*Shabbes,* 1953), in which he hymned the glory of heaven and earth, God and the Jewish people, sanctified by the weekly day of rest. There was Mattes Deitch (1894–1966), another Chicago poet who was active since 1916 in the Yiddish cultural life of the midwestern metropolis. There was Levi Goldberg (b. 1893), a lyric realist, whose songs and ballads appeared in three volumes between 1923 and 1948. There was Israel Goichberg (b. 1894), whose songs for children were often set to music by Jewish composers. There was Celia Drapkin (1888–1956), whose poem "The Boundary" in one of the last issues of *Gezelten* summed up her contentment with having lived a full life and in which she extended her hand without fear across the thin boundary that separated her from the enchanted land of death. Only a single volume of her lyrics appeared during her lifetime and only a single volume of her collected poems and stories posthumously. Both bore the same title, *In Hot Wind* (*In Haisen Vint*, 1935, 1959).

In young years at Kiev, Celia Drapkin wrote in Russian and was encouraged to continue by A. N. Gnessin (1879–1913), the Hebrew narrator. After her coming to America in 1912. Abraham Liessin recognized her talent and influenced her to change from Russian to Yiddish. "Die Yunge" welcomed her in their periodicals and the "Insichisten" opened the columns of *In Sich* to her lyrics.

These lyrics were characterized by intense feeling, pure longing and passionate fulfillment. She compressed in rhymed quatrains uncomplicated experiences: the submission of a wife to a beloved husband, the happiness of a mother, the blessedness of living without pain or guilt. Her lullabies to her infant children delighted with their simple charm and her songs for her more grown-up sons and daughters expressed motherly care and tenderness.

Among the frequent contributors to *Gezelten* was Berish Weinstein (1905–1967), whom critics called the most American of the Yiddish poets. After an adventurous youth in Galicia, Bohemia and Vienna, during which he accumulated a basic knowledge of Polish, German, Hebrew and Yiddish, he arrived in New York at the age of nineteen and was enriched by English and American influences. He began his Yiddish literary career in 1927. His lyric volume *Fragmentation* (*Bruchvarg*, 1936) was hailed as a significant achievement in Yiddish letters by S. Niger, A Mukdoni, S. Margoshes and Moshe Nadir. This volume was later incorporated in the more important collection *Songs and Poems* (*Lieder un Poemen*, 1949). Weinstein's chief claim to fame, however, was the trilogy which unfolded in colorful imagery and grand rhythmic panoramas the three stages of his inner evolution: *Raishe* (1947), *America* (1955), *In King David's Domains* (*In Duvid Ameilekhs Giter*, 1960).

In Weinstein's earliest lyrics non-Jewish subjects were dominant and much use was made of Christian symbolism. Several poems dealt with Negro toil and Negro suffering. Others sang of sad-robed, soft-treading nuns who never felt the touch of a man's hand. Still others centered about Sheeps-head Bay, a harbor district in Brooklyn, where salt-blown fishermen anchored their ships and through whose streets sailors sauntered in search of pleasures and female company.

The opening lyric of *Fragmentation,* entitled "Beetho-ven's Bust," revealed Weinstein's early virtuosity. Just as a physicist converts one form of physical energy into another and the second into a third, so, said the poet, the emotional and spiritual energy which found expression in Beethoven's musical accords was transmuted first by a sculptor's hand to inert bronze, until the metal became vibrant with it, and then by the poet into verbal imagery, ultimately living on again in rhythmic stanzas.

Although Weinstein attempted to reproduce in lyrics the moods of Brahms, Tchaikovsky, Sibelius, César Franck and Dvorak, his chief love continued to be Beethoven. In a series of poems, he reviewed the various stages of this com-poser's career, his abysmal loneliness, his cosmic sadness and his one moment of supreme ecstasy when he wanted to em-brace millions and kiss the macrocosm.

With the rise of Hitlerism, Jewish themes came to the fore. Repercussions of 1933 are to be found in lyrics such as "Hangmen" and "Hakenkreuz." In the poem "Jews," Weinstein recalls tensions in his own Polish town, a pogrom he had witnessed, a desecrated Sabbath when Jewish chil-dren with dazzling white Sabbath loaves in their hands were set upon by stone-hurling neighbors and when churchgoers wielding canes caused blood to flow from wise Hassidic brows upon Sabbath robes of velvet and satin.

When news of Maidanek and other extermination camps reached the poet, he felt that the martyred sons and daughters of his Jewish people had prior claim upon his muse. In tones reminiscent of the biblical *Lamentations,* he bewailed his slaughtered kinsmen and all the holy ones of Israel whom God deserted in years of wrath. Maidanek was for Weinstein not only the altar upon which Jews went up in flames but also the gallows upon which God himself was hanged.

To expiate his own guilt in not having been with the victims in their hours of agony, the poet devoted his volume

Raishe to a reconstruction of their vanished world, the world he had known in his childhood. An entire civilization parades before our eyes. Shadowy figures are quickened into being and move about in work-a-day and in holiday moods. The streets and marketplaces of the Galician town come to life and hum with activity. His Raishe becomes symbolic of every town in which East European Jews dwelt in tolerable security and semi-poverty for many generations until they were overtaken in our century by ever increasing pressures. He stresses the experiences of his own contemporaries who were uprooted from traditional ways and forced to set out on endless wanderings along the highways and bylanes of this globe. A few of them managed to get to Palestine and to pioneer a new life for themselves and their people. More got to America, even as he himself did. With his crossing of the Atlantic, the first epic of his trilogy comes to an end. By not continuing the narrative to the final catastrophe, the almost total liquidation of the many who remained behind in Raishe or on the European way-stations, the poet leaves the reader sad but not crushed, unhappy but not bitter.

Weinstein's second epic, *America,* begins with the landing of the young immigrant upon the strange new soil and describes his gradual integration into American culture. At first the loneliness, indifference and cruelty of New York fill him with longing to return to the warm hearth of his childhood. He comes in contact with the crushed victims of the sweatshops, the flotsam and jetsam of the Bowery, the bankrupt souls of the Great Depression. These pass before him, each with a grim tale of frustrated hopes. After his first difficult decade of adjustment, however, he responds to the resurgent ideals instilled by Franklin D. Roosevelt's New Deal and he establishes new roots. In Whitmanesque verses, he sings of America's vast spaces, rich history, pioneers of freedom. The idealism of Lincoln, the Great Emancipator, fills his soul, displaces older dreams, and gives him temporarily the feeling of being truly at home. Standing on the once blood-drenched field of Gettysburg, he accepts the ringing phrases of the Gettysburg Address as the genuine voice of democratic America, the blessed land of his children though not of his forefathers.

As for himself, the yearning for a complete Jewish life, such as he knew in his pre-American youth, still lingers with him. Israel reborn draws him irresistibly. In the third epic of his trilogy, *In King David's Domains,* he records the impact of his first visit to the land beside the Jordan. Cabalist Safed is not strange to him. Nor is Tiberias by the Sea of Galilee. He remembers them from tales of his grandmother and from legends of his grand uncle. To stand on Mt. Carmel is to relive childhood dreams of Elijah which were submerged for many years. In the orchards and vineyards of Zion he finds his classmate Sanya, who tended them while he himself was busy tending alien orchards and vineyards. He realizes that Raishe and America were long way-stations. In the domains of King David is his yearned-for home. There the stones talk to him and the trees whisper to him reminiscences of ancestral deeds and daring.

With a reiteration of the biblical vow "If I forget thee, Jerusalem, may my right hand wither" and with the annually repeated hope "Next year in Jerusalem," Weinstein ends his poetic trilogy, the main achievement of his life-long wrestling to find himself and to attain a stable relationship to his people's past and present.

His epic *Homeriade* (1964) sought to capture in dactylic hexameters the sunny spirit of carefree Hellas, but his Jewish heart was with the conquered and despoiled Trojans, with Hector, Priam and Hecuba, far more than with the wily Odysseus, the fleet-footed Achilles and the other well-greaved Achaians. In three cantos, he recreated Homeric legends of the "Radiant Helen," the "Wrath of Achilles," and the "Homecoming of Odysseus." But by far the finest legend retold was that of the blind bard Homer, with whom the contemporary poet identified himself.

In the volume *Songs Granted Me (Basherte Lieder,* 1965), American themes were again dominant, especially New York with its subway scenes, wharfs, beaches, parks, avenues, saloons. The poet's characters ranged from sailors and drunkards to Hassidim and visionaries, bronze, yellow, black and white human beings of all social strata. But there were also repercussions of his trip to Israel in 1952, verses of the fields of Galilee and the tents of Jacob. In every European city en route to Israel he felt himself a stranger and longed for the sight of a Jewish face. He recalled how in his younger years he had wished to walk along the boulevards of Basel, Bern, Brussels, Paris. Now these cities were for him merely foreign places leading on to the land of his heart's desire. It was not granted him, however, to tarry long in Israel. "In New York I shall always be sad with yearning for you, Jerusalem; I shall never forgive myself for leaving you, Jerusalem, for leaving only a tear in you."

Weinstein belongs to the epigones of Yiddish literature. He opened no great new vistas. He did, however, reduce to rhythmic utterance and vivid imagery the physical and spiritual migration of his Yiddish-speaking generation from its origins in Eastern Europe through the squalor and glamor of America onto an autumnal rejuvenation in Israel.

To this generation belonged Aaron Nissenson (1898–1964), who was brought to the United States at the age of thirteen and who in his personality combined Lithuanian melancholy and New York's turbulent joy.

In his first volume, *One Hundred Songs* (*Hundert Lieder*, 1920), he described his final moments in the townlet of his birth, his young friends asking him not to forget them in the distant trans-Atlantic continent, his last view of a golden-haired maiden at the well. Thereafter, memories of an idyllic, lost boyhood paradise accompanied him and he tried to recover this paradise in poetic visions. In the storm of restless days, he yearned for simplicity and kindness. In the depths of the Great Depression, he composed his dramatic poem *The Road to Man* (*Der Veg Tsu Mensh*, 1934), in which the central hero was the Socialist leader Eugene V. Debs, symbol of immaculate man. Amidst the barbarity of the Hitler years, he sang of a coming reign of pure goodness. In twelve scenes of *The Promised Land* (*Dos Tsugesogte Land*, 1937), he depicted man's efforts to evolve toward moral perfection. Beginning with Pharaoh and Moses, in whom antithetical forces of evil and goodness, matter and spirit, were embodied, the poet traced the struggle of these forces in various transformations throughout historic times and voiced his faith that science would soon end man's schizophrenic tendencies and bring him closer to the radiance of God.

While the Second World War was at its height, Nissenson entitled his lyric volume *Life Sings Even in Death (Dos Leben Zingt Afile In Toit,* 1943) and, after the war, he entitled his last volume *In the Footsteps of the Righteous (In Tzaddiks Trit,* 1950), thus continuing to voice optimism in the triumph of life over death and of righteousness over wickedness, despite temporary horrors and bloodshed. Instead of blasphemous accusations against God, he pointed to the wondrous structure of God's universe and to those recent scientific achievements that could pave the way for the compassionate, just human beings who would evolve from the imperfect creatures of the past and the present.

Benjamin Jacob Bialostotsky (1893–1962) came to America in the same year as Nissenson and also retained throughout life an abiding faith in man's inevitable progress and perfectibility. Though memories of his childhood in a Lithuanian townlet were reflected in his poetry, he preferred to direct his gaze more often upon the American metropolis. He felt that Jews must accept the fact that they had outgrown the townlets which cradled Yiddish culture and that they had become to the largest extent city dwellers. The task of a Yiddish poet should be, therefore, to reproduce the sights and rhythms of urban, industrialized civilization. He should be forward-looking, sensitive to the new era in which he lived, without letting himself be entirely consumed by it.

Bialostotsky's early model was Morris Rosenfeld, to whom he dedicated adoring essays and whose influence was paramount in the social songs of *Along the Highway (Beim Breiten Veg,* 1920). These songs depicted the poverty and sadness of the immigrant generation. He too sang of the sallow, white-bearded operator who sat bent over a machine day and night, the mother who sewed a shroud for her only child, the homeless drunkard asleep on a park bench, the blind beggar, the Bowery vagabond, the bleary-eyed derelict.

In his later lyrics, the picturesqueness of New York's East Side came more to the fore, but also its rebellious mood. The old house on Cherry Street, doomed to demolition, reminded him of the toiling tenants of earlier decades who chanted Rosenfeld's pathetic lyrics and whose eyes glowed with visions of a juster world for which they were prepared to strike and to hunger. In Ludlow Street, the poet still found bearded Jewish pushcart-peddlers and aging Jewesses who spoke the earthy, unadulterated Yiddish of Vilna, and he enclosed in rhymes their honest efforts to earn their bread by their own labor. The lyrics, which allied him to the proletarian poets of the 1920's and 1930's, failed to survive the ravages of time. His simple children's songs, however, set to music by Solomon Golub and Michel Gelbart, continued to be sung in Yiddish elementary schools and his poetic tales of Noah, Moses, Elijah and Chelm long fascinated young audiences. His masterpiece for children, however, was *Bienele* (1940), the story of a little boy who set out in search of the land of the eternal holiday and who, after many adventures past the river of tears, the maelstrom of blood and the mountain of dead bones, finally arrived at the terrestrial paradise, where people worked and enjoyed the full products of their labor and where sadness, distress and death were unknown. Only three days were granted to Bienele to be there, but the memory of the experience remained with him ever thereafter and his days were irradiated by his faith in the inevitability of such a utopia for all the inhabitants of this globe.

In his last years Bialostotsky retold for grownups Jewish tales and legends from Babylon and Rome, parables of the famed Maggid of Dubnow and jests of legendary merrymakers and contemporary humorists. Though originally written for newspaper readers, they were based on thorough research as well as memories retained from the folklore with which his father, a famed preacher, regaled audiences during the poet's youth.

Mark Schweid (b. 1891), an actor by profession and a poet by inclination, began under the influence of Peretz in Warsaw. At twenty he arrived in New York from Vienna and began an illustrious career on the Yiddish and English stage. He also translated and adapted for the Yiddish repertoire from German, Polish, Russian and English dramatists. But his original contribution was in the lyric. Using simple words, pure rhymes and traditional metrical stanzas, he stressed the need for drinking deep of momentary joy even though pain was more universal and enduring. He found joy in the transitory fragrance of a flower, in the loaf of bread earned by the sweat of one's brow, in a bit of love that glowed for an instant, in Jewish festivals that infused bright colors into gray seasons.

While Schweid's early, Viennese, romantic poems betrayed the influence of young Heine, his later, more realistic, American poems were lightened by humor and deepened by contemplation. The sonnet became his favorite vehicle for expressing immediate insights and recollections of past moments. For decades there recurred in his verses the longing for his parental home and his native townlet where he did not feel himself to be a superfluous, lonely individual but a vibrant Jewish cell functioning within a living Jewish communal organism. After the Nazi destruction of his Polish-Jewish birthplace, he recognized the futility of nostalgia, vented his anger at the destroyers of his kin, and contented himself with expressing in verse his ripe autumnal experiences and distilled impressions. Under the title of *Complete Poems* (*Ale Lieder un Poemes,* 1951), he included in a single volume all his poems which he cared to preserve.

Meir Zimel Tkatch (b. 1894), a native of the Ukraine, began as a Russian poet in New York on the eve of the First World War and did not publish his first book of Yiddish songs and fables until 1927. Eight additional volumes followed. The best of his verse narratives, fables, parables, sonnets, triolets, serious and humorous lyrics, songs for children and translations of Russian and American poetry were collected in the two volumes of *My Possession and Gift* (*Mein Hob un Gob,* 1963).

Tkatch is at his best in his fables. These are superb miniature dramas. Each teaches a lesson by means of a vivid, verbal encounter between animals or things. Their dialogues

afford bitter insight into motivations. Tkatch does not indulge in moral abstractions, but a moral code fit for creatures endowed with reason emerges from watching the behavior and listening to the conversations of things and beasts
not so endowed. The tree that wants to reach up to heaven
rebukes the roots that hold it fast to earth and is then accused of ingratitude by the roots, for is it not by sucking at
their juice that the tree has the strength to aspire to the
heights? When the sour Miss Lemon turns green with cha-
grin because Mr. Orange does not call her by the more
aristocratic name of Citrus, she receives the answer that the
fairer name will not change sour to sweet. The neutralist
Hyena steers clear of the combat that rages between neighbors, but when the battle is over it feeds leisurely, with the
appetite of a neutral, on the casualties left on the field.

Tkatch loves earth and sky, man and worm, and he sings
in happy tones of this love. He says yea to life, though it be
a tangled skein of good and bad. He wants to weed this earth
of its noxious growths and convert it into a paradise. The
optimist is shocked, however, as he becomes aware of his
people's tragedy during the years of conflagration. His light
verses are then tear-stained as he demands a reckoning of
God for Jewish blood that cries up from the ground.

Aba Stolzenberg (1905–1941) came to New York in 1923
from eastern Galicia. His first poems appeared during the
following year. A friendship with Meyer Stiker (b. 1905)
and Abraham Tabachnik (b. 1901) led to a common literary
striving. This found expression in the journal *Feilen,* published between 1928 and 1931. Although Stolzenberg in his
earliest poems sought to follow the example of the undisciplined *Khaliastre* poets then in fashion, he soon came under
the influence of their antipode, the poet Reuben Iceland, a
pillar of "Die Yunge." Iceland taught him to tame his exuberant imagination, to eschew Expressionism and to encase
his strong emotions in few words and carefully chiseled lines
which produce a unitary mood.

Stolzenberg tried to curb his restlessness and to control
the fire that burned within himself, but his heart continued
to yearn for storms and raging billows. Chained to poverty,

he turned his eyes to his Galician past, irretrievable save for idealizing, dream-drenched memories. He sang of young hopes no longer realizable, of first love whose flaming breath once seared him, of beauty that faded all too soon, of cold autumnal rains that fell upon gray days. Romantic melancholy enveloped him. Compassion filled him for bankrupt souls, for girls with extinguished eyes, for women with bent shoulders, sad and obedient under the yoke of unending toil, for a Yiddish poet who had hanged himself and an Irish drunkard clubbed by police.

In the largely autobiographic poetic cycle "The Diary of the Straw Knight," Stolzenberg set out to recount the evolution of a Galician Jewish intellectual of his generation. The twenty-four lyrics and ballads of this cycle bore dates from January 1, 1900 until March 14, 1909. Had he been able to complete this work, upon which he labored until his death, it would have given a colorful panorama of a typical Galician townlet both before and after World War I. According to his fellow poet Abraham Tabachnik, to whom he confided his innermost thoughts, the cane-twirling Straw Knight, who went forth to adventure in the wide world, would have wandered among many ideologies and would have returned at the end, exhausted and disillusioned, to die on the soil of his Galician birthplace.

Tabachnik, who wrote the finest evaluation of Stolzenberg, was primarily a literary critic and essayist, even though he contributed to poetic journals and published two volumes of lyrics. In his first volume of 1936, he let his songs dance like painted puppets on a string and used rhythmic words to build castles in the air. He toyed with concepts ranging from God to estheticism and was eclectic in his choice of subjects and forms. He characterized himself as a cup full of wine that poured itself out before every swine. However, this wine was pressed from a mixture of grapes of varying quality.

In his second volume of 1949, Tabachnik again immersed himself in the essence of other poets and sought to reproduce their uniqueness in lyric portraits. By selecting poets to whom he reacted sympathetically, such as Morris Rosenfeld, Joseph Rolnick, Mani-Leib, Zishe Landau and Aba Stolzenberg, he was able to blend his own emotions with theirs. Lacking naiveté and endowed with fine taste, he recognized his limitations as a poet. Nevertheless, he did create a few lasting poems as in "God's Bunker-Weeping." In this poem, he presented the beaten God fleeing from heaven and finding refuge in a ghetto bunker among a dozen Jewish children. For them He was father and mother, grandfather and grandmother. He began to teach them the alphabet and He regaled them with wonder tales of heaven. But before He got to the end of the alphabet, all the children had perished. God alone survived and His weeping in the bunker resounded throughout the universe.

The best of Tabachnik's essays were collected under the title *Poets and Poetry* (*Dichter un Dichtung,* 1965), a volume of discerning insights in impeccable prose.

Meyer Stiker was the third of the closely knit poets who appeared as a group in the issues of *Feilen.* Unlike Stolzenberg and Tabachnik, who only rarely included American themes in their verses, Stiker was not indifferent to his New World environment. Although his first volume, *Songs* (*Lieder,* 1945), sought to rescue from oblivion types and scenes of his native Galician townlet before its destruction, his more significant second volume, *Yiddish Landscape* (*Yiddishe Landshaft,* 1958), roamed across the entire range of contemporary Jewish life, from Eastern Europe to Israel and America. But it also touched on eternal problems, on the lure of life and the inevitability of death, on the alternation of the seasons with their varying moods, on the reality of dreams and the dreamlike quality of even trivial, normal experiences. Like Tabachnik, he too lacked naive freshness and compensated for this lack by subtlety of language and utmost refinement of verse. He was well acquainted with the most modern currents of German, French, English and American literatures, but preferred rhymed quatrains and severe traditional forms to free verse and undisciplined rhythms.

Chaim Krull (1892–1946) stood under the shadow of death for many years. As a result, the theme of death predominated in his poems, which included elegies to a dead child, to a deceased friend, to his mother to whom he was deeply attached and who passed away at a young age. Death was welcomed by him as the redeemer from life's pain and loneliness.

A single, unhappy love left its impact upon him, saddening him prematurely. In short impressionistic verses, he reproduced a rich variety of sensations, emotions and nervous excitations which this love, more longing than fulfillment, aroused in him. *About Myself (Arum Sich, 1930)* contained not only cycles of love poems but also a prose romance about this girl of his adolescent dreams who left for America before he could win her in reality and whose traces he could not find when he landed in New York. The volume also included essays on Yiddish writers in which he, the Impressionist, displayed less interest in facts than in the atmosphere about each of his subjects.

Krull's closest affinity was for J. I. Segal (1896–1954), the Montreal poet, who also invoked death in many a poem, following upon the loss of his young daughter. Indeed, the literary critic Baruch Rivkin (1883–1945) characterized them as two poets who prayed from the same *siddur*.

While Krull was economical in his use of words and left but a modest literary legacy, J. I. Segal was extremely prolific and only a part of his prose and verse has been collected in the dozen published volumes. Through most of them there resounded the mournful refrain of the fading of beauty along with the fading of the traditional Yiddish way of life. He undertook the task of preserving in his own poetic idiom whatever could be preserved of the liturgical style of Tchines and to make retrospectively fascinating whatever could be retained of the folk habits of the Yiddish townlets. He averted his face from the Canadian metropolis in which he spent his post-adolescent decades. He preferred to mingle in imagination with simple, quiet, silver-bearded Jews who walked in the paths of piety. He sang of the holiness of the Sabbath in Podolian Jewish communities where God's spirit hovered closely over a chosen, obedient people. He retold tales of the Prophet Elijah, the Baal-Shem, and less well-known, humble, saintly personalities. The poet's mother was for him the symbol of the goodness that inhered in poor, hard-working, uncomplicated souls and he repeatedly invoked her in his lyrics.

While Segal spent his mature years in Montreal, Leon Feinberg roamed over lands and languages and ideologies before he attained to stability as a person and as a poet. Born in 1897 as the youngest child of an impoverished cabalist in a Podolian townlet, he was reared in traditional learning, but began his literary career as a Russian lyricist under the name of Leonid Grebniov. He dreamed of becoming another Pushkin, or at least another Soloviev or Yessenin, poets he admired. When the Revolution of 1917 broke out, he exchanged the pen for the gun and fought for three years against the anti-Semitic Ukrainian bands. Then followed restless wandering from Bombay to Jerusalem, through North Africa and Europe, until he landed in 1923 in New York, his more enduring home. He then made Yiddish his primary linguistic medium and continued with Russian as his secondary medium.

In the poems of *Metropolis* (*Groisshtut,* 1928), he groped his way to original perceptions through a vast variety of literary influences with which he had come in contact. He assimilated Russian mystic and revolutionary strains, American Imagism and Yiddish Insichism. He alternated between warm reminiscences of his pious heritage and a desire to help the forward march of the new redeemers. The epic *Bolsheviks* in the volume *Light and Bread* (*Likht un Broit,* 1931) represented the climax of his proletarian poetry. In the ballads of *Comrade Life* (*Khaver Leben,* 1938), he still prided himself on being a class-conscious, belligerent poet. He still wove a ring of sonnets about Soviet Russia, the motherland he loved with an unabating love. Then came the Stalin–Hitler Pact of 1939 and brought him sobering disillusionment. In the volume *The Inheritors of the Earth* (*Die Yorshim Fun der Erd,* 1941), his infatuation with Soviet Russia was replaced by an ardent affection for the Jewish people. He felt that forces of destruction had overwhelmed the creative revolutionary forces which had once sought to bring salvation to Adam's children, and he found new com-

fort in the Bible and its teaching that the wicked would
ultimately be destroyed and that those who put their trust
in God would inherit the earth. In his poem *Yiddish* (1950),
he drew his self-portrait. From the alien idols he had formerly served so faithfully, he had escaped back to his own
fold. Thereafter he would guard his own vineyard; he
would seek his inspiration in the Hebrew prophets; he
would be the harpist of Jehovah; he would be the guardian
of the Yiddish tongue and heritage.

There then followed four novels in verse, each of them
autobiographical, illuminating under various disguises the
poet's inner conflicts. *The Doomed Generation (Der Far-
mishpeter Dor,* 1954) portrayed a hero who was disappointed
with the Communist ideal. *The God of Wrath (Der Gott
Fun Tsorn,* 1957) showed the heretic Elisha Ben Abuya vacil-
lating between Hebraism and Hellenism, seeking a synthesis
between Greek beauty and Jewish ethics under Roman power. But, Apollo, Shaddai and Jupiter were mutually contradictory forces and could not be reconciled. The heretic, who
opposed the revolt of Bar Kochba, could not witness the
martyrdom of his people at the hands of the conquering
Romans without repenting his heresies and returning to
them in their hour of affliction. *The Blessed Generation (Der
Gebentshter Dor,* 1962) reverted again to Feinberg's own
generation, which achieved maturity in the decade between
the abortive Russian Revolution of 1905 and the First World
War. In the hero, Lulik Adler, the poet relived the events
of his early years, the pogrom by the Black Hundreds in
Kiev in 1905, the feverish weeks of liberation in 1917, the
visions and emotional ecstasy of his youthful striving for the
laurels of a Russian lyricist, his struggle for survival in communities ravaged by Denikin and Petlura, his escape from
chaos, epidemics, massacres and the horror of Odessa in
1920, his unsuccessful attempt to adjust to the hard realities
of the re-Promised Land where the heroic pioneers were
shepherds and kibbutz tractorists. Finding himself mute and
useless among the Jewish colonists, Feinberg's hero resumed
his odyssey, experienced Parisian loves and hells, and shed
the non-Jewish layers of his soul. However, unlike his au-

thor, he resisted the temptation to settle in America. Tired of wandering, he returned to kibbutz life in the Emek. The bankrupt Jewish Don Quixote, erstwhile worshiper of Apollo and the Muses, finally found happiness and fulfillment as a tiller of the soil in the land of his forefathers but still dreaming vivid Messianic dreams, a creative member of the blessed first generation of Jewish redemption. The final cantos of this verse epic were filled with yearning for a world which the author could not make his own, for an Israel Feinberg could only experience in glowing verses that stirred imagination, mind and heart in the autumn of his life.

The last of Feinberg's poetic epics of the Russian Jewish intellectuals with whom he shared his early years was *The Ruined Generation* (*Der Khorever Dor*, 1967). In this work, which followed the pattern and the stanzaic form of Pushkin's *Eugene Onegin*, he dealt with the Communist idealists who did not leave their native land, since they had faith in the vistas of freedom and equality apparently opened up by the Revolution of 1917. These Jews fought, even as Feinberg did, in the ranks of the Bolsheviks against the pogrom bands of counter-revolutionists. During the early years when Lenin held sway, some rose to high rank in the Soviet hierarchy. However, their Jewish origin, which they sought to forget, continued to render them vulnerable, and under the Stalin dictatorship the Kremlin realists wreaked havoc among them. Some perished before firing squads, others languished and died in Siberian labor camps. In the Jewish youth Pinie Yolles, who rose to the rank of Marshal of the Red Army and who was then liquidated, Feinberg drew a sympathetic portrait of Jan Gamarik, who was his friend and a brother-in-law of Chaim Nachman Bialik and who in 1937 received an order from Stalin's secret police to shoot himself. Only a single survivor of the Ruined Generation, the poet's alter ego, succeeded, thirty years after the Revolution, in escaping from Russia and in penning a fierce condemnation of the entire oppressive system. The tortured lives and unsung death of the Jews who remained found late expression in Feinberg's poetic laments completed shortly before his death in 1969.

The most controversial figure among the American Yiddish poets was Elihu Chaim Sheps, who wrote under the adopted name of A. Almi (1892–1963). Born in Warsaw and experiencing a difficult childhood amidst poverty and misunderstanding, he early attracted the attention of I. L. Peretz, H. D. Nomberg and Abraham Reisen. He published his first lyrics at fifteen. After sojourning in Cracow and Vienna, he returned to Warsaw and wrote for its influential daily *Moment*. At twenty he left for the United States. In New York he was welcomed by editors and literary colleagues and reached the height of his popularity during the following decade when he published more than a dozen books of prose and verse. He translated the sayings of Buddha. He introduced Yiddish readers to the poetry and philosophy of China. He made the mythology of Japan and India intelligible to wider audiences. However, his non-conformism and his bitter humor estranged friends and nurtured antagonists. He had keen insight into Jewish life and, since he did not hesitate to call attenton to social ills, literary shams and religious hypocrisy, he was constantly engaged in feuds, in the course of which he inflicted many wounds and received more in return.

In his two autobiographic volumes, *Moments of a Life* (*Momenten fun a Leben*, 1948) and *Spiritual Balance* (*Kheshbon un Sakh-Hakol*, 1959), he detailed his spiritual odyssey, his espousal of anarchism, spiritualism, vegetarianism and various esoteric doctrines, his suicidal tendencies and his quarrels with his fellow men, whose weaknesses he had a talent for ferreting out. As he aged, loneliness gathered about him. Reacting against neglect, he found relief in sardonic outbursts against God and man, dominant ideologies and popular idols.

On Almi's seventieth birthday, a volume of appreciations by critics who admired him appeared, but by then his mood had become thoroughly nihilistic and his self-destructive urge could no longer be arrested. A decade before his self-willed end, he took leave of the lyric muse in his volume *Last Songs*

(*Letzte Gesangen,* 1954), in which his cosmic despair found raging expression. He felt that God's show would go on interminably but he did not want to be part of it. The role of a marionette dancing to the whimsical tunes of a supreme puppeteer did not appeal to him. He looked up to the stars and saw them smiling, while human beings squirmed here below. The heavens were praising the Lord while hearts bled on earth and fists were raised in vain protest against a callous Almighty. The faith of the pious, the verses of the poets, the destiny of the entire human race, the pain of all species mattered nothing in the wild whirl of galaxies. With all our weeping and imprecations, we still remained insignificant dust in the vast expanse of time and space. The God was dead who had once proclaimed "Let there be Light'" and we were groping with blind fingers in a blacked-out universe. The poet hurled curses at the cosmic slaughterer who led the Jewish people to the sacrificial altar and had them go up in flames. He repeatedly called Him to judgment and proclaimed Him guilty.

Almi's principal theme was death. He invoked it in a thousand shapes. Death was final wisdom and ultimate truth, while life was folly and illusion. He toasted death and faced it fearlessly—"Only a fool fears death." What did worry him, however, was the possibility that souls might survive physical extinction, as his cherished Oriental philosophers asserted. In that case, he prayed that an exception might be made for him and that his bruised soul might share total extinction together with his body.

Death and pessimistic insight also permeated the poetry of Alter Esselin (b. 1889), who maintained a lonely vigil as a Yiddish lyricist in Milwaukee, Wisconsin. His best elegy was on the death of a tree, his companion for eighteen years, his sympathetic friend that peered into his window, listened to his verses, shared his melancholy on wintry nights, and let him partake of its joy in blossoming April days. Another unforgettable poem portrayed the death of an ox in the snow, its impotent rage, its struggle against the implacable Almighty, its last roar of despair before it sank into the whirling white heap.

Esselin described himself in a poetic epitaph as a lyricist who poisoned himself with songs in which honey and arsenic were mixed. He was born in Chernigov, Ukraine. At ten he lost his father and, as the oldest of five children, he had to face mature responsibilities. He worked as a carpenter's apprentice. At sixteen he emigrated to America and labored in several mid-western communities before settling in Milwaukee. His poems, beginning with *Knots* (*Kneitn,* 1927) and continuing with *Songs* (*Lieder,* 1936) and *Songs of a Desert Poet* (*Lieder fun a Midbernik,* 1954), voiced his pride that he was earning his bread with saw and hammer and that he was endowed with the physical stamina to stand up against all the blows of fate. He wrote stirring social poetry and boasted of his proletarian uncouthness. Nevertheless, he could not mask his tender sensitivity. He felt the pain of all creatures, the pain of the hungry dog and the frostbitten cat no less than of the drunkard in the gutter and the Negro beaten to death in a lynching. In sick dawns and solitary nights, he raged at God through tears. In his loneliness he found companionship in the realm of dreams and in his poverty he found wealth in the silver of the moon and the diamonds of the stars.

The American epigones and eclectic poets suffered from the fact that they were uprooted from their Yiddish base in Eastern Europe at an early age and were compelled to spend most of their years in an English-speaking environment. They witnessed the gradual aging and diminution of their reading public and they were plagued with doubts as to the meaningfulness of their literary creativity in Yiddish. These doubts arose at a time when Yiddish had attained a richness of vocabulary, a flexibility in syntax, a stylistic artistry which enabled it to express the subtlest thoughts and feelings with utmost refinement. A reassessment of the role of Yiddish in Jewish life was necessary and was undertaken by ideologists of the post-Classical generation.

12

Yiddish Ideologies

THE MATURING OF YIDDISH as a linguistic medium, its refinement by literary innovators, its strengthening by educational networks, its nurture by philologists and academic scholars called forth an intense ideological debate which did not abate until a majority of the Yiddish-speaking persons were annihilated by the Holocaust.

The various attitudes toward Yiddish were in large measure dictated by the main ideological positions which were already well established before the First World War and which continued to flourish after the war. Epigones sought to adapt earlier systems of thought to the reality of the postwar and post-revolutionary generation and eclectics sought to effect a synthesis of the original ideas inaugurated by the pioneering intellectual giants since the 1880's.

The political Zionism of Theodor Herzl, which found incorporation in the World Zionist Organization and was developed at various Zionist congresses from 1897 on, came increasingly under the influence of Hebraists and hailed the revival of spoken Hebrew as a major achievement of the Jewish renascence. The cultural Zionists, led by Ahad-Haam, were even more militant in their advocacy of Hebrew as the sole national tongue of the Jewish people. But there also persisted ideologies that laid stress upon Yiddish as a unifying national factor. Shimon Dubnow's theories of Diaspora Nationalism found wide repercussion in Eastern Europe, where post-war treaties guaranteed minorities, including the Jewish minority, the right to develop autonomous cultural and educational institutions in their own languages. His followers included both Hebraists and Yiddishists. The Bundist philosophy attained notable successes in Poland and the Baltic states, where its representatives, largely Yiddish-speaking, could at last function legally after the collapse of the Czarist regime. Chaim Zhitlowsky's Yiddishism, which celebrated its first triumph at the Czernowitz Language Conference of 1908, reached the peak of its influence with the founding of YIVO, the Yiddish Scientific Institute, in 1925. In the Soviet realm, the Communist approach, implemented by the *Yevsektsie* with ever greater severity, called for a complete banning of Hebrew and favored Yiddish as the language of the common man.

The various ideologies differed in their attitude toward Yiddish but none, not even the extreme Zionists, completely negated it as an instrument for contemporary Jewish survival. Among the Zionists, Jacob Klatzkin (1882–1948) and Chaim Greenberg (1889–1953) gave clearest expression to the viewpoint of those who sought the Hebraization of the Jewish people but who also acknowledged the need for the preservation of Yiddish in the Diaspora until such time as Jews would be fully ingathered in their national homeland.

Klatzkin did not believe that Jews could survive much longer in the Diaspora. Nationalism had replaced religion as the strongest unifying force. If Jews wished to survive as Jews, they would have to concentrate their efforts upon reestablishing themselves as a Jewish nation upon their historic soil, with Hebrew as their common national tongue. His essays, written in Hebrew and German, roused greater interest after their translation into Yiddish, since Yiddish ideologists could not be indifferent to their challenging logic.

Klatzkin equated Diaspora with *Galut*, exile. He held

that Jews everywhere and at all times have yearned for release from their anomalous existence, for a return from exile to their original homeland and for the rebirth of their own tongue. Their strong religious attachment sufficed to keep them distinct from their neighbors and enabled them to maintain themselves as a dispersed historic community with national characteristics, as a viable nation in exile. With the weakening of religious bonds since the Enlightenment, a process of Jewish de-nationalization set in. Increasingly Jews were absorbed in the various nations in whose midst they dwelt. Jewish values and ideals, such as monotheism, Messianism, optimism, absolute justice, became the common property of a large sector of mankind and offered an inadequate basis for the further survival of Jews as a distinctive group. All environments of the Diaspora became inimical to Jewish continuance, some more so and some less so. Philo-Semites sought to assimilate Jews. Anti-Semites sought to eject them as a foreign body. To maintain their group uniqueness, Jews would have to will against their Diaspora environments. They would not be able to do so successfully without the hope of a renewed normal life in the future. Should the goal of national restoration in Zion be abandoned, then Jews would have to reconcile themselves to an acceptance of their various alien lands as their own fatherlands. This would be especially so in Western Europe and America where anti-Jewish forces were not sufficiently virulent to compel Jews to remain outsiders. There the normal process of acculturation would erode Jewish differences and lead to continual decline and ultimate dissolution. But even in Eastern Europe Jews could not maintain their national strongholds indefinitely. They might be able to do so as long as the peoples about them had not yet reached national maturity. Once nationalism ripened there, assimilation would increase. Equality of rights included the right to assimilate to the majority population and Jews would undoubtedly make use of this right. They would assimilate to the language and the culture of their host peoples. The concept "assimilated Jew" was, however, pure nonsense. It denoted a Jew who was not a Jew. It persisted only because Jews were in the anomalous position of a people without a national home of their own. Once Palestine became such a national home, Jewishness would be nationally determined. A Jew would be a person whose fatherland was Israel and whose language was Hebrew. All other persons of Jewish origin or Jewish faith who lived outside of Israel's borders, who were rooted in a non-Hebraic tongue, and who fought and died for another commonalty would no longer be able to misuse the name Jew. Nor would it be forced upon them. Their Jewish descent would have merely archival, genealogical interest. After the stabilization of the Jewish State, such designations as German Jew, French Jew, American Jew would sound as absurd as German Frenchman, American Spaniard, or Russian Englishman. Jewish concentration in Israel must result in a gradual withering away of Jewish communities elsewhere. National rebirth in Israel spelled national death for Diaspora Jewry.

To those who argued that the Diaspora might be able to maintain a Jewish national existence with Yiddish as its unifying language, Klatzkin replied that, if this were to happen, two distinct groupings would emerge, a Hebrew people in Israel and a Yiddish people in the Diaspora. These would grow ever further apart until their distinctiveness would be as clear as that between Germans and Englishmen, two peoples who evolved from a common Germanic stock. There was, however, no likelihood of an evolution of a Yiddish nation anywhere, because *Galut* Jewry, weakened by the departure of its best sons to Israel, would not be viable.

Despite insistence on Hebrew as the only national language of the Jews, Klatzkin deprecated the struggle against Yiddish waged by some well-meaning but ignorant Hebrew fanatics. He was prepared to concede that Hebrew could never become the vernacular of Diaspora Jews, not even to the limited extent that Yiddish still was. National wisdom, therefore, dictated the preservation and strengthening of Yiddish as a bulwark against the destructive force of assimilation. Yiddish must be nurtured as the Jewish vernacular insofar as possible in order to safeguard Jewish distinctiveness during the transition period until the ingathering of Jews in their homeland would be completed and Hebrew firmly established there. In the long run, however, the position of Yiddish was hopeless, as hopeless as the survival of Jews as Jews in the Diaspora.

Chaim Greenberg was no less militant than Klatzkin in his advocacy of political Zionism, but he was more sympathetic to the cultural forces which found their expression in Yiddish. Fluent in many languages and active as editor and writer in Russian, English and Hebrew, he was most eloquent in Yiddish both on the lecture platform and as an essayist. When the *Yevsktsie* sought to suppress Hebrew after the Communists attained to power in Russia, Greenberg resisted their efforts and mobilized influential support for this endangered tongue. But when the Histadrut, Palestine's Labor Confederation, sought in 1933 to ban public speeches in Yiddish, he vigorously opposed such a resolution and called for the teaching of Yiddish in the land of Israel.

In an essay on *Cultural Problems of American Jewry* (1930), Greenberg gave clearest formulation to his attitude toward the language problem. He declared himself to be a lover of Yiddish. At the same time he recognized the tragic fate of this language which was trying to maintain itself against attacks on two fronts. On the one hand, it was assailed by Hebrew, which had the sanctity of religion and of millennial historic continuity and, on the other hand, it had to ward off the inroads of the more useful languages of the Diaspora. But even as a folk language, its decline could not be arrested despite the high level of its contemporary achievements. It was no longer the spoken language of Jewish youth. It was becoming converted into a literary and academic tongue. In America, which harbored the largest concentration of Jews, it was doomed. If American immigrants of German or Italian origin were unable to retain German or Italian as the vernacular of their children against the competition of the dominant English speech, despite strong cultural bases in Germany, Austria, Switzerland and Italy, was there a likelihood that Yiddish-speaking immigrants would be more successful? Undoubtedly, language was the best vehicle for transmitting a people's values and traditions. A Jewish educational system, however, could at best hope to intensify Jewish experiences by exposing the younger generation to one Jewish language in which Jewish religious, literary and cultural treasures were imbedded. In that case, was not Hebrew to be preferred to Yiddish, if, as was apparent, the latter could not be retained as a natural, intimate, spoken tongue? As a book language, Hebrew certainly had more to offer.

Greenberg could not accept Klatzkin's extremist views which negated the Diasporo *in toto* and which must logically lead to the voluntary expatriation of all Jews outside of Israel, their denaturalizing themselves, if not legally then at least morally, their withdrawing themselves completely from all positions of influence in their native lands. He rather held that Diaspora Jews were bi-cultural. American Jews were culturally both Americans and Jews. Cultural dualism was not incompatible with political monism. He granted that cultural monism was certainly a more normal experience for human beings, but Jews were not granted by history such a normal group experience. There was, however, nothing disloyal about Jews proclaiming themselves to be cultural dualists. They had a right to nurture their Jewishness as well as their Americanism. Amnesia, forgetfulness of one's antecedents, was not a prerequisite for citizenship in a democracy. On the contrary, enriching one's life with Jewish content should enable a Jew to be a more wholesome personality and a more valuable member of the American community. While Jewish content could best be imbibed through Hebrew, it could also be absorbed through Yiddish and even through so-called alien tongues which were really not alien to millions of Jewish individuals.

In an address at the inauguration of a Yiddish Chair at the Hebrew University in 1951, Greenberg moved his audience with his remarks on the role of Yiddish in the past and the role it should occupy in Israel: "Yiddish weeps for its children. It mourns the millions of its sons and daughters, the annihilation of its heirs and spokesmen. A short while ago, Yiddish was the modest ruler of an entire empire. Without royalty and sovereignty, it throned over millions of men, women and children. The sabras of Israel must imbibe the spiritual values of their Yiddish ancestors and the Yiddish language is one of the jewels in the crown of Jewish martyrdom."

In contrast to Klatzkin and Greenberg, Abraham Golomb (b. 1888), spokesman for Integral Jewishness, asked that linguistic primacy be given neither to Hebrew nor to Yiddish. He saw these languages as twins who supplemented each other. Both were containers in which the wine of Jewishness was stored. They were not the wine itself. To make a cult of a language was idolatry. Content was more important than form. A priest who mastered Hebrew and a Gentile maid who learned to speak Yiddish did not thereby become Jews. Golomb defined a Jew as a person whose daily life was interpenetrated with Jewish traditions and values. Not Zionism or Bundism, not Jewish theology, prophecy or philosophy were in themselves the essential ingredients of Jewishness. These were merely fruits of the Jewish tree. Daily rootedness in Jewish cultural habits and daily nourishment from the Jewish collective experience were needed to keep the Jewish tree strong and healthy. This collective experience included language, festivals, religious observances, family relationships, ideals carried into practice, taboos, social activities, group discipline.

Golomb held bi-culturalism to be unwholesome, and preferred maximum autonomous development of Jewish communal life and institutions. A person who participated in two cultures was, in Golomb's opinion, schizophrenic, in constant conflict with himself. Such a Jew, growing up in a predominantly non-Jewish environment, was bound to develop an attitude which Ahad-Haam called "servility in freedom." He was bound to regard the mores of the majority as more important, of a higher rank, obligatory, and his own mores as less important, unnecessary, superfluous. He would discard them if he could, if he were not constantly reminded by his neighbors of his otherness. His egophobia or self-hatred must lead him to assimilate to the majority cultures rather than to enrich his own group with the cultural products of others. Assimilation was, therefore, synonomous with de-Judaization, with the loss of one's own cultural configuration.

To stem de-Judaization, all conflicts must cease between Hebrew and Yiddish, Zion and *Galut*, religion and secularism. No aspect of Jewish culture should be discarded, because the excision or even weakening of any Jewish organ endangered the vitality of the entire organism. Continuity did not exclude evolution of forms or modification of content to bring these up to date with ever new realities. For example, the urbanization of the Jewish group, the change from a *shtetl* culture to a metropolitan culture, necessitated certain adjustments. These adjustments and reforms, however, should be directed toward strengthening Jewish cohesiveness and guarding Jewish group distinctiveness. This involved greater efforts to maintain Yiddish and Hebrew, because the loss of common media of communication spelled disintegration for a people. Individuals might write about Jewishness in all languages, even as archeologists wrote about Sumerian or Hittite, but such writing by Jewish scholars in German, French, Russian, Spanish and English merely added archival material and helped to embalm Jewishness. It did not change habits of living to any significant extent.

Golomb, therefore, arrived at the conclusion that all alien languages adopted by Jews in order to integrate more successfully with other peoples brought about a decrease in Jewish cohesiveness. On the other hand, the languages Jews spoke in order to differentiate themselves from others led to the group's preservation and growth. Diaspora communities which were giving up Yiddish were becoming fossilized and incapable of future growth. Without Yiddish, the Jewish people would be fragmentized into scattered, dying remnants of a people. A people created its language and the language united the people. Hence, losing a language meant loss of peoplehood, because language was more than a mere collection of words. It was intonation, melody, logic, psychology, aroma, the storehouse of the collective memory of many generations.

Golomb devoted his creative years in Vilna, Kiev, Winnipeg, Mexico City and Los Angeles to teaching, writing and agitating for the retention of Yiddish as the international medium of communication among Jews. He founded schools and teachers' seminaries, he trained disciples to agitate for Integral Jewishness. He enriched the Yiddish vocabulary of science and psychology. He supplemented his theoretical discourses with practical texts useful for classrooms. He often aroused strong antagonism, but he also found fervent followers. Wherever he dwelt, he was a pillar of strength for the Yiddish structure.

During Golomb's Vilna period in the 1920's, while he was devoting himself to training Yiddish teachers at the Jewish Teachers' Seminary, a movement arose to found an academic institute to further research and scholarship in Yiddish as an additional essential factor in assuring the creative viability of the Jewish people. The ideologists who stressed Yiddish as the principal cohesive force of Diaspora Jewry saw Vilna as the most desirable center for such an institute. It was there that YIVO flourished from 1925 until the Second World War.

The original proposal for the *Yiddisher Visnshaftlikher Institut,* which was better known under its initials YIVO, stemmed from Nochum Shtif (1879–1933), a Yiddish linguist and editor who often wrote under the pseudonym of Baal Dimion.

Shtif had begun as a Russian writer, a Zionist and a Socialist. He had helped to organize a Jewish self-defense group in Kiev after the Kishinev Pogrom of 1903. He had suffered imprisonment by Czarist authorities, had escaped to Switzerland, and had returned to Russia after the Revolution of 1905. He soon discovered that he could propagate his doctrines of Zionism and Socialism among the Jewish masses far better in Yiddish than in Russian. In 1916 he championed the cause of Yiddish in a memorable debate with Chaim Nachman Bialik, the champion of Hebrew. The following year, immediately after the Czar was overthrown, he immersed himself in political activities and helped to found the Jewish People's Party in the Russian capital.

In 1919 he abandoned politics and devoted himself solely

to Yiddish research. He published his polemic pamphlet *Jews and Yiddish* (*Yiedn un Yiddish*, 1919), in which he formulated the ideology of the Yiddishists with great eloquence. He explained that Yiddishism arose as a reaction to a century of anti-Yiddish agitation. This agitation was begun by the pioneers of Enlightenment in Eastern Europe. When these obtained their first glimpses of Occidental culture, they became aware of the backwardness of their own Jewish people in the Czarist realm and of the low esteem in which this people was held by its neighbors. They believed that they could elevate their religious and ethnic group by changing its occupations to more productive ones, closer to the soil, and by changing its distinguishing speech, which they labeled a "jargon," to the more esteemed languages of the majority populations, Polish, Russian, German.

While the early men of Enlightenment were genuinely concerned with the plight of their people, Shtif pointed out that their children were far less concerned. These children were, to a large extent, no longer raised in traditional schools, whose curriculum stressed holy texts and whose language of instruction was Yiddish. They attended government schools which stressed secular subjects and whose language of instruction was Russian. They acquired a feeling of superiority toward their bearded, kaftaned kinsmen. They were ashamed to speak the Yiddish "Jargon" in public and avoided doing so even at home. Some became careerists, interested solely in their own advancement; others, more idealistic, were caught up in various radical and revolutionary movements, and were ready to sacrifice themselves for the common good, for Russia's glory and Poland's emancipation. They opposed Jewish separatism. They were horrified when the pogroms of the closing nineteenth and early twentieth centuries hurled them back to their own "benighted" people, from which they had been estranged. Repentants among the assimilationist idealists then went to the opposite extreme. They became fiery Jewish nationalists. They espoused a return to Zion and a resumption of pre-*Galut* Jewishness. They held that Yiddish, as the language which arose in *Galut*, should make way for Hebrew, the language of the Bible and of the

ancient Jewish sovereignty, whose renewal the Zionist movement would bring about. Until the resumption of sovereignty
in a distantly envisaged Jewish state, the rebirth of Jewish
nationalism could best be accelerated by the renascence of
Hebrew as a spoken tongue and not merely as a literary
medium. Hebraists, therefore, joined Russifiers in the struggle against the "Jargon" of the people. The slogan of the
intellectuals was Hebrew or Russian or Polish but by no
means Yiddish. The common folk, however, continued to
speak the Yiddish vernacular. The growing awareness of the
dignity of the common man led to the rise of Yiddishism as
a movement of teachers and writers to counter the attacks
of the Hebraist visionaries and the self-hating Russifiers.
Yiddishists wanted Jews to be sound personalities, educated
in their mother tongue and satisfying their cultural needs
in it.

The post-war treaties that followed the break-up of the
Russian and Austro-Hungarian Empires guaranteed Jewish
minority rights in several European countries. If Jews wanted
national autonomy, they could not claim it on the basis of
a common territory but primarily on the basis of a common
language. "Yiddish does not have to be resurrected or implanted or strengthened. It is alive, it is deeply rooted, it is
strong among the people . . . The time has come to proclaim
to the world and to ourselves: Yiddish is and will remain
our language."

Shtif, as spokesman of the Yiddishists, therefore called
for Jewish secular schools in which all subjects would be
taught in Yiddish, the natural language of Jewish children
and their parents.

In 1922, Shtif left for Berlin, where he found a group of
ardent disciples of Yiddish, including young Max Weinreich,
who was then completing his dissertation on the history of
Yiddish philology, and the historian Elias Tcherikover, who
was using Yiddish material for his studies of Ukrainian
Jewry. Upon the urging of these and other Yiddish scholars,
Shtif published in 1925 a booklet on the organization of
Yiddish scholarship, in which he proposed the immediate
formation of a Yiddish academy and outlined its program

and principles. He pointed out that Yiddish scholars were carrying out their research without any central direction and with no coordinating organ for their publications. He singled out the achievements of Mordecai Venger, Haim Tchemerinsky, Ber Borochov, Noah Prilutzky, Zalman Kalmanovitch, Max Weinreich, Zalman Reisen, J. L. Cahan, Jehuda Elzet, S. Anski, Jacob Leshchinsky, Mark Wischnitzer, Abraham Menes and Elias Tcherikover. Some of these scholars found themselves in Berlin in August 1925, at a conference that accepted the proposals of Shtif as the basis for a Yiddish research institute which was to function from a main center in Vilna, with subsidiary centers in Berlin, Warsaw and New York. Although Shtif left for Kiev in 1926 and became the guiding spirit of the Kiev Institute for Proletarian Culture, YIVO continued to flourish in Vilna. Within a decade after the founding of YIVO, its influence spread to many lands with a sizable Yiddish-speaking population. Before World War Two there were YIVO groups in Argentina, Austria, Brazil, Chile, England, France, Latvia, Rumania and Palestine. The apex of YIVO's Vilna period was reached at the tenth-anniversary conference in 1935, which was attended by scholars from several continents. This was also the climax of Yiddishism before catastrophe struck and destroyed its base in Eastern Europe.

Meanwhile, YIVO succeeded in collecting and preserving books, letters, manuscripts, diaries, and priceless documents mirroring Jewish life. It rescued from oblivion the Jewish folklore of Eastern Europe. It standardized Yiddish spelling. It trained young scholars. It published books and periodicals of value. It initiated significant projects, exhibits and conferences to shed light upon the Jewish past and present. It attracted to its ranks the historians Elias Tcherikover, Shimon Dubnow, Saul Ginsburg, Abraham Menes and Jacob Shatzky; the psychologists and educators Leibush Lehrer, Abraham Golomb, H. S. Kasdan and A. A. Roback; the economists and demographers Jacob Leshchinsky, Ben-Adir, Liebman Hersh and Moshe Shalit. Its strongest section dealt with Yiddish linguistic and literary phenomena. Its director was Max Weinreich and among his earliest co-workers were J. L.

Cahan, Alexander Harkavy, Judah A. Joffe, Selig Kalmano-vitch, Shmuel Niger, Noah Prilutzky and Zalman Reisen.

The principal contribution of Jehuda Leib Cahan (1881–1937) was in the gathering and publication of folktales and folksongs and in the training of researchers in Yiddish folk-lore. Alexander Harkavy (1863–1939) was primarily a lexi-cographer. His *Complete English-Yiddish Dictionary* (1893) was for more than half a century an important reference work for Yiddish readers and writers of the immigrant gen-eration in America. His *Hebrew-Yiddish-English Dictionary* (1926) was less widely used. Judah A. Joffe (1874–1966) specialized in Old Yiddish and published numerous articles in YIVO's journals on the origin, history and development of Yiddish. Zalman Reisen (1867–1941), younger brother of the poet and narrator Abraham Reisen, was a noted gram-marian, linguist and literary historian. His encyclopedia of Yiddish literature, press and philology appeared at first in a single volume in 1914 and then in four volumes, 1927–1929. It was the main reference source in its field. Reisen was also a distinguished editor and the inspirer of the literary group "Young Vilna." His liquidation by the Soviet authorities after their occupation of Vilna deprived YIVO of one of its strongest pillars.

The ideology that underlay YIVO's projects from its inception was an acceptance of Jewish peoplehood the world over and of Jewish scholarship as a means for enrichment of Jewish life and of maintaining Jewish identity. YIVO's prin-cipal periodicals were *YIVO Bleter,* published since 1931 and *Yedies fun YIVO,* since 1929.

When the Nazis overwhelmed Vilna, YIVO's New York branch became the main center with the Buenos Aires branch as the most important subsidiary. The greater part of YIVO's library and archives, carried off to Germany and intended to be used for anti-Semitic studies by Nazi racial scientists, sur-vived the war and was retrieved for YIVO's North American center. The directors of all four research sections of YIVO—Elias Tcherikover (1881–1943), Jacob Leshchinsky (1876–1966), Leibush Lehrer (1887–1964) and Max Weinreich —either were in America or were able to reach America's shores and to resume their productive work. In 1941, *Yiddishe Shprakh* began to appear under the editorship of Yudel Mark (b. 1897). It dealt with problems of Yiddish usage and paved the way for the *Great Dictionary of the Yiddish Language (Groiser Verterbukh fun der Yiddisher Shprakh)*, edited by Yudel Mark, with Judah A. Joffe as co-editor of the first two volumes, which appeared in 1961 and 1966 and defined 40,000 words out of a projected total of 200,000 words. In 1946 the *YIVO Annual of Jewish Social Studies* was founded for English readers, under the editorship of Shlome Noble (b. 1905).

YIVO also published, sponsored and supervised many basic books on linguistics, folklore, literature, psychology, labor, economics, demography, history and education. YIVO's exhibits, conferences, seminars and training program for Yiddish teachers and scholars stimulated and enriched the Jewish cultural scene. YIVO's collection of a million volumes of Judaica and more than two million archival items made its New York headquarters the most important center in the Western Hemisphere for the study of Eastern European Jewry.

YIVO's research director, Max Weinreich (1894-1969), became in 1947 the first professor of Yiddish at an American institution of higher learning, New York's City College. When American universities followed City College's pioneering example and introduced courses in Yiddish, YIVO's texts were used in American classrooms. The most popular text for students was *College Yiddish: An Introduction to the Yiddish Language and to Jewish Life and Culture,* by Uriel Weinreich (1926–1967), son of Max Weinreich and a professor of Linguistics at Columbia University. His Yiddish-English, English–Yiddish dictionary, published posthumously in 1968, was the first adequate replacement for Harkavy's dictionary, which had appeared three-quarters of a century earlier and which had been out of print for decades.

While YIVO specialized in research, YKUF—Yiddisher Kultur Farband, founded on an international scale in Paris in 1937, sought to stem the decline of Yiddish by the publication and dissemination of Yiddish belles-lettres. As the cultural voice of the radical Left, it published more than two hundred Yiddish works during the following three decades and disseminated more than half a million copies of Yiddish books. Its principal organ was *Yiddishe Kultur,* edited by Nachman Maisel (1887–1966) from 1939 until he settled in Israel in 1964 and thereafter by Itche Goldberg.

The Congress for Yiddish Culture was founded in New York in 1948 in order to strengthen Jewish manifestations in Yiddish throughout the world. Allied with CYCO, the Central Yiddish Culture Organization founded in 1938, it published many Yiddish books and supported the oldest and most influential American Yiddish literary monthly, *Die Zukunft,* founded in 1892. Its most grandiose project, begun in 1954, was the publication of the eight-volume comprehensive *Biographical Dictionary of Modern Yiddish Literature (Lexikon fun der Nayer Yiddisher Literatur).* This dictionary included more than 8,000 Yiddish writers of the nineteenth and twentieth centuries, and is an indispensable reference work for Jewish literary historians.

Buttressed by the efforts of YIVO, YKUF, CYCO, the Congress for Yiddish Culture and by an ever increasing number of departments of Jewish studies at universities, the decline of Yiddish was slowed down, though not arrested. At the close of the 1960's, however, Yiddishism, as an ideology, was no longer at the forefront of discussion.

13

The Rumanian Center

RUMANIA ENTERED UPON the Yiddish literary scene in 1876 when the folksinger and wedding-bard Velvel Zbarzher Ehrenkranz (1826–1883), who stemmed from Galicia, sang and acted out his dramatic verses in Rumanian towns, and when Abraham Goldfaden (1840–1908), who came from Russia, began in Jassy his first experiments in Yiddish dramatic performances. The enthusiastic reception given to Goldfaden in Rumania prompted him to expand his dialogues and scenarios into full-length comedies and his two or three acting assistants into large troupes that wandered through the length and breadth of Eastern Europe.

Of Yiddish folk poets indigenous to Rumania, the best known was Yakov Psanter (1820–1900), who was born in Botoshani and reared in Jassy. Self-educated and talented in music, he became a wedding bard, adapting the verses of famed *Badchonim* to his Rumanian audiences. For years he roamed with a gypsy band and performed on cymbals at non-Jewish festivities. Compelled to listen in aristocratic homes to constant slurs against Jews as foreigners and undesirable intruders, he wrote a two-volume history in their defense.

This history set out to prove that some Jews had lived in Rumania since the days of Nebuchadnezzar and that a large contingent had arrived while the provinces that later became Rumania were still under Roman rule. The first volume, published in 1871, ended with the fall of the Byzantine Empire in 1453. The second volume, published in 1873, continued the narrative until his own generation. Psanter's history is no longer accepted as an authentic source, but it performed a valuable service during the decades of the struggle for Jewish rights in Rumania, from the Berlin Peace Conference of 1878 to the First World War. It was often quoted as evidence of the antiquity of Rumania's Jews.

The Czernovitz Language Conference of 1908 stimulated Yiddish cultural activities throughout Eastern Europe, and had repercussions in Rumania. Among the pioneers of Yiddish letters on the eve of World War I were Jacob Groper (1890–1966) and Jacob Botoshansky (1892–1964). They were also the most talented contributors to the first Rumanian Yiddish literary journal, *Licht,* published in Jassy during the two years preceding Rumania's entrance into the war in 1916.

Groper began to write Yiddish poetry while still a student of law at Jassy University and while serving in the Balkan War in 1913. His poems appeared in periodicals and anthologies since 1914, but not until twenty years later were they collected in a slender volume, *In the Shadow of a Stone (In Shutn Fun a Shtein,* 1934). These poems are romantic in tone and replete with youthful melancholy. The poet wants to grasp the glad moments of spring's blossoming because he is aware that cold winds will soon nip the blossoms and it will be too late to be glad. He sees his bright dreams dissolving and his heart becoming filled with pain, but he is still young enough to wait for the flowering of new dreams and for the heart to recapture its buoyancy. Groper's lyrics, once on the lips of Rumanian Jewish youth, both in the Yiddish original and in Rumanian translation, are today forgotten. They did, however, help to raise the prestige of Yiddish. His admirer, the literary critic Shlomo Bickel, said of him: "As a creator of Yiddish Jacob Groper was in Rumania the start; as a Jewish intellectual he was the zenith; as a spiritual personality he was the full day of the Old Rumanian Jewish community."

Jacob Botoshansky participated in the upsurge of Yiddish in Rumania from 1914 to 1926 as critic, essayist, journalist and dramatist before emigrating to Buenos Aires. There he edited Argentina's most influential Yiddish daily *Die Presse,* and for more than a third of a century he was a central figure in Jewish cultural activities. His survey of Rumanian Yiddish literature in the volume *Mother Yiddish* (*Mame Yiddish,* 1949) anticipated the more detailed analysis in Shlomo Bickel's volume *Rumania* (1961).

After World War I, Bessarabia, Bukovina and Transylvania, with their large Yiddish-speaking populations, were added to Rumania. Only then did a reading public arise of sufficient magnitude to support quality journals and Yiddish publishing ventures. From these newer provinces rather than from Old Rumania stemmed most Yiddish writers of the next half century. The single town of Lipcani, in Northern Bessarabia, was the birthplace of the fabulist Eliezer Steinbarg (1880–1932), the dramatist Jacob Sternberg (b. 1890) and the novelist Moishe Altman (b. 1890).

Steinbarg, the most original writer of fables in Yiddish, attained international fame only after his death. His fables, which had appeared solely in periodicals during his lifetime, were collected in a posthumous Yiddish volume. It had a large vogue, and was translated into Hebrew and into half a dozen European languages. Steinbarg was an educator in Lipcani, Rio de Janeiro and Cernauti. His *Tales for Children,* (*Meiselekh,* 1936), combining Yiddish folk treasures, imaginative animal lore, light humor and simple vocabulary, furnished attractive reading material for Yiddish schools.

His fables are generally in the form of dialogues. The characters are inanimate objects more often than animals or plants. To all of them he assigns human traits and has them engage in disputes as to proper behavior. Each object experiences far more suffering than joy; through each the author emphasizes the tragedy and the injustice inherent in the structure of the world.

Steinbarg is pessimistic, yet compassionate. He holds that heaven may perhaps punish sinners, but that earth certainly punishes the virtuous. He illustrates this conclusion in the fable of the good-natured piece of soap which cleanses and purifies, but is penalized for this virtue by becoming ever thinner and nearer to dissolution. In another fable, that of the knife and the saw, he points out that on this imperfect planet the *shochet's* knife is blessed, strutting about as a glistening aristocrat because its function is to cut living throats, while the saw is looked upon as an ugly plebeian because it busies itself with the menial task of sawing dull, wooden blocks.

Steinbarg opposes docile submission to the dominant order, which he regards as an evil order. He advocates resistance to it under all circumstances. He illustrates this view by means of the fable of the cow that appears before heaven's judgment seat as complainant against the butcher Shloime Zalman, murderer of the cow and its offspring, the young innocent calves. The court's decision is in favor of the defendant. It is the cow, not the butcher, which has horns, teeth, hoofs, and yet lets itself be milked dry and slaughtered; the cow deserves to be sent to Gehenna because by not resisting it tempted this servant of God, the butcher, to apply the knife to its throat. In the fable of the hammer and the iron, Steinbarg agrees that there may perhaps be no way of escape from being beaten, if one is caught between hammer and anvil, but one should at least cry out at such a merciless destiny. The unctuous hammer advises the bar of iron to be patient under the undeserved blows. It is true that the striking hammer and the struck iron are both God's children fashioned of the same metal, but God has assigned a different function to each. The hammer is carrying out its divinely ordained assignment by hammering its brothers until the sparks fly. It bears no malice. It is acting under compulsion, under the command of the smith, who is himself merely doing his duty as a craftsman, restoring to health a wagon's broken axle. The wagon too acts under compulsion, since it is enslaved to the horse that compels it to turn the wheels unceasingly. But the horse also cannot be blamed, for it is lashed by the whip which in turn carries out the orders of a higher authority, the driver—and so on *ad infinitum*. Despite the logical reasoning of the aggressive hammer, the iron, writhing in agony, still cries out, as it properly should, against its apparent fate.

Steinbarg makes use of all the riches of Yiddish, the spoken idiom as well as the written. He borrows phrases of the Hebrew prayerbook and the Talmud and adapts them in startling, original combinations. Nor does he hesitate to invent a multitude of neologisms whose meaning evolves from their strange sound effects. He ranks with Itzik Manger as Rumania's greatest master of Yiddish.

Jacob Sternberg, who edited Steinbarg's *Fables*, began in 1908 with lyrics and short stories that immediately won recognition. Toward the end of World War I he wrote and produced, in collaboration with Jacob Botoshansky, nine playlets and satiric revues for the Bucharest Yiddish Theatre. During the following two decades he forged ahead as the most popular theatre director of Rumania. His lyrics gradually eschewed Neoromantic, Symbolistic characteristics and evolved into the grotesque Expressionism of his volume *Profile of a City (Shtot in Profil,* 1935). Fleeing from the Nazis in 1941, he spent his later years in Soviet Russia. Until 1945 he was a refugee in the Asiatic province of Uzbekistan. After World War II, he directed Yiddish plays in Kishinev. He served as the most prominent Rumanian member of the Jewish Anti-Fascist Committee in Moscow until its liquidation in 1948. He spent the following five years in a Siberian Labor Camp. After Stalin's death he was rehabilitated as an innocent sufferer and became a much respected contributor to *Sovetish Heimland.* His poems were translated into Russian in 1959. His critical articles of the 1960's carried great weight with the younger Soviet Yiddish writers. His memoirs resurrected for them the pre-Revolutionary period that had already become historic.

Moishe Altman, a townsman of Sternberg and born in the same year, excelled in the 1920's with short stories that had a moral undertone. He also wrote in the 1930's two novels of Bessarabian Jewish life. The chronicler in both novels is Mottel Unruh, his alter ego, who experiences many disappointments and little joy. While most of Altman's characters, including Mottel, are but vaguely delineated, a few are so clearly etched that they captivate the imagination for a long time. There is the beautiful, robust, sophisticated, honey-voiced, sex-driven peasant girl Marianna, whose body exudes fragrant magic like a tree in blossom and who is prepared to outrage her family and to marry the Jew Yosef, if there is no other way to satisfy her longing for him. There is her rival and antipode, the dutiful, virtuous, silent, brooding Jewish maiden Rita, whose calmness is ruffled when Yosef appears upon the scene. And there is Yosef himself, the emaciated, tubercular young Jew, whose ascetic saintliness seeps like a poison into the veins of the women about him, inflaming them, even while his own thoughts and dreams still bear the scars of the pogrom which killed his wife and child and hurled him far from his native Ukrainian province.

Altman's love for Bessarabia's earth and its toiling Jews and rugged peasants led him to remain there when it was occupied by Soviet forces in 1940. The following year, however, he was forced to flee before the German invaders. After the war he returned and resumed his writing of tales glorifying the tillers of the soil. Despite his proletarian proclivities, he was not spared years of hardship in a Siberian camp from 1948. After Stalin's death he was rehabilitated and permitted to publish again, but the only available periodical in the post-Stalin era was *Sovetiṣh Heimland*. In it appeared his story *A Tale with a Name* (*A Meisse Mit A Nomen*, 1968), in which the principal character is again a restless Mottel who possesses many skills and is helpful to his fellow men, Jews and non-Jews, but who has learned to be silent, undemanding and unobtrusive. Like his author, who had undergone many trials in the course of a difficult life, Mottel has become an enigma to every person with whom he is in contact.

Shlomo Bickel (1896–1969), the best interpreter of Rumanian Jewish culture, did not stem from Rumania but from eastern Galicia and he reached the climax of his career in

New York as literary critic of the Yiddish daily *Der Tog,*
as co-editor of the Yiddish monthly *Die Zukunft* and as head
of the research activities of YIVO. However, during the two
decades before his arrival in the United States on the eve
of the second World War, he was in the center of the Yiddish literary revival in Cernauti and Bucharest. At the former
city he studied law after his demobilization from the Austro-
Hungarian army and edited *Die Freiheit,* the weekly of
Bukovina's Labor Zionists, from 1920 to 1922. Upon obtain-
ing his doctorate in jurisprudence, he moved to Bucharest,
where he practiced his legal profession and at the same time
edited Yiddish literary periodicals together with Jacob Sternberg and Moishe Altman.

The best essays of Bickel's Bucharest period were collected
in his book *In Me and Around Me* (*In Zich un Arum
Zich,* 1936). His nine other volumes belong to his American
period, but much of their content deals with Rumanian and
east Galician Jewry. The vanished culture of the Galician
town of Kolomea, where he spent his boyhood, is depicted in
his two books *A City of Jews* (*A Shtot Mit Yiedn,* 1943)
and *We Were Three Brothers* (*Drei Brieder Zeinen Mir
Geven,* 1956). In his book of history, literary criticism and
reminiscences, entitled *Rumania* (1956), he surveys the struggle for Jewish rights since the 1870's, he sketches portraits
of half-forgotten political, social and literary figures of three
generations, he depicts the Jewish uniqueness of Bucharest,
Marmoresh, Kishinev and Cernauti. In his historical novel
Family Artshik (*Mishpokhe Artshik,* 1967), he recalls to life
Bukovina Jewish villagers of the mid-nineteenth century and
the problems and legal disabilities Jews had to overcome
when seeking to eke out a living among peasants.

As a literary critic, Bickel is impressionistic as well as
deep-delving. He does not content himself merely with re-
cording the facts and ideas of writers. He also frames them
within their specific cultural environment and communicates
the unique atmosphere about each of them. In the two volumes *Writers of My Generation* (*Shreiber Fun Mein Dor,*
I, 1958; II, 1965), he reveals great sympathy for skeptics who
harbor religious longings, for Soviet Marranos who sublimate

their love for Jewish traditions in the deepest recesses of the heart, for Israeli poets who continue to create in Yiddish in completely Hebraized kibbutzim, and above all for Rumanian contemporaries with whom he shared earlier, happy years and who either perished or were scattered in all directions. His greatest admiration is reserved for Itzik Manger, whose beginnings he acclaimed and whose growth he accompanied with interpretative essays.

Although Manger was born in 1901 in Czernovitz, the capital of Bukovina, when this province was still part of the Austro-Hungarian Empire and when its name had not yet been transmuted to Cernauti, and although his family stemmed from Kolomea, Galicia, he is nevertheless generally associated with the Rumanian literary group because he left at 16 for Jassy, the important Jewish center of Old Rumania, and because the Rumanian editors were the first to recognize his talent and to publish his poems in their periodicals. Warsaw, Paris, London, New York and Tel Aviv were other way stations in the creative experience of this last and greatest of Yiddish troubadours.

From his father, a master tailor who dabbled in Yiddish verse, Manger imbibed Yiddish folklore from childhood on. At the secular high school of Czernovitz, which he attended until he was expelled for his pranks, he acquired a knowledge of German literature. At Jassy, he worked at various callings without much success. The founding of several Yiddish journals in Greater Rumania after World War I supplied the young craftsman with an opportunity to publish his early lyrics and ballads. The first of these appeared in 1921, but it was not until he arrived in Warsaw seven years later and published his earliest book of poems, *Stars On the Roof* (*Shtern Oifn Dakh,* 1929), that he was recognized as more than a regional poet.

In these early lyrics, Manger succeeds in combining the simplicity of folksongs and folk ballads with the sophisticated structures derived from German classical and romantic poets. Quatrains alternate with sonnets. Echoes of popular Galician bards like Velvel Zbarzher, Berl Broder and of the theatrical innovator Abraham Goldfaden resound alongside of remi-

niscences of Bürger's *Lenore*, Goethe's *Erlkönig*, and young
Heine's ghostly ballads. Monks, nuns and gypsies appear
alongside of pious Jewish maidens and the biblical figures of
Rebecca, Joseph and David. Jesus is invoked but far less
often than the Baal Shem. Unlike the Christian Messiah, who
bears the pain of the world, the Baal Shem hymns the joy
of all creation and proclaims: "The world is holy and three-
fold beautiful." The poet joins in this refrain. He too sings
out his joy on all occasions and seeks to get to God over the
bridge of ecstasy. "My song is my gold," he proclaims in a
poem that bears the characteristic title "Happiness" *(Glik)*
and in which he likens himself to rich Croesus because whatever he touches turns to lyric gold. Elsewhere he speaks of
himself as a simple tailor's wildly lost son whose young
years wandered in the wind until he found the thin golden
ray that lit up the dark alleys. It was the ray of joyous poesy
which revealed to him beauty in every nook and corner,
which converted reality to fantasy, and which made of
dreams reality. Looking at the world through the blue lantern of illusion, he finds everything beautiful and good and
holy, delight in every tear, a spark of love in every eye, a
bright end to every road.

In Manger's second book of poems, *Lantern in the Wind*
(Lamtern In Vint, 1933), the troubadour of light and joy
matures to perfection. All nature is personified and throbs
with vitality. The cloud becomes a wanderer who visits him
in ever new attire and talks to him throughout the night
about adventures amidst stars and winds. The bird brings
him greetings of the world's crossroads and of the changing
seasons which return more lovely each year. The rain that
knocks at his window is an enchanted prince who can resume
youthful charm when greeted by a smile.

In most poems gaiety mingles with ironic wisdom. But
there also creep upon him sad and tired moods when he is
emptied of lyric intoxication, when he feels that he has
frivolously squandered golden youth, when he becomes aware
of loneliness amidst adulation, when he weeps for the God
of his fathers toward whom he yearns but whom he cannot
grasp.

In these moods Manger turns to the Book of Books, the eternal text of his people, and it lives for him again as intimately as in his childhood imagination. Just as a child in its daydreams and night fantasies envisages characters of long ago and far-off places in terms of immediate family relationships and familiar childhood experiences, so too does Manger read into the souls of biblical figures from Adam and Eve to David and Abishag thoughts, feelings and motives which might indeed have been theirs, had they lived in his generation in East European townlets still permeated with traditional lore.

In Manger's biblical songs, published in 1935 and 1936, patriarchal figures become contemporary Jews, with all their foibles and all their charm. The mythical figures are no longer embalmed and enshrined in Torah scrolls. They are flesh of our flesh, our grandfathers and grandmothers, our brothers and sisters. We lose our awe of them but we love them even more. Father Abraham scolds his nephew Lot for getting drunk every night in the tavern, thus ruining the family's reputation and making it impossible for the two grown-up daughters to get decent husbands. Hagar, the maid, washes the kitchen dishes during her last evening in the house of her boss Abraham and laments the faithlessness of men, whose love floats away like the smoke of a railroad engine. On the following morning, Abraham sees her off on her journey into the unknown after haggling with the coachman who has come to drive her to the railroad station. Hagar comforts her crying baby Ishmael by telling him that he will have to learn to adjust to the ways of the world: "That's how patriarchs with long, pious beards behave." Fortunately for her, the Turkish Sultan, passing by with his caravan, recognizes little Ishmael as the ancestor from whom Allah's worshipers and even he himself stem.

When Joseph walks in his silk blouse along the boulevard, girls with blue parasols and May fragrance walk past him smiling, casting sly glances, and wondering how they could entice him as husband or lover. Samuel, the lonely old bachelor who claims to be wedded to prophecy, foresees for the shepherd lad David a crown, a sword and a collection of psalms. He asks Reb Jesse to pack a valise for David, the youngest son, who is to be taken to the train and brought to King Saul's court.

The peasant girl Abishag of the village of Shunam dreams of silks, muslins, golden chariots, awaiting her in the marble palace of the legendary David, whose portrait hangs over her mother's bed. However, when she comes to live in the vicinity of the old king, she is miserable and bewails her lot as his hot-water bottle. She finds no comfort in learned men's assurance that she will earn a line in the Bible. An inked line on parchment cannot compensate for her wasted years and her misused young body. By heaping anachronisms upon anachronisms, Manger constantly moves from the bib-lical to the contemporary level and produces original poetic effects, a combination of religious reverence, skeptical satire and sly folk humor. He is a superb master of romantic irony.

As the last Yiddish troubadour, Manger has an affinity for earlier minstrels. He penned penetrating sketches of Berl Broder, Yakov Psanter, Velvel Zbarzher, Eliakum Zunser and Abraham Goldfaden. To Zbarzher he devoted a cycle of twelve songs in the form of lyric letters which this bard supposedly wrote to Malkele the Beautiful and which ex-pressed the sad longing of the roaming Galician minstrel for his idolized beloved in far-off Constantinople. Zbarzher's golden dreams of her are transmuted into song. He is aware that golden dreams end in illusions. While they last, how-ever, they warm the heart and should not be lightly dis-carded.

Manger voices in these Zbarzher letters his own person-ality, his own feeling that everything wants to become song, everything which breathes, laughs and blossoms, wind, bird and cloud, teardrop and wine drop, chimney sweep and blind beggar, mother and child, milkman and flower maiden, above all, the longing that can find no other form of ful-fillment.

When Manger lived in Jassy, the tradition of Velvel Zbarzher, who had acted out his songs in its wine cellars, was still alive in the memory of its inhabitants. Folk plays, especially Purim plays written and directed by amateurs,

still delighted Yiddish audiences. Manger recalls that his own
father, the master tailor, once assembled the tailor apprentices and led them to put on a performance of the Esther
story at Purim festivities. Manger's *Megilla Songs* (*Megilla-
Lieder,* 1936) retell the Purim episodes in the form of dramatic lyrics to be sung and acted out by various biblical
characters. But the poet also introduces characters and incidents which are not found in the original source, such as
the unhappy love of a tailor apprentice named Fastrigassa
for Queen Esther both before and after her coronation and
his attempt to assassinate his rival, King Ahasverus, an attempt for which he paid with his life. These lyrics were produced as a tragi-comedy thirty years later in Israel and were
eminently successful, reviving in Israeli towns the almost
extinct tradition of the Purim plays.

As the ablest successor of the folk dramatists, Manger
was invited by a Warsaw theater to adapt Goldfaden's plays
for a post-Goldfaden generation. These adaptations proved
to be theatrically successful. Indeed, he reworked one play,
Koldunia, so completely as a comedy in three acts and fourteen tableaux that he afterwards published it as his own
work *Hotzmach,* (1947), giving Goldfaden credit for the
theme and inspiration. To the original characters which had
delighted audiences for half a century, Bobbe Yakhne, Hotzmach, Mirele and Eliakum, he added others of his own creation; and to popular Goldfaden arias and duets he added new
ones of his own composition.

Manger paid eloquent tribute to Goldfaden in a narrative
depicting the final hour of the creator of the Yiddish theater.
He let pass before Goldfaden's dying eyes for the last time
colorful scenes of an eventful life and stage characters from
the hilarious Shmendrik and Kuni-Leml to the tragic Shulamith and the heroic Bar Kochba. The Angel of Death
appeared to the theatrical pioneer in a theatrical mask and
carried on a stylized conversation that, in Goldfaden's opinion, would have guaranteed success on any Yiddish stage.

Manger also paid tribute to other predecessors in the
volume *Endeared Figures* (*Noente Geshtalten,* 1938). He
showed Eliakum Zunser, the famed bard of Vilna, moving

wedding guests to laughter and tears with rhymed improvisations. He showed Berl Broder intoning at an inn sweet, sad melodies and verses about poor craftsmen who toiled for a pittance and retained unwavering faith in God, the ultimate bringer of light to this dark world in which they were enshrouded. He showed the impact made by the wise jester Hershele Ostropoler upon the masses who adored him for his merry ancedotes and who, even while accompanying him to his grave, recalled his cheerful, comforting aphorisms in which he castigated the hard-hearted rich and the respected leaders of the community. In the various portraits painted by Manger, his own features, his own experiences, and his own love for the common man peered through.

Manger's most charming, fantastic, grotesque tales were, however, those he told about authentic life in the Garden of Eden. These tales were published in Warsaw in 1939, a few months before bombs rained down upon this city and destroyed Jewish light-heartedness. He put these stories in the mouth of the newborn babe Shmuel-Aba Aberval.

According to Jewish lore, when children have to leave their heavenly home in order to be born on earth, they are shorn of their angelic wings and are given a fillip on the upper lip or nose. This causes them to forget their former existence. The clever and impish Shmuel-Aba of Manger's narrative succeeds in eluding the drunken angel who is to administer this fillip and he therefore retains, after birth, memories of his experiences in the Jewish paradise and even of a temporary excursion into the Christian sector of heaven. Night after night the precocious baby Shmuel-Aba regales his earthly parents and their three invited guests with his adventures among patriarchs and saints in the realm of the immortals. All of these immortals retain in their superterrestrial home the traits and interests they displayed before their terrestrial death. Their quarrels and reconciliations, their appetites and expectations, their escapades and flirtations, their tragedies and amusements are portrayed in most vivid colors by the artistic conjurer, Manger, at the height of his creative power.

The author planned more than a single volume of these

stories but was interrupted by the war, which caught up with him in France. He succeeded in escaping to London, which became his temporary home for a decade and which he exchanged for New York in 1951 and for Israel in 1967.

In 1967, two years before his death, Manger took leave of his readers in the volume *Stars In the Dust* (*Shteren in Shtoyb*). The title was meant to be symbolic: the stars that once sparkled on the roof were now rolling in the dust and the last promenaders on the dusty road were not even stopping for them. These last songs, in what he called "the murdered language," were indeed sad. He felt the shadows lengthening about him and the night coming on. In a world of woe and weeping, his sole consolation at life's twilight was the mirage of past days which shimmered in his verses.

Throughout the post-war period, Manger's songs of joy and wine and his ballads of love and death continued to be chanted by Yiddish survivors as an antidote to nightmarish memories. His triumphant appearances in Warsaw, New York and Tel Aviv were holidays for overflow audiences that flocked to hear him. He remained in the post-war decades as in the pre-war years the poet of his people in their gay moods, even as he alleviated with his playful, yet sophisticated humor their tragic moods. He was their bridge to joy, beauty and a strange kind of holiness.

In the wake of Rumania's Yiddish pioneers, a galaxy of aspiring writers arose on the eve of the second World War. Many of them perished during the catastrophic years when Rumania became involved in this war. The survivors scattered in all directions. Among the surviving young poets were Jacob Friedman, Chaim Rabinsohn, Freed-Weininger and Motl Sakzier. Prose writers included the historian and editor Joseph Kissman, the literary critic and essayist Yitzkhak Paner, and the philologist Chaim Gininger.

Friedman (b. 1910), a descendant of the Hassidic dynasty of Rizhin, began writing in 1934, spent the war years in a Transnistrian camp, attained artistic maturity in Israel, and reached the summit of his creativity with his dramatic poem *Titans* (*Nefilim,* 1963).

Rabinsohn (b. 1910), also of rabbinic descent, began with

Yiddish lyrics in the same year as Friedman, but after his arrival in Israel in 1945, he gradually changed to Hebrew. His collected songs *Earthly Days* (*Yemai Haadamah*, 1966) revealed that he had mastered the nuances of Hebrew style to an even greater extent than Yiddish.

Freed-Weininger (b. 1915) also began with lyric contributions in 1934. He was encouraged by Shlomo Bickel and, like Bickel, was able to reach the United States shortly before the Holocaust. His poetic collections *Evening Along the Prut* (*Ovent Baim Prut*, 1942) and *Along the Prut, the La Plata and the Jordan* (*Baim Prut, La Plata un Yarden*, 1966) ranged in content from themes of Bukovina, North and South America and Israel to cosmic visions and philosophic meditations, and in style from restrained sonnets to meandering free rhythms.

Motl Sakzier (b. 1907), son of a Bessarabian tailor, wrote primarily social poetry. In his verses he often recalled his father, who sewed new clothes for rich customers but remained poor and yet content with dreams of a nighing Messianic salvation. He himself escaped from a stifling workshop to a Parisian garret and then to Vienna and Bucharest. His elegies of his attic existence, *Therefore* (*Derfar*, 1936), mingled sentimentalism and irony. They showed him in languid, melancholy moods, drinking of love wherever he could find it. Nevertheless, this spinner of dreams about Parisian boulevards and Viennese streets could not liberate himself from images of Jewish tailor lads in his native province who went to their martyrdom singing hymns of the Bund and songs of freedom penned by Vinchevsky, Bovshover and Edelstadt, the adored poets of tailor workshops. After years of Asiatic entombment, he survived Stalin's purges, returned to Kishinev and continued to pen proletarian poems there in the 1960's.

Soviet Kishinev in the post-Stalin era was also the home of the Yiddish writers Yekhiel Shreibman and Yankel Yakir, the former excelling in short sketches and the latter in longer stories of Bessarabian Jewish life. At the same time, Soviet Cernauti harbored not only Moshe Altman after his liberation from a Siberian labor camp but also the younger writers Meyer Kharatz, Hirsh Bloshtein and Chaim Melamed. Their contributions were published in the 1960's in the only available Soviet Yiddish organ, *Sovetish Heimland*.

In the truncated Rumania of the post-Holocaust decades, the quantity and quality of Yiddish literary activity continued to decline. The severance of Bessarabia and Bukovina from Rumania, the migration of Jewish intellectuals to other Soviet centers, the large *aliya* to Israel, the pressure for integration into the culture of the majority population, the decrease of the Yiddish reading public were major factors accounting for this decline. Though some literary activity was still being maintained toward the end of the 1960's and a Yiddish theatrical company was still functioning and even undertaking guest performances in Israel in 1968, the outlook for a Yiddish resurgence, such as Rumania experienced three decades earlier, was bleak.

14

Yiddish Literature
in South Africa

JEWS DID NOT EMIGRATE to South Africa in significant numbers before the second half of the nineteenth century. The earliest Jewish settlers were mainly from England
or Germany. While a few Jews of Eastern European origin
whose mother tongue was Yiddish arrived in the 1870's in
the Cape Colony, it was not until after the Russian pogroms
of the early 1880's that Lithuanian Jews began to stream to
South Africa, attracted by tales of freedom and prosperity.
To meet their needs a Yiddish press arose during the quarter
of a century before World War I and a Yiddish literature
began to flourish soon thereafter.

The earliest pioneer of Yiddish journalism was Nehemiah Dov Baer Hoffmann (1857 or 1860–1928), who founded
the short-lived *Der Afrikaner Israelit* in 1890. When this
weekly ceased publication, he successively launched four
other weeklies and a monthly. His book of memoirs, *Sefer
Hazikhronos* (1916), was the first Yiddish book printed in
South Africa and ushered in the most productive period of
Yiddish literature in this southern outpost.

Hoffmann was a picturesque, talented personality. He

stemmed from a townlet of Kovno Province. In his youth he came in contact in Vilna with the pillars of enlightenment, the *Maskilim* Abraham Ber Gottlober, Shmuel Joseph Finn and Abraham Baer Lebensohn. Kalman Schulman and Zvi Nissun Golomb encouraged him to write. In 1879, Michel Levi Radkinson, editor of the Hebrew weekly *Hakol* and the Yiddish weekly *Kol l'Am,* invited him to Koenigsberg as editorial assistant. Although he remained under Radkinson's tutelage for less than half a year, he acquired literary and journalistic experience which was most useful to him in subsequent years.

Hoffmann's first books were in Hebrew. When Golomb and the Vilna publisher Matz suggested to him that he try his skill at writing story booklets in Yiddish for the less sophisticated readers, he completed about twenty such booklets in a few months. These followed the tradition established by Isaac Meir Dick and Shomer, the most popular narrators of the early 1880's, and bore sensational titles such as *Life in a Harem, Poisoned Love, Innocently Convicted, To the Gallows.* In 1882 he was engaged by the Hebrew editor Haim Zelig Slonimsky to write for the Warsaw journal *Hatzfira.* Three years later Kasriel Zvi Sarasohn brought him to New York to work for the Yiddish weekly *Die Yiedishe Gazetn* and the newly founded first Yiddish daily, *Tageblatt.* After nine months in the United States, however, longing for his wife and children caused him to return to Europe. In 1886 he was called upon to edit the Hebrew weekly *Hamagid.*

When the Jews of his native Lithuania began to emigrate to South Africa, he too was persuaded by his brother-in-law Barnett Millin to exchange Czarist Russia for a freer life in Capetown. But when he arrived there in 1889, he at first experienced the hardships to which most Jewish immigrants were subjected. Unacquainted with the language of the Boers, he yet took to peddling among them, traveling from farm to farm with horse and wagon. Despite Millin's encouragement, he was singularly unsuccessful.

In 1890, Hoffmann brought over the first Hebrew-Yiddish type to South Africa and was thus able to print the first Yiddish weekly, *Der Afrikaner Israelit.* While this periodical lasted only half a year, his second weekly, *Ha-Or,* lasted from April 11, 1895 to July 5, 1897 and his third weekly, *Der Yiedisher Herold,* an additional two years. His fourth weekly venture was *Der Afrikaner Telegraph,* 1898 to 1892; his fifth venture was the weekly *Yiedishe Folkszeitung,* which suspended publication after only two months in 1905; his final venture was the monthly *Der Afrikaner,* from January 1909 to April 1914.

In his articles and, above all, in his book of memoirs, Hoffmann gave a colorful picture of the pioneering generation of Lithuanian Jews in South Africa. In his *Sefer Hazikhronos,* whenever he refers to a friend or acquaintance—and these included outstanding personalities on three continents—he adds a biographic sketch and a subjective evaluation. His facts are not always accurate, but his pen portraits are vivid and illuminating. He writes with great facility in a popular but somewhat archaic style and retains the interest of his readers, despite a moralizing tendency which constantly interrupts his narration of events in his own life and in the life of others.

David Goldblatt (1866–1945), who was co-editor and co-owner with Hoffmann of *Der Afrikaner Telegraph,* was another early pioneer of South African Yiddish journalism and a most ardent champion of the Yiddish language and literature. He had grown up in Radom, Poland, and had lived in Warsaw, Berlin and London, before emigrating to South Africa. In London he had mingled in the circles of the Russian revolutionary writer Prince Peter Kropotkin, the English socialist idealist William Morris and the Yiddish poet Moritz Vinchevsky. In the British capital he acquired his first journalistic experience as a writer for the Yiddish organ *Der Arbeiter-Freind.*

In 1898, Goldblatt arrived in Capetown and was invited by Hoffmann to write for *Ha-Or,* the only existing Yiddish weekly. The following year he founded the first Yiddish daily, *Der Kriegstaphet.* It appeared from October 16 to December 13, 1899. Each issue consisted of a single page and brought reports of the Boer War, an editorial and news of interest to Jews.

Goldblatt's most successful journalistic venture, however, was the weekly *Der Yiedisher Advokat,* which appeared regularly from 1904 until 1914, when he left for the United States. In South Africa, Goldblatt is best remembered for his struggle to gain recognition for Yiddish as a European language. The immigration law of 1902 restricted admission to the Cape Province and Natal to persons who could pass a written examination in a European language. Jews whose mother tongue was Yiddish were in danger of being refused admission. Authorities claimed that Yiddish was a jargon and not a language, that it was not the national language of any European country, and that it was written in Oriental characters, from right to left. Goldblatt and the eloquent advocate Morris Alexander were the leading figures in the successful struggle for Yiddish. Goldblatt's pamphlet *Yiddish, Is It a European Language?* marshaled the arguments for Yiddish and influenced the legislators of the Cape House of Assembly to accord it equal legal status with the other European languages.

During World War I, Goldblatt came to the United States in order to gain support for a projected twenty-volume Yiddish encyclopedia on which he worked for thirty years. He succeeded in completing and publishing the first volume in 1920 and the second volume in 1923, but the unfavorable reaction of the Yiddish press and insufficient financial backing forced him to abandon the project. Nevertheless, his militant advocacy of Yiddish continued unabated until the end of his long life and found expression in many essays and also in the Yiddish volume *In Kamf Far Der Yiddisher Shprakh* (*In the Struggle for Yiddish,* 1942) and in the English volume *The Jew and His Language Problem* (1943).

Hyman Polsky (1871–1944) was five years younger than Goldblatt. He grew up in a townlet near Grodno. To avoid impressment in the Czarist army, he left for London in 1891 and became a successful photographer. It was not until his fortieth year that he emigrated to South Africa. In order to make a living in his profession of photography, he traveled through many towns and villages and had an opportunity to observe Jewish life in its many varied aspects. He recorded his impressions in sketches for Yiddish periodicals. He was a regular contributor to the Johannesburg Yiddish weekly *Der Afrikaner* and was its editor from 1920 to 1923, when it was merged with the *Afrikaner Yiddishe Zeitung.*

Unlike the militant Goldblatt, Polsky avoided controversy and shunned loud, sensational effects. He was at his best in sketching the transformation of the character of Lithuanian Jewish immigrants under the impact of the harsh struggle for survival in pioneering communities. These immigrants usually arrived with illusions of golden opportunities awaiting them in the land of gold mining. Having no experience in any trade and knowing neither English nor Afrikaans, they had to begin as peddlers of miscellaneous wares. When they did acquire a sufficient knowledge of the spoken languages, they opened little country stores, trading with the Boers and more often with the natives. Years passed before a new immigrant could save enough money to bring over his wife and children from the Old Country. Often when they finally did come, estrangement had set in because of the long separation and led to many domestic tragedies. Polsky wrote of these tragedies with a deep understanding of all the human frailties involved. Kindness permeated his depiction of Jewish men and women. He reproved their failings but without bitter denunciation.

Polsky is most compassionate in portraying the Jewish woman as mother, wife or beloved. As mother, she takes pride in giving her children the best moral education at home and tries against great odds to inculcate in them respect for traditional Jewish customs and values. As wife, she waits patiently through interminably long years in the Lithuanian townlet until her husband is in a position to send for her. Meanwhile she works hard to raise children of whom he can be proud. In her new home, she is a faithful helpmate, comforting her husband when he despairs, assisting him in his country store or farm, joining him in scrimping and saving for a better tomorrow, understanding him even in his aberrations. As beloved, she seeks to bring happiness to her man, even if he is an old bachelor who has already spent his younger years in the bush or semi-desert toiling to gain an economic foothold which would enable him to marry. Often she marries him in order to help support her poor parents or needy brothers and sisters in the old country. She finds contentment in living for others and bringing a bit of sunshine to the aging, much-tried man who has chosen her.

Polsky is less tolerant of the more prosperous, assimilated Jewish men who flaunt their newly gained wealth. He castigates the vice of card-playing to which many of them are addicted. He has no sympathy for the Jewish pseudo-Boer or the would-be English sportsman who shed his Yeshiva values, or the son who is ashamed of his father, the cobbler, and his uneducated mother, after these had toiled for years to see him complete medical school and gain a respected social position as a doctor.

Polsky's satire is mild. He prefers the happy ending. He rewards the good even if only at the end of their sad, wearisome years. He punishes the wicked but not too severely. A son who brings his old father to South Africa and then unwittingly hurts him by abandoning traditional piety, thus forcing him to seek refuge and understanding in an old-age home, is himself punished by discovering his own children becoming estranged from him.

Morris Hoffman (1885–1940) was another keen-eyed observer and talented chronicler of the immigrant generation. Born in Preil, near Vitebsk, he emigrated to South Africa in 1906 and lived for many years in the Karu, a semi-desert of Cape Province. After eight years of loneliness and hardships, during which he was buoyed up by his romantic dream of the youthful beloved left behind in Europe, he voyaged to her on the eve of World War I, married her and settled to a happier existence as a storekeeper in De Aar. She encouraged him to record his pioneering experiences and he did so in the poetic volume *Chants of a Wanderer* (*Voglungsklangen,* 1935) and in short stories which appeared posthumously under the title *Under Africa's Sun* (*Unter Afrikaner Zun,* 1957).

The best poems of the former volume were the early ones that deal with Malpenheim—"Monkeyhome"—his designation for Hopetown, his first home in Cape Province. Hoffman emphasizes the tragedy of idealistic young Lithuanian Jews who succumb to primitive African conditions which reward the strong, the brutal and the unscrupulous and which crush the gentle-hearted, the visionaries and the intellectuals. He depicts the decay of morals in an inhospitable environment, the desecration of love, the mad life of the newly rich. When his immigrants attain to affluence, they generally take on the values of their Boer neighbors, but a last vestige of Jewishness still clings to them and makes them sensitive to the pain of their servants and employees. They are on the whole more humane in their dealing with their customers of darker hue. The daughters of immigrants are often fascinated by the robust, earthbound, Bible-loving Boer youths among whom they grow up. However, when these youths embrace Nazi doctrines, they recover from assimilationist delusions and revert to the Jewishness of their parents. There is a moral tone in Hoffman's tales as in those of most South African Yiddish writers.

Jacob Mordecai Sherman (1885–1958), who came to the Transvaal in 1903, began with sad poems that reflected his early hardships. More than half a century later, when he collected his poems in the volume *In Quiet Hours* (*In Shtile Shtunden,* 1957), he recalled his years of stress, wandering and changing callings. He was *shochet,* storekeeper, farmer, bookkeeper, before he attained stability and maturity and accepted his fate. A poem of the nineteen-year-old, entitled *Lonely* (*Elent,* 1904) reveals him in a despairing mood wondering how much longer he can survive the all-encompassing loneliness. In another poem of the same year, he dreams of the poor but warm home he left behind; this old-fashioned Jewish home takes on the hues of a paradise when compared to his wretchedness in his new, strange abode. In still another melancholy poem, he wonders what happened to the ideals he once nurtured and he replies that they remained with his real self when he sailed forth on the Atlantic and that only a shadow of himself survives in the land of his present exile.

Sherman participated in many Yiddish publications and edited several Yiddish periodicals, including the bi-weekly

Dorem Afrike. He was the author of the first Yiddish novel of South Africa, *Land of Gold and Sunshine* (*Land Fun Gold un Sunshein*, 1956), as well as of a volume of tales and lyrics *On Transvaal's Soil* (*Oif Transvaler Erd,* 1949).

Sherman's novel is largely autobiographic. His hero, Meir, comes to South Africa in the same year as did the author himself and goes through a similar metamorphosis from butcher's assistant to storekeeper before finally integrating completely into his strange environment and living as a farmer on his own soil. Stress is laid on the friendly relations between Boers and Jews, the respect of the religiously oriented Afrikaner for the Jews as the people of the Bible. By answering the needs of the non-Jewish farmers and plantation owners, the Jews prosper as traders in outposts far from the large towns and in the course of years help to develop these outposts into viable communities. Sherman gives detailed, sympathetic consideration to the problem of mixed marriages between Jews and Afrikaner. He recognizes that the paucity of Jewish girls among the immigrants faced young men with the dilemma of marriage outside of their faith or no marriage at all. Though Jews as White were associated with the dominating sector of the population, they are portrayed by the novelist as extremely solicitous of the welfare of the Blacks, who formed a majority of the population.

The relations between Blacks and Whites formed the main subject of Richard Feldman's narratives. Feldman (1897–1968) was brought by his parents from Lithuania to South Africa at the age of thirteen. He played a prominent role in the liberal and labor movements of the Transvaal. For eleven years he served as a Labor member in the Transvaal Provincial Council. His book of short stories, *Black and White* (*Shvarts un Vays*), was first published in 1937 and was republished twenty years later, the only Yiddish work in South Africa which experienced a second edition.

Feldman stresses the dignity, the warmheartedness, the cheerfulness of the Blacks. He shows their exploitation for the sake of gold and diamonds and their physical and moral decay when detribalized. He depicts the suffering and the ostracism meted out to the so-called White Kaffirs, the few

Whites who intermarry with the Blacks and raise families in Zulu villages. Feldman also calls attention to the precarious position of the Jewish settlers in cities in which racial strife was reaching a climax after World War I. The volume includes a playlet about Jewish hawkers whose livelihood depended upon the good will of all racial groups and who, when subjected to crucial tests in the racial conflict, remain true to the Jewish values inculcated in them in pre-African years by the Bible and the Talmud.

In the writings of Leibel Feldman (b. 1896), the older brother of Richard Feldman, there is also a tendency to depict the "noble savage" as somehow more moral than the civilized European, a romantic tendency which harks back to Rousseau and his idealization of the natural man. This tendency comes to the fore in his impressionistic sketch of a temporary sojourn among the Bechuanas in the village of Mochudi and in his narrative of his brief experience as a diamond-digger.

Leib Feldman recounted the economic, social and cultural development of the Yiddish-speaking pioneering generation in his early study *Jews in South Africa* (*Yiedn in Dorem Afrike,* 1937) and in his study of 1941 on the rise and decline of the Jewish community of Oudshoorn, once famed as the Jerusalem of South Africa and until World War I a most important center of ostrich-breeding and of a flourishing trade in ostrich feathers. His later studies dealt with the Jews of Johannesburg (1960), the Indians of South Africa (1961), Israel (1965) and an analytical survey *My View of History* (*Mein Kuk Oif Geshikhte,* 1967).

With the founding of the Yiddish Cultural Federation in 1947, its monthly organ *Dorem Afrike* in 1948, and the publishing venture Kayor in 1949, South African Yiddish literature reached its crest.

Kayor began with the lyric volume of Michel Ben Moshe (b. 1911). A journalist by profession, Ben Moshe arrived in South Africa in 1931, wrote for Hebrew periodicals, co-edited the Hebrew monthly *Basad* in 1932, changed to Yiddish in 1936, and collected his Yiddish poems under the title *Fragment* (*Opris,* 1949). These were impressionistic lyrics full of despair, with only now and then a glimmer of a distant light beyond the encompassing gloom.

Kayor also published the sketches of Hyman Ehrlich, *Dankere* (1956), and his verses for children, *Grow, Flowers, Grow (Vaksen, Vaksen, Blimelekh,* 1964), as well as the epic poem of Johannesburg by Nathan Berger, *The Golden Rand (Beim Rand Fun Gold,* 1966).

Ehrlich, who was born in Dankere in 1888, revivifies in his sketches this Latvian townlet which bordered on the three provinces of Vitebsk, Courland and Lifland and whose Jewish inhabitants remained poor, pious and picturesque, generation after generation. He describes their weddings and funerals, their superstitions and their stubborn resistance to change. By means of a single characteristic episode or anec-dote, he illustrates the uniqueness of each figure. The cob-bler, the tailor, the grave-digger, the thief emerge as more sympathetic human beings than the town's only patrician or the reputedly miracle-working rabbi.

Although Ehrlich came to South Africa in 1906 and spent most of his mature years in Johannesburg, his prose and verse do not reflect the slightest influence of this land and its largest metropolis. Berger (b. 1910), on the other hand, was enamored of the Rand. His epic poem of Johan-nesburg consisted of two cantos in rhymed quatrains. In the first canto, he sang of his beloved Transvaal metropolis which arose from the bush eighty years earlier and which became ever more resplendent in luxury and ever more troubled in spirit. This canto ended with the dream-musing of an old Swazi watchman, who traversed in imagination the long road from his former tribal krall to his present detribal-ized, lonely vigil far from his kinsmen. In the second canto, the poet gave a composite picture of Johannesburg's Jews, their rise to affluence, their transmigrated culture, their grad-ual yielding to the assimilationist forces of their glamorous environment. He concluded sadly that this much-tried Jew-ish community, which fought long and stubbornly to retain its own group personality, was becoming ever more alienated from healthy, traditional roots and was giving up long-defended cultural positions—"because life so demanded."

The Jewish bard of the second canto was not unlike the Swazi watchman of the first canto. He too was nostalgically recalling the *shtetl* which he exchanged in his youth for the glittering South African metropolis and he too felt emptied of his earlier radiant dreams and was also now holding a lonely vigil surrounded by mountains of dead sand from which the gold had long since been extracted.

South Africa's finest Yiddish poet was David Fram (b. 1903), who began in 1923 with idyllic poems of Jewish life in Lithuania, before emigrating to Johannesburg in 1927 and moving on later to Salisbury in Rhodesia. His *Songs and Poems* (Lieder un Poemes, 1931) was the first lyric collection by a recognized poet based in part on South African experiences. His later poems, however, reverted to the vanished world of his Eastern European childhood and youth. Two decades after the end of World War II, he still raged at God and could not reconcile himself to the Almighty who let His most faithful followers go up in flames.

Among South African Yiddish writers of considerable significance after World War II were Levi Shalit (b. 1916), editor of the *Afrikaner Yiddishe Zeitung* since 1953 and author of a study on H. Leivick's Messianism (1947) and of memoirs recalling his ghetto and concentration camp experiences, *Thus We Died* (*Azoi Zeinen Mir Geshtorben*, 1948); Hersh Shishler (b. 1903), author of four volumes of humorous sketches; Bernard Mirwish, author of the satirical tales *The Glory Seekers* (*Die Koved Zukher*, 1946); Mendel Tabachnik (b. 1894), the talented author of the songs and poems *In Late Hours* (*In Shpehte Shtunden*, 1965); Sarah Aizen, the lyricist of Capetown, whose *Selected Songs and Poems* (*Geklibene Lieder un Poemes*, 1965) ranged in subject matter from Kovno to Israel and Africa but who was at her best in her simple verses of woman's longing and tender sadness; David Wolpe, poet, essayist, narrator, and editor of *Dorem Afrike;* and Zalman Levi, a pillar of the Yiddish Cultural Federation and a contributor to its publications.

Yiddish plays were staged in South Africa since 1895 but they were generally written by dramatists from other lands, of whom the most popular was Abraham Goldfaden. American Yiddish actors frequently toured South Africa both before the Boer War and throughout the twentieth century. The dramatist Peretz Hirshbein spent several months in South Africa in the course of his world tour, 1920–1922, and aroused great interest with his lectures and dramatic readings.

South African playwrights whose Yiddish dramas and comedies were published between the two world wars included David Fram, I. M. Sewitz (1896–1939), Hersch Bril (1891–1925), Mendel Tabachnik, Shlomo Kartun (b. 1895). The demand for Yiddish plays subsided with each decade and only guest performances by visiting actors and amateur productions now and then still attracted significant audiences after the mid-century.

Because of the negligible immigration of Jews to South Africa after the founding of Israel and because of the aging of the pioneering generation, Yiddish literature could no longer thrive in its former intensity and vigor. Jews born and reared south of the Zambezi were English-speaking and to a lesser extent Afrikaans-speaking. In the 1960's the best Yiddish poems about the South African landscape were written not by indigenous poets but by Abraham Sutzkever, the poet of Vilna and Tel Aviv. The outstanding Jewish novelists of South Africa, Sarah Gertrude Millen, Nadine Gordimer, Lewis Sowden and Dan Jacobson, wrote in English, and the finest lyricist, Olga Kirsch, wrote in Afrikaans before her settling in Israel.

15

Young Vilna

YOUNG VILNA WAS THE YOUNGEST and most promising Yiddish literary group on the eve of the Second World War and from its ranks stemmed writers who influenced the Yiddish scene in the United States, Argentina, France and Israel during the post-Holocaust decades.

Vilna was known as the Jerusalem of Lithuania before the destruction of its Jewish community. During and after the First World War it changed hands repeatedly before it finally came under Polish jurisdiction. Its population contained Russians, White Russians, Poles and Lithuanians, but the Jews predominated. By 1939 they numbered more than 200,000.

Vilna could look back upon a century of Hebrew and Yiddish Enlightenment. It harbored magnificent library collections, the best of which was that of Mathias Strashun (1817–1885), deeded to the Jewish community after his death. Pioneers of Yiddish literature in Vilna included Isaac Meir Dick (1814–1893), the storyteller with the largest reading audience of his generation, Michel Gordon (1823–1890), the militant lyricist of the Haskalah, and Eliakum Zunser (1836–

1913), the most popular bard or *badchen*. From Vilna stemmed also Abraham Cahan (1860–1951), who became the most influential Yiddish editor in the United States, Abraham Reisen (1876–1953), the poet of the poor and the narrator of Jewish sorrow, Shmuel Niger (1883–1955), the literary critic famed throughout the Yiddish world.

During World War I and under the German occupation, Yiddish writers continued their literary activities. A notable product of those years were the two volumes of *Vilner Zamelbukh* (I, 1916; II, 1918), edited by the physician and communal leader Zemach Shabad (1864–1935) and the critic Moshe Shalit (1885–1941).

Hardly was the war over, when plans were set afoot for more ambitious literary projects. The dramatist A. Veiter (1878–1919), liberated from Siberian entombment by the Russian Revolution, the folklorist S. Anski (1863–1920), the historian S. M. Zitron (1860–1930) and the critic S. Niger were among the dynamic figures in the reorganization and coordination of Yiddish literary activities. Unfortunately, Veiter was shot in April 1919 by Polish legionnaires during their rampage when they recaptured Vilna from the Bolsheviks, Niger emigrated to the United States a few months later, and Anski died the following year. However, their efforts, brief but intense, bore fruit in several directions. The Yiddish daily *Der Tog* was founded under the editorship of Niger from May to August 1919 and of Zalman Reisen thereafter. Within a few years Vilna could boast of five Yiddish dailies. The Vilna publishing house of Boris Kletzkin (1875–1937) eclipsed the century-old Vilna publishing firm of the Romm family, whose Yiddish booklets had reached hundreds of thousands of readers. The Vilna troupe of actors, first organized in 1916, attained its artistic peak with the performance of Anski's *Der Dybbuk* in Warsaw in 1920 and then went on to celebrate triumphs in other communities. In Vilna's Yiddish schools and Teachers' Seminary, youth was inspired by the literary historian Max Erik (1898–1937), the poet Moshe Kulbak (1896–1940) and the educators Falk Heilperin (1876–1945) and Abraham Golomb (b. 1888). After 1928, YIVO offered an hospitable home for aspiring intellectuals who streamed to Vilna to be trained by YIVO's scholars under the direction of Max Weinreich, Zelig Kalmanovitch and Zalman Reisen.

Reisen, journalist, scholar, editor of the Vilna *Tog,* is generally credited with being the discoverer and inspirer of Young Vilna. On October 11, 1929, he introduced the group to the readers of his daily under the headline "Young Vilna Marches into Yiddish Literature" and during the following years he encouraged beginners by printing their poems, which were often immature but which contained sparks of talent. Soon the group, constantly augmented, gained confidence and published its united efforts in periodicals and individually in books of verse and fiction.

The writers associated with Young Vilna had no common platform and issued no manifestos. What united them was a common cultural background, youthful enthusiasm, a love of Yiddish and a desire to use it as a medium for self-expression. Leiser Ron and Elias Schulman, two members of the group who later chronicled its achievements, listed more than three dozen adherents who participated to a greater or a lesser extent in its publications. However, the only ones among them who matured to perfection were Chaim Grade (b. 1910) and Abraham Sutzkever (b. 1913). Others perished during the Second World War or soon thereafter, while still others, deprived of the Yiddish-saturated atmosphere of Vilna, failed to fulfill adequately the promise of their first years. Among the former the most talented were Leiser Wolf (1910–1943), Hirsh Glick (1922–1944), Shimshon Kahan (1915–1941), Moshe Levin (1907–1942) and Schmerke Kaczerginsky (1908–1954).

Wolf was a protégé of Reisen. He contributed to all three annuals of *Yung Vilna,* 1934–1936. His first verse booklet, *Eviningo,* was printed in Latin characters in 1936. It consisted of sixteen pages and imitated the sonorous rhythms and the picturesque imagery of Longfellow's *Hiawatha.* Far more important was the selection of his lyrics, *Black Pearls* (*Shvartse Perl,* 1939), which appeared just before the outbreak of the war. Wolf succeeded in escaping to Soviet Russia, where his third poetic booklet, *Lyric and Satire*

(Lyrik un Satire, 1940), was published with an introduction
by the Moscow Yiddish poet Aaron Kushnirov. When the
Germans invaded Russia in 1941, he was evacuated to Uzbekistan. Enduring hardships in this Asiatic region and undernourished month after month, his health deteriorated and led
to his death at the age of thirty-two. Shortly before his end
he was hailed by Peretz Markish as the Yiddish Heine. In
his mingling of melancholy sentimentalism, romantic irony
and social satire, he did indeed resemble the German poet.
Besides, he often modeled his early lyrics after Heine, as
in "The Weavers" *("Die Weber,"* 1935), an anti-Nazi song
in which the members of the Underground were depicted as
weaving amidst curses a net to enshroud the "Brown Vam-
pire."

In a poem of 1936, Wolf described with subtle irony the
only meeting of Heine and Goethe, and identified himself
with the young singer of sorrows rather than with the old
Olympian sage of Weimar. Wolf's Heine resented Goethe's
patronizing tone and coldness of spirit, his smug pursuit of
sweet calmness, his dwelling in a palace of fortune, his
insufficient familiarity with pain. Wolf's Goethe, on the
other hand, saw in Heine a young upstart, a borrower of
artificial pain, a dispenser of hate, a poet of little talent.
When Goethe politely inquired: "What are you now creating, my dear?" Heine answered in hot anger: "A Faust!"
And both eyed each other, sensing themselves to be worlds
apart.

Wolf assimilated influences from German, Russian and
American poets. He felt a kinship to Byron, Pushkin, Nietzsche, Spinoza, literary rebels and heretical philosophers. But
the Jewish heritage meant far more to him and he was well
versed in Yiddish literature of preceding generations. Above
all, Vilna scenes, figures and incidents supplied him with
rich subject matter. In one poem, he contrasted the Vilna
Gaon with the Baal Shem. In a verse dialogue, the aged
Vilna storyteller Isaac Meir Dick came to life. In a poetic
tribute to the Yiddish classical triumvirate, he showed them
seated on golden thrones in paradise, with silver-haired,
steel-eyed Mendele in the center, flanked by Peretz of the

mighty brow and fiery dark eyes and Sholom Aleichem with the brown curls, resplendent blue eyes and the open mouth always laughing, laughing, laughing.

In 1939 Wolf headed a group of very young Vilna writers who collaborated in publishing the modest journal *Yungwald.* The war ended this venture and dispersed the group. Wolf left for Dniepropetrovsk and there penned anti-Nazi lyrics. Moshe Gurin (b. 1921), who participated in all four issues of *Yungwald,* survived the liquidation of Vilna's ghetto and Latvian concentration camps and reached Israel in 1947, where he continued with lyrics of the new landscape. Hirsh Glick, a cousin of Gurin and the youngest member of Young Vilna, was only seventeen when he joined the *Yungvald* group and only twenty-two when he died fighting with the partisans after escaping from Vilna's ghetto and from an Estonian concentration camp. Nevertheless, he succeeded in attaining immortality with a single lyric, his "Song of the Partisans" (*Partizanerlied,* 1943). This stirring song, set to the melody of a Cossack march, instantly won the hearts of resistance groups. Its five stanzas lent courage in darkest hours and instilled faith that the struggle of the doomed would not be vain. It began with the admonition not to despair: "Say not, you're going on the last road, even if leaden skies obscure blue days." It continued with the assurance that the longed-for hour of deliverance would yet come, the golden sun would dissipate the gloom, and the song of the heroism of the Jewish people, fighting amidst tumbling ghetto walls, would resound from generation to generation. Translated into the principal languages spoken by Jews, this song has been sung at memorial meetings for the Nazi victims year after year. The young author was the subject for poems by Peretz Markish, Abraham Sutzkever, Shmerke Kaczerginski, Moshe Gurin and Peretz Miranski.

Shimshon Kahan belonged to the original group discovered by Reisen in 1929. He earned a living as a teacher in a village near Vilna, as a toiler of the soil, as a prompter with a troupe of wandering actors. He associated with gypsies, learned their language and translated their songs into Yiddish. His own lyrics were generally shrouded in sadness and appeared only in periodicals.

Moshe Levin was a portrait painter and storyteller. He participated with naturalistic tales in all three annuals of *Yung Vilna*, 1934–1936. He wrote and illustrated stories for children. His volume *Spring in a Cellar Den (Frihling in Kellershtub,* 1937) contained gloomy sketches of honest craftsmen who suffered from chronic unemployment, anti-Jewish discrimination, filth and vermin. While his pious characters accepted their apparently God-given destiny, which condemned them to hunger, sickness and anti-Semitism, his younger characters revolted against poverty and social degradation and engaged in Socialist activities to undermine the existing regime. As the son of a glazier, Levin wrote a moving story of the unfair competition to which Jewish but not Christian glaziers were exposed. In *Motie Droshke* he chose as the representative of the older, tradition-bound generation a driver of a droshke, who was dull-witted, good-natured and submissive to authority. The driver's younger daughter, however, rebelled against tradition, read Marx and Engels, fought against the reactionary Polish regime and endured arrest with a smile.

When the Soviets overran Vilna, Levin contributed to Communist publications. When the Nazis later captured the town, he escaped to Minsk and was active in the underground of the Minsk ghetto. When Jews in 1942 were led to the Minsk prison courtyard to be liquidated, the German commander offered to spare Levin's life because of his usefulness as a painter, but he preferred to share the fate of his coreligionists and was shot together with them.

Shmerke Kaczerginski began with militant proletarian lyrics and sketches, participated in the annuals of *Yung Vilna* under the pseudonym of C. Shmerke, and survived the horrors of the Vilna ghetto and the dangers of a partisan behind the battlefront, only to perish in an airplane accident on a flight from Argentina. During the early years of the war he was employed by the Nazis to classify YIVO's collection of books and manuscripts so that the most valuable items could be transported to Germany and used for anti-Semitic studies after the war. In the process of making the selection, he succeeded, with the assistance of Abraham Sutzkever, in hiding and burying many precious items. When the work neared its end and his liquidation seemed imminent, he fled with Sutzkever to the surrounding forests. There the poets fought, gun in hand, until the day of liberation. At the same time Kaczerginski kept a diary of his experiences, while Sutzkever reduced the group's perilous and heroic deeds to flaming verses. After the war both returned to Vilna. They succeeded in finding and digging up the hidden YIVO material amidst the rubble of the destroyed ghetto. Kaczerginski found a temporary refuge in France and a permanent one in Argentina before his fatal accident. His post-war volumes of Vilna's ruined community and of the partisan struggles chronicled Jewish heroism and Jewish martyrdom. These volumes are among the most moving, authentic sources for the Holocaust years.

Among the survivors of Young Vilna was the symbolist poet Elchanan Rozhansky, who wrote under the pseudonym of Elchanan Wogler (1907–1969). He chose this pseudonym because *Wogler* is the Yiddish word for "wanderer" and it symbolized his homelessness ever since he was orphaned at an early age. While earning his meager bread as a sign-painter, Wogler came under the influence of Moshe Kulbak but soon developed his own original lyric style. In his first booklet, *A Leaf in the Wind* (*A Bletl in Vint,* 1935), he animated natural phenomena. The theme of this idyl in rhyming quatrains was the poet's marriage to the Plum Orchard. This marriage took place after he fell in love in the spring. It flourished throughout the summer. It ended in red autumn, when the beloved died of tuberculosis, leaving her orphaned children, the plums, at the mercy of cannibalistic humans. The road beside the orchard was depicted as an old, withered bachelor, who moaned whenever a heavily laden truck passed over him. The neighboring rose garden was personified as a beautiful young maiden who was wooed by many attractive birds and bees. When she was caught at a rendezvous with a male butterfly, the jealous bees challenged the latter to a duel, which ended fatally for him.

They then proceeded to bite the maiden's lips, to tear her silken dress and to rape her. The wind was portrayed as a happy fiddler. When his yellow wife, the grain, passed away, he mourned her for seven full days and then set out in search of a new mate. He played a tearful elegy for his orchestral comrades, the rivers, before they were locked up in an icy prison for the winter.

Wogler was shaken out of his poetic allegories when the Nazis neared Vilna in June 1941. He fled to Alma Ata, in the Asiatic region of Kazakhstan. After the war, he was permitted to return to Poland, and from there he emigrated to France. In Paris he felt lonely and lost. There he wrote his nostalgic recollections of Young Vilna and published his collected lyrics, *Spring on Earth (Frihling Oifn Trakt,* 1954). Some of these lyrics harked back to pre-war scenes, to idyllic characters such as the bearded drayman Moshe, who disputed with God while driving along the village road, or the Lithuanian shepherd Nikite, who reigned over an empire of sheep, commanding their obedience with the sounds of a flute. The poet still personified phenomena of nature as, for example, the Old Wind who survived three wives, was wooing a fourth wife, and was raging at his son, the Young Wind, who was no less amorous. In Wogler's war and post-war verses, new tones came to the fore: elegies on the poet Shmuel Rossin and on the martyred Vilna hero Itzik Wittenberg, laments for the children of Vilna's ghetto, sad echoes of his Lithuanian homeland lost to him forever, pessimistic images of Parisian garrets where painters, musicians and poets consorted.

Another survivor of Young Vilna was the poet Peretz Miranski (b. 1908), a cousin of Hirsh Glick. He joined the group in 1934 and participated in its annuals with fables and parables in the manner of Eliezer Steinbarg but with a grimmer undertone of social satire. Fleeing before the Nazi invaders, he reached Samarkand in Central Asia. There he wrote in 1943 his apocalyptic poem "War," depicting a city at night as it waited with darkened eyes for its doom. Then death flew over it on silvery, icy wings and sealed the streets with blood. The terror-stricken houses collapsed under thun-

derclaps and fiery rain. When pale morning dawned, the
smoke-filled city lay in ruins, its trees corpses, its windowless,
roofless dwellings mounds of fresh graves. In the ballad "The
Gaon and the Partisan," the poet let the Vilna Gaon arise
from the Old Cemetery and encounter a Jewish partisan who
came to avenge murdered kin. Despite the Gaon's compassion
for man and beast, he blessed the avenger, since such mon-
strous crimes as the Nazis had perpetrated must be atoned
for.

Returning to Vilna in 1945, Miranski saw his own house
in ruins while the house of his non-Jewish neighbor stood
intact. His own father, mother, sister were dead, but this
neighbor enjoyed their few belongings. Then the latter's
proferred glass of water seemed to drip drops of blood and
the cherries in the garden seemed to have been reddened by
his sister's life when it oozed away. He could no longer stay
on in post-war Vilna and fled to a German Displaced Persons' camp. In 1949 he reached Canada. There his only
volume, *A Candle for a Penny* (*A Likht Far a Groshen*,
1951), appeared. It included the fables of his Vilna period,
the lyrics of his war years, and the poems of his post-war
impressions in Berlin, Paris and Montreal.

Abraham Lev (b. 1910) participated in the earliest of the
publications of the Vilna group but emigrated to Palestine
as early as 1932 and later became one of Israel's finest lyricists.

Abraham Karpinovitch (b. 1918) also began in Vilna in
the pre-war decade but did not succeed in getting to Israel
until 1950. In his volume *In Vilna's Courtyard* (*Beim Vilner
Durchhoif,* 1967), he recreated the splendor of Vilna's Jewish culture before its destruction.

The splendor of Jewish Vilna also emerges from the
poems and novels of Chaim Grade (b. 1910) and the poems
of Abraham Sutzkever (b. 1913).

Grade stemmed from a family that was long rooted in
Vilna. In a poem of 1936, "The Cry of Generations," he
portrayed the three generations that preceded his own: his
great-grandfather of pre-Napoleonic days who still suffered
from medieval disabilities imposed by a fanatical church,

his grandfather who hailed Napoleon as the world liberator, his father, a Hebrew teacher who turned from the mysticism of the Cabala to the rationalism of Moses Mendelssohn, who became a social incendiary, hating the pious patrician whose children he taught, and who died prematurely. Grade inherited from his father a shelf of books and a rebellious temperament. His mother insisted that the seventeen-year-old orphaned lad continue to study at Yeshivot, while she eked out a bare living for herself, peddling fruit in Vilna's marketplace.

Grade was most influenced in his adolescence by a great and saintly teacher, the Hazon-Ish, under whom he studied for seven years. What this sage meant for him he later recorded in an elegy composed in 1954 after his teacher's death in Israel. He called him an angel who hid his wings while among mortals, a pillar of radiance who shed the light of compassion upon pupils. "Though he did not want to bless my way of life, yet do I shine by the reflection of his great love."

While dreaming of beauty, young Grade consorted with the adherents of the Musar movement, whose ideal was spiritual purity and who despised the pursuit of beauty as sinful, seductive, vanity of vanities, time ill spent. This movement was originally launched by Rabbi Israel Salanter in the nineteenth century and its tenets continued to be practiced with great zeal and severity between the two world wars in the Navaredker Yeshivot. Grade depicted his experiences in such a Yeshiva in his epic poem *Musarnikes* (1939). He emphasized the disputations of his classmates who strove for moral perfection. He mirrored himself in the figure of Chaim Vilner, a twenty-year-old, pale, emaciated, grimly serious student, who conducted himself like a person long past his youth. He was perpetually hounded by a sense of guilt, a fear that he had sunk into a morass of moral impurity, and he tried desperately to work his way out of this morass. He felt himself attracted to secular books rather than to ethical tracts. The former books were taboo in this ultra-religious institution and yet he could not resist the temptation to peer into their forbidden contents. For a time he joined in the self-flagellation and the constant confessions indulged in by the Musar youths, but finally he gave up his unsuccessful straining for extra-mundane holiness. The bird that sang in the sunlight enchanted him and the wind that rustled in the forest tore him away from his Talmudic tomes. He became aware of social injustice. He began to resent economic inequality. He threw himself into the struggle for political renovation, as did so many poets of Young Vilna.

From 1932 he joined these poets in their publications. His first lyric booklet, *Yea* (*Yo*, 1936), gave expression to his affirmation of active striving, after he had torn himself away from the pursuit of contemplative asceticism. The volume began with tributes to his mother who was still supporting herself by marketing her basket of apples all day. He idealized her in many lyrics as a model of integrity, self-effacing, deeply devoted to her God and her children. Various aspects of her personality also emerged from the poetic volume *My Mother's Testament* (*Der Mames Tsvue*, 1949) and from his prose volume *My Mother's Sabbaths* (*Der Mames Shabosim*, 1955). When the Nazis entered Vilna, she remained and perished together with many of her townsmen on the Day of Atonement, 1941. The poet succeeded in escaping by joining the refugees that streamed eastward. He found safety throughout the war years in towns of Asiatic Russia. From there he launched poems of hatred against the invaders and calls for vengeance. Some of these were included in the volume *Generations* (*Doires*, 1945) and others in the lyric collection *Refugees* (*Pleitim*, 1947). However, far more numerous than the accusations he hurled against the Nazi foe were the poems of love and comfort he directed toward his own people. The Yellow Badge had united Jews. Common wandering and common suffering had obliterated the dissentions long raging between Jewish groups. The fratricidal strife between Hebraists and Yiddishists was over. The language of the Bible was being rejuvenated in the ancestral Holy Land and the Yiddish speech of the masses was being sanctified by their martyrdom. Grade prayed for prophets to arise in both tongues to uplift the hearts of Jews who would survive the Holocaust.

Grade survived the difficult war years in central Asia. In 1945 he trekked westward to Moscow, then on to ruined Vilna after its liberation from the Nazis. In the early chapters of *My Mother's Sabbaths,* he gave the finest literary description of pre-war Vilna as seen through the eyes of his mother's generation and his own, and in the closing chapters a most moving narration of his post-war homecoming to Vilna's empty houses and full graves. When he learned that his wife, a nurse in the Vilna ghetto, had been led to her death together with the last Jews when the ghetto was liquidated in September 1943, he could no longer linger amidst Vilna's ghostly memories and he continued on to Paris. In Paris he was active among the surviving Yiddish writers but, when most of them left their temporary French asylum for more permanent homes in Israel and the Americas, he too left for New York to rebuild his shattered existence.

In the United States, Grade found admirers of his poetry, audiences for his lectures and readings, publishers for his narratives of the Vilna he had experienced but which had already become historic. The three novelettes of *The Synagogue Courtyard (Der Shulhoif,* 1958) brought back to life the narrow, teeming streets of Vilna's poorest district in which his early years had been spent. Though the houses had turned to rubble and their inhabitants had been exterminated, they were still vivid in his memory and he fixated them for posterity in beautiful narrative prose.

The longest novelette is *The Well.* It narrates the efforts of the district's water carrier, Mende, to get the well of the courtyard repaired so that the poor inhabitants would not have to trudge to a distant part of the town for their water or to pay the monastery, which had the nearest functioning well, for the precious liquid needed to sustain their lives. In addition, there is the constant danger that the whole neighborhood might go up in flames if a fire were to break out and no water be available in the courtyard to extinguish it.

Most chapters deal with Mende's experiences, successes and reverses as he tries to scrape together from the townsmen the sums needed for this repair job. His chief ally in his

solicitations is the ascetic Reb Bunim, who continues throughout the narrative to mourn his two children who perished of
hunger during the war and his oldest son who succumbed
soon after the war. Bunim wants desperately to absolve God
of guilt in their deaths. He seeks an answer by studying the
Book of Job and pondering the destiny of this biblical father
whose reverses paralleled his own and who yet remained
faithful to the Lord. Mende shows him how to find consolation by joining in the charitable project of gathering funds
for the well.

Grade depicts these crotchety, good-natured, trusting characters and their more practical wives with sympathy and sly
humor. The townspeople with whom they come in contact
range from superstitious old women to rebellious workmen,
from an attractive merry widow and a robust red-cheeked
merchant, her suitor, to the widow's pale daughter, who hovers between three suitors, an aging Torah scribe, a youthful,
dreamy-eyed skeptic, and an immature, irreligious apostle of
revolution.

The novelette reaches its climax in the assembly of the
Polish rabbis convoked by a saintly sage, the revered, ninety-
year-old Chofetz Chaim. Each rabbi is portrayed in his individual traits and carefully differentiated from the others.
This great assembly is brought to a pause in its deliberations
of weighty political and religious problems in order to help
the humble water carrier in his simple, charitable deed. At
the dedication of the repaired well, the principal characters
are brought together in a final scene of rejoicing and festive dancing. The author's kindness constantly leads him to
mitigate stark tragedies by deflecting attention to acts of
moral greatness by those whom God afflicted. He feels that
trust in a divine order helps one to bear adversity and to retain an optimistic attitude amidst ups and downs of fortune.

Grade's longest and most significant narratives composed
at the height of his creativity in the United States are *The
Agunah* (*Die Agune,* 1961) and *Tsemakh Atlas* (1967).

An *agunah,* in Jewish law, is a woman who is legally
barred from entering into a new marriage because she has
not been granted a *get,* a bill of divorcement, by her husband.

Though the husband may have disappeared during the sinking of a ship on which he was sailing or in the course of a pogrom or in the midst of battle, Jewish law considers him alive unless there are credible witnesses and adequate testimony establishing his death beyond the possibility of doubt. The unmerited cruel fate of living widows always aroused sympathy. Down the centuries rabbis have, therefore, differed in the strictness of their interpretation as to the amount and quality of evidence necessary to establish the fact of certain death.

Grade's novel deals with the struggle of two schools of rabbinical thought in the case of a woman of Vilna whose husband did not return from the First World War and whose entire squadron was reported to have been wiped out. Though nobody actually saw him die, yet fifteen years passed since his squadron came under fire and not a single one of its soldiers was known to have survived. It could therefore be presumed that he was killed in action, but presumption was not sufficient proof in the opinion of most rabbis to justify freeing the woman so that she could remarry. A compassionate religious judge was found, however, who was prepared to take upon himself the responsibility of giving the Vilna *agunah* a *get* in order to mitigate her loneliness and suffering and to let her wed a pious *hazzan*. As a result, this dissenter was hailed before a *Bet Din*, a rabbinical judicial assembly, and was subjected to persecution by the more literal-minded rabbis and Jewish officials.

Grade unrolls a rich panorama of Jewish religious life in Vilna and the struggle between traditionalists and innovators in the 1930's, the final decade of Vilna's eminence as a center of Jewish learning. The further this city receded in time, the more did the novelist discover a kaleidoscope of attractive colors in its apparent grayness, the more beauty did he ferret out in its simple, poor Jews, the more tolerance did he display toward the religious extremists, whose fanaticism he deplores with ever increasing mildness.

Grade's poems of the post-Holocaust period, *The Man of Fire* (*Der Mentsh Fun Fayer,* 1962), continued to revolve about his people's tragedy. In the silence of nights he was haunted by visitors who had long since been turned to smoke, dust and ashes. They called upon him to resurrect them in people's memories by writing about them. Since he saw the hill of shoes at Maidanek and the heaped ashes that were once the feet to which these shoes belonged, he went about with bowed head and felt that he must pen epitaphs for the burned victims. In the course of years, however, as the poet became rooted in his new home beyond the Atlantic, he also included joyous New World themes. He sang odes to the Grand Canyon, Yosemite, Niagara, the mountains of California, the desert of Arizona and the islands of the Pacific. But when confirmation reached him that the Russian Yiddish writers with whom he had consorted in Moscow had been liquidated by Stalin's hangsmen, he again reverted to his earlier mournful tones. In his magnificent elegy "I Weep for You in All the Letters of the Aleph-Beth," he paid tribute to these martyred friends: Bergelson, Der Nister, Kushnirov, Hofstein, Kvitko, Michoels, Dobrushin, Fefer and above all Peretz Markish. He likened his dearest friend Markish to Jonathan, David's dearest friend, and he lamented him in biblical tones reminiscent of David's dirge for the Prince who fell at Mt. Gilboa. In Grade's happiest moments, shudders would come over him, reminiscences of destroyed Vilna, and he reverted to the scenes, the moods and the figures of his youth, embodying them in poignant images and unforgettable stanzas.

Abraham Sutzkever was only twenty-six when the idyllic period of "Young Vilna" came to an end. His more important works were written after 1939 in the Vilna Ghetto under Nazi surveillance, among the Partisans behind the Front after his escape from the Ghetto, and above all in his creative decades in Israel after his arrival in 1947. However, the roots of his personality were laid in the vast spaces of Siberia, to which he was brought from Smargon in White Russia as a two-year-old, when his family fled before the German invasion of World War I. Then came his years of storm and stress during which he matured. These were spent in Vilna, to which he returned with his mother after his father's death in 1920.

The Siberian landscape and childhood experiences found poetic repercussion in the lyrics collected under the title *Siberia (Sibir,* 1936). The city of Omsk, the Irtush River, the vast expanse of snow-covered forests lived on in his memory and imagination long after his carefree boyhood had come to an end and he was confined to the cramped quarters of Vilna's Jewish district. His early lyrics reflected the joy of life and the longing for liberty which were implanted in him during the Siberian years close to nature. He recalled that he often drove with his father to fetch wood from the forest. Then he came to know fox and wolf, the setting sun in fiery fur and the harp of the moon that accompanied his homeward-bound sled.

In the dank quarters of Vilna he yearned for light, beauty and freedom. Failing to find these in reality, he sought to conjure them into being through the magic of rhythmic incantation. In his verses, the grass babbled, the roots laughed, the skies brightened, the dewdrops kissed. He was like a freshet gushing forth young, joyous lyrics. He wove legends of the changing seasons, from intoxicating spring and star-studded summer to fading autumn and chilly winter. In these legends were intertwined visions of the ethereal beloved, who also blossomed, changed, ripened and faded with the seasons. In forest, field and brook he did not yet sense fear or hostility. The passing cloud implanted kisses on the forest. The village lass dreamed beside her sickle which rested in the field. Trees slept peacefully. The poet embraced with his loving glance a twig of ripe cherries and a fiery blond apple until he entered into the essence of each. Life to him was rhythm and cosmic fire. He wanted to drain his earthly time to the last drop, to soar like an eagle in the wind, released from taboos and conventions, to peer into all animate and inanimate objects with pristine, wondering eyes like Adam when he first set out upon his terrestrial adventure.

Sutzkever's optimism was irrepressible. He felt sunny music in his veins and sparks of joy impinging upon all his senses. "Ecstasies" was the title he gave to a series of twenty-eight lyrics because their dominant mood was ecstatic. What if clouds and storms at times obscured bright sunlight! What if earth also contained gray steppes and stinging thorns! The poet came, even as did the rainbow after the thunder and the lightning, to color the steppes with rosy hue and to feed the thorns with beauty. The poet harmonized discords and brought a holiday mood to the dreariest days.

Then came the war. It locked the poet in the Vilna Ghetto and gave the lie to his optimistic faith. During his two years of living entombment, 1942-1943, his Utopian dreams went up in smoke and his light-hearted verses gave way to elegies for the dead and the doomed. He sang of the self-sacrificing courage of the teacher Mire, who continued to brighten the school hours of her pupils with the humor of Sholom Aleichem, with melodies of spring and hope, and with preparations for a dramatic pageant, even while their number dwindled from day to day until she and her last wards were liquidated. He sang of the ghetto Orpheus who dug up his buried fiddle and awakened the dead with his playing. He gave a rhythmic description of a wagonload of shoes transported by rail from Vilna to Berlin: bridal shoes, children's shoes and his own mother's Sabbath shoes. These shoes twitched and rattled, though the feet and bodies to which they adhered were no longer alive.

In February 1943, Sutzkever composed the poetic monologue *Kol Nidre,* which ranks with Katzenelson's *Song of the Murdered Jewish People* and Segalowitch's *There* among the most memorable verse records of the Holocaust years. It described the raid of an extermination squad on Yom Kippur eve, when the Jews of Vilna were assembled for Kol Nidre prayer in the synagogue. The worshipers are dragged off to prison pens for final processing on the following day. Among them is an old man whose father, wife, five sons and grandson preceded him in death. He is ready for the end, since he has nobody to live for and nobody who will miss him save perhaps his oldest son who left home twenty years earlier and who may still be alive. During the night the old man encounters a wounded Red Army prisoner who has been brought in to share the fate of the Jews and whom he comes to recognize as his long lost son. When a Gestapo officer mocks and humiliates the doomed Jews, this prisoner revolts against such treatment and hurls a stone at the brown-shirted tormentor. To save the son from torture and Nazi vengeance, the father stabs him. When the death wagons lead forth the Jews and the bullets mow them down, the old man somehow survives the hail of bullets and tells his tale of woe to the poet on the following Yom Kippur.

By the spring of 1943 the elegiac verses of the mild-mannered poet were being replaced by cries of defiance and calls for vengeance. No longer was he willing to wait for miracles. The time had come to rely on weapons of iron and not merely on prayers to God for deliverance from the oppressor. He felt that every hand must hurl itself against the annihilating foe. Revolt was in the air. In September 1943, on the eve of the final liquidation of Vilna's Jews, when the last men were being transported to Esthonian camps and the last women and children to the Auschwitz crematoria, the poet, along with a few survivors, fought his way, weapon in hand, to a forest beyond the doomed town and joined the Partisans. He participated in the military activities of a Jewish group. "The Avengers," until March 1944, when a Soviet military airplane brought him from his forest base to the Russian capital. Over the Moscow radio he broadcast first-hand information about German atrocities in the Vilna area. In Moscow he also began his longest epic poem, *Secret City* (*Geheimshtot,* 1948). In it he described the struggle for survival of a group of ten Jews in the city sewage canals, a dark realm of mice and mud but irradiated by the will of these Jews to remain moral personalities and to preserve their group identity.

In 1946 Sutzkever returned to Poland. He testified at the Nuremberg Trial of the Nazi war criminals. He went on to Paris and to Switzerland. With his arrival in Palestine in 1947, his period of storm and stress came to an end. A new creative period began for him. Themes of the Holocaust gradually gave way to Israeli themes based on his experiences in the Jewish homeland and on his observations during Israel's three wars for survival. His search for lyric perfection continued and his creative vitality was undiminished during the following decades. In him as well as in Chaim Grade, the generation of "Young Vilna" reached its apex.

"Young Vilna" is gradually becoming a legend. It is a legend of the dynamic striving of a Yiddish-speaking youth that was born before World War I, that matured during the post-war struggle for the retention of Jewish minority rights in Eastern Europe and that was filled with enthusiasm for the new literary medium forged to perfection by the classical Yiddish triumvirate and standardized by the scholars of YIVO. This youth, endowed by an abundance of talent and united by a common will to express its subtlest emotions and deepest insight in Yiddish, was rich in fulfillment and richer in promise. It never fully ripened because most of its members perished during the Holocaust. The survivors, uprooted from their native soil in the Jerusalem of Lithuania, continued against overwhelming odds a valiant struggle to arrest the decline of Yiddish and to retain a reading public for the products of their pen. In their prose and verse Yiddish still bears fruit of fine literary flavor.

Bibliography

Yiddish bibliographies of writers discussed in the text are available in Zalman Reisen's *Lexikon fun der Yidisher Literatur* (4 vols., 3rd ed., Vilna, 1928) and in the more recent *Lexikon fun der Nayer Yidisher Literatur*, of which seven volumes appeared from 1956 to 1968 under the auspices of the Congress for Jewish Culture.

A bibliography of books on, and translations from, the Yiddish literature available in English until 1940 is appended to A. A. Roback's *Story of Yiddish Literature*, published by YIVO in New York. *The Jewish Book Annuals*, 27 vols., published by the Jewish Book Council of America from 1941 to 1969, list the more recent translations of Yiddish books. The bibliography *Yiddish Literature in English Translation*, compiled by Dina Abramowitz (New York, 1967) lists books published 1945-1967.

The present bibliography serves primarily as a guide to further reading in English on literary movements and on writers discussed in the present volume. For writers who appeared on the Yiddish literary scene before 1914, English translations are listed in the author's earlier volume *The Flowering of Yiddish Literature* (New York, 1963).

GENERAL REFERENCES AND ANTHOLOGIES

Bellow, Saul, ed. *Great Jewish Short Stories,* New York, 1966.
Biletzky, I. C. *Essays on Yiddish Poetry and Prose Writers,* Tel Aviv, 1969.
Charles, Gerda, ed. *Modern Jewish Stories,* London, 1963.
Cooperman, J. B. and S. H., eds. *America in Yiddish Poetry,* New York, 1967.
Dawidowicz, L. S., ed. *The Golden Tradition,* New York, 1967.
Goodman, Henry, ed. *The New Country,* New York, 1967.
Howe, Irving and Greenberg, Eliezer, eds. *A Treasury of Yiddish Stories,* New York, 1953.
Landis, J. C., ed. *The Dybbuk and Other Great Yiddish Plays,* New York, 1966.
Leftwich, Joseph, ed. *The Golden Peacock,* New York, 1961.
Leftwich, Joseph, ed. *Yisroel,* New York, 1963.
Lifson, D. S. *The Yiddish Theatre in America,* New York, 1965.
Madison, C. A. *Yiddish Literature,* New York, 1968.
Rosenfeld, Max, ed. *A Union for Shabbos and Other Stories of Jewish Life in America,* Philadelphia, 1967.

INDIVIDUAL AUTHORS

Ansky, S. *Dybbuk,* New York, 1926; Winnipeg, 1953.
Glatstein, Jacob *Homecoming at Twilight,* New York, 1962.
Grade, Chaim *The Well,* Philadelphia, 1967.
Greenberg, Chaim *The Inner Eye,* New York, 1964.
Manger, Itzik *The Book of Paradise,* New York, 1965.
Opatoshu, Joseph *The Polish Woods,* Philadelphia, 1938; *The Last Revolt,* Philadelphia, 1952; *A Day in Regensburg,* Philadelphia, 1968.
Raboy, Isaac *Nine Brothers,* New York, 1968.
Singer, I. Bashevis *The Family Moskat,* New York, 1950; *Gimpel the Fool,* New York, 1951; *Satan in Goray,* New York, 1955; *The Magician of Lublin,* New York, 1960; *The Spinoza of Market Street,* New York, 1961; *The Slave,* New York, 1962; *Short Friday and Other Stories,* New York, 1964; *In My Father's Court,* Philadelphia, 1966; *Selected Short Stories,* New York, 1966; *Zlateh the Goat and Other Stories,* New York, 1966; *The Fearsome Inn,* New York, 1967; *The Manor,* New York, 1967; *Mazel and Shlimazel,* New York, 1967; *The Seance, and Other Stories,* New York, 1968.

Singer, I. J. *The Brothers Ashkenazi,* New York, 1933; *The Sinner,* New York, 1933, reprinted as *Yoshe Kalb,* New York, 1961; *Spring and Other Stories,* New York, 1937; *The River Breaks Up,* New York, 1938; *East of Eden,* New York, 1939; *The Family Carnovsky,* New York, 1943.

Sutzkever, Abraham *Siberia,* London, 1961.

Weinper, Zisha *At the Rich Man's Gate,* New York, 1935.

Index